Contents

SPARKNOTES™ 101

American Government

SPARK PUBLISHING

Spark Publishing
A Division of Barnes & Noble
120 Fifth Avenue
New York, NY 10011
www.sparknotes.com

ISBN-13: 978-1-4114-0516-5
ISBN-10: 1-4114-0516-1

Please submit all comments and questions or report errors to www.sparknotes.com/errors.

Library of Congress Cataloging-in-Publication Data available upon request.

Printed and bound in the United States.

10 9 8 7 6 5 4

Chapter 5

Chapter 9

Chapter 10

Acknowledgments

SparkNotes would like to thank the following writers and contributors:

Paul Glenn, PhD in Political Science

Joshua Cracraft, Graduate Student, American History
Brandeis University

Andrew J. Waskey, MA in Theology
Professor, Division of Social Sciences
Dalton State College

John W. Sutherlin, PhD in International Relations
Assistant Professor, Department of History and Government
University of Louisiana at Monroe

A Note from SparkNotes

Welcome to the *SparkNotes 101* series! This book will help you succeed in your introductory college course for American government.

Every component of this study guide has been designed to help you process the material more quickly and score higher on your exams. You'll see lots of headings, lists, and charts, and, most important, you won't see any long blocks of text. This format will allow you to quickly learn what you need to know.

We've included these features to help you get the most out of this book:

Introduction: Before diving into the major chapters, you may want to get a broader sense of American government as an academic discipline. The Introduction discusses the components of American government; discusses the relationship between American government and political science; explains the relationship between political science and the other social sciences; and describes some possible career paths for students interested in pursuing further study.

Chapters 1–14: Each chapter provides clarification of material included in your textbook, as well as the following:

- **Shaded Text Boxes:** These call out main points and provide related information.
- **Examples:** These clarify main points and show you how concepts from political science work throughout the world.
- **Key Terms:** Important terms are bolded throughout each chapter for quick review. Definitions for these terms are compiled in the glossary at the back of the book.

- **Sample Test Questions:** The study questions, including true/false, multiple choice, and short answer, show you the kinds of questions you're most likely to encounter on a test and give you the chance to practice what you've learned. Answers are provided.

- **Suggested Reading:** This list makes recommendations for enhancing your knowledge with further research in notable books.

- **Useful Websites:** This list shows you where to go on the web to get more information or explore a topic in depth.

A+ Student Essays: These are the real thing. These essays show you how to pull together the facts and concepts you've learned in your course to make a compelling argument. They also show you the kinds of concerns scholars grapple with. We should point out that the essays do not reflect the political opinions of the writers or contributors of this book, SparkNotes, or the publishers.

Glossary: Review new terms and refresh your memory at exam time.

Index: Turn to the index at the back of the book to look up specific concepts, terms, and people.

Your textbook might be longer or look different than our study guide. Not to worry—we've got you covered. Everything you need is here. We've gone for concision to make your studying easier. The material is organized in a clear, logical way that won't overwhelm you—but will give you everything you need to know to keep up in class.

We hope *SparkNotes 101: American Government* helps you, gives you confidence, and occasionally saves your butt! Your input makes us better. Let us know what you think or how we can improve this book at **www.sparknotes.com/comments.**

Introduction

As an academic field, American government encompasses not only the study of the systems, institutions, and policies of the United States government but also the political ideals and beliefs of the American people. The field falls within the broader discipline of political science, the study of government and power. Students and scholars of American government try to answer questions concerning the political culture, the distribution of power, decision-making processes, government policies, and laws, among other issues and behaviors. American government and political science often overlap with other social sciences, including economics, psychology, sociology, and anthropology.

Components of American Government

The United States is a constitutional democracy, a type of government characterized by limitations on government power spelled out in a written constitution. Written in 1787, the U.S. Constitution is both the oldest and shortest written constitution in the world. It serves as the supreme law of the United States.

The Constitution outlines a federal government with three separate branches: the legislative branch (Congress), the executive branch (the presidency), and the judicial branch (the courts). Over time, however, other key elements of government have developed and become just as important, such as the federal bureaucracy, political parties, interest groups, the media, and electoral campaigns. We will cover these components in detail in upcoming chapters.

THE LEGISLATIVE BRANCH

Congress is the legislative branch of the federal government and is responsible for creating laws. Congress consists of two chambers, an upper chamber called the Senate and a lower chamber called the House of Representatives. Congress has the sole authority to make laws, levy taxes, declare war, and print money, among other powers. Congress also controls the federal budget.

THE EXECUTIVE BRANCH

The presidency is the executive branch of the federal government. The president is elected every four years and is responsible for enforcing the laws that Congress makes. The president is also the commander-in-chief of the armed forces and has the power to conduct foreign relations.

THE JUDICIAL BRANCH

The federal courts make up the judicial branch of the federal government, which consists of regional circuit courts, appeals courts, and the Supreme Court. The Supreme Court is the highest legal authority in the country and has assumed the power of judicial review to decide the legality of the laws Congress makes.

THE BUREAUCRACY

The term *bureaucracy* refers to the various departments and agencies of the executive branch that help the president carry out his or her duties. There are fifteen departments within the executive bureaucratic branch, including the Department of State, the Department of Labor, the Department of Homeland Security, and the Department of Education. Each of these departments is also responsible for a number of small government agencies, such as the Federal Bureau of Investigation, the Central Intelligence Agency, and the Food and Drug Administration.

POLITICAL PARTIES

A political party is an alliance of like-minded people who work together to win elections and control of the government.

Political parties work to win as many offices in the government as they can so that they can put the party's policies into effect. Like most presidential democracies, the United States has only two powerful political parties: the Democrats and the Republicans.

INTEREST GROUPS

An interest group is an organization of people who share a specific common interest and work together to promote that interest through government via lobbying or grassroots activism. Interest groups give voice to the people outside of elections, but can sometimes skew government policy.

THE MEDIA

The media refers to the private organizations that keep the public informed about politics and current events through newspapers, magazines, television, radio, and the Internet. The media also keep the government in check and can even influence the government agenda by deciding what to cover.

CAMPAIGNS AND ELECTIONS

Because the United States is a democracy, the president, vice president, members of Congress, state governors, and many state, county, and city office holders must campaign for their positions in an election.

Themes in American Political History

Americans tend to view their history as a success story and as a victory for democracy. A number of themes recur in how Americans think about their history, including the mythical founding of the United States, the struggle against tyranny and injustice, and the sense of history as progress. Popular culture, especially movies and television shows, constantly reinforces these themes and this view of American history.

MYTHICAL FOUNDING

Most Americans re-imagine the founding of the United States in mythical terms, as the triumph of wisdom over tyrannical ignorance and as the creation of something new and important in the world. Likewise, many American citizens tend to revere the Declaration of Independence and the Constitution, and the Founding Fathers are seen as paragons of virtue and political acumen. The iconic image of George Washington on the one-dollar bill or the statue of Abraham Lincoln inside the Lincoln Memorial fits in with this heroic vision of the founders.

STRUGGLE AGAINST TYRANNY AND INJUSTICE

Most Americans often think of their country as the champion of democracy and justice. Many events in American history are therefore seen as part of this struggle. Americans tend to think of the Civil War, for example, as the battle to end slavery, World War II as the defeat of evil tyrants, and the Cold War as a triumph of democratic values over communism and totalitarianism. Today, many Americans see the fight against terrorism as the latest example of the United States standing up for what is right in the world.

HISTORY AS PROGRESS

Although the United States is not a perfect democracy, many Americans interpret its history as progress toward a better democracy. In this view, America has improved from century to century, getting better and more democratic over time. The expansion of the right to vote is the best example. At the start of the republic, the right to vote was restricted in most places to older, wealthy, white landowners. Over time, however, all citizens won the right to vote, including the middle classes, the poor, people of other races, women, and younger people. American democracy has thus grown as more people have been allowed to participate.

The Other Social Sciences

Social sciences study how people interact with and relate to one another. The study of American government, with its emphasis on political systems and the distribution of power, falls into this larger academic category. Like other disciplines within political science, the study of American government draws from some other social sciences, including sociology, economics, psychology, and anthropology.

SOCIOLOGY

Sociology studies social life and human interactions, from how groups form to how large organizations run to how people interact with one another. In their analyses of American government, scholars make use of sociological studies and methods when examining, for example, how small group dynamics affect the decision-making process, how people acquire and maintain power, and how political culture shapes our attitudes.

ECONOMICS

Politics and economics often intersect. Studying government without also studying economics, especially in free-market societies such as the United States, is not possible. Scholars in this field examine such economic issues as the effects government policy has on the economy, the role money plays in campaigns, and how nations arrive at trade agreements.

PSYCHOLOGY

Psychology studies the way the human mind works, helping us to understand why people behave the way that they do. The insights of psychology are sometimes used to analyze a president's or voter's behavior or to explain why some people are more prone to supporting certain governments and ideologies.

ANTHROPOLOGY

Anthropology examines cultures within a society and theorizes about how those cultures affect society. Anthropologists also explore how people acquire cultural values. Because culture often has a strong effect on behavior, scholars rely on anthropological studies and methods to draw conclusions about American political culture and behavior.

What Political Scientists Do

Scholars of American government are known as *political scientists.* A background in political science generally and American government specifically is useful in many different fields.

PUBLIC POLICY

Government policy affects nearly everything that we do, so public policy experts can work in a variety of areas:

- Issue advocate
- Government official
- Activist
- City planner
- Legislative analyst

CAMPAIGNS

Many political science majors spend time working on campaigns, which can lead to one of several careers in politics:

- Pollster
- Event organizer
- Public opinion analyst
- Communications director

LAW AND LAW ENFORCEMENT

Many students of political science go on to choose one of the following careers in law and law enforcement:

- Attorney
- Judge
- Police officer

- Parole officer
- FBI or CIA agent
- Prison administrator

BUSINESS

Although political science does not deal directly with business matters, it does teach the analytical and data interpretation skills needed for many careers in the private sector. Political scientists interested in working in business might take the following kinds of jobs:

- Bank executive
- Career counselor
- Corporate economist
- Government relations manager
- Management analyst
- Systems analyst

EDUCATION

Many political scientists earn a PhD and do specialized research and scholarship at a "think tank." Still others may choose one of the following jobs :

- Professor
- High school teacher
- Educational curriculum developer
- Journal editor

This list covers just a few of the careers open to students of political science majors. As you will see in your studies of political science, the discipline teaches many skills, including critical thinking and analytical reasoning, which can be applied in many fields.

AMERICAN POLITICAL CULTURE

1

Overview

Defining the label *American* can be complicated. What makes someone an American? Citizenship status? Residency? Paying taxes, playing baseball, speaking English, eating apple pie? The United States is a nation of immigrants—almost every one of us has ancestors who came to America from other parts of the world, and immigrants continue to arrive today. Citizens and residents of the United States demonstrate tremendous diversity with regard to religion, culture, native language, beliefs, and tradition. As the old adage goes, America is one big melting pot. So, if we're all different, how do we define our national identity? What does it mean to be American when Americans are so diverse?

Now that the United States stands as the world's only superpower, defining "American" has become all the more important. Many of our leaders wish to export American ideas and values abroad, but which ideas and values are distinctly American? What are the basic factors that influence and define our political identity? Before turning to the finer points of American government, we need to explore the principles and core values that define America.

The Importance of Geography

The United States covers a large chunk of the North American continent, incorporating a variety of climates and bound on two sides by ocean. The country's unique geography has given it a number of benefits:

- **Isolation from conflict:** For much of its early history, the United States was able to keep out of political and military entanglements with the rest of the world. Separated from Europe by one ocean and from Asia by another, America avoided the conflicts and wars among states in those regions. Peace provided a rich environment for the development and growth of the new nation.

- **Vibrant trade:** Although vast oceans separate the United States from much of the world, access to these oceans allowed for the development of lively trade routes in the eighteenth and nineteenth centuries. The United States traded regularly with Europe and increasingly with Asia as the nineteenth century wore on. America also possesses a number of long navigable rivers (including the Mississippi River) that allowed for extensive trade within the country.

- **Rich farmland:** Large parts of the United States contain excellent farmland. By producing more food than necessary, the United States could trade excess food to support a growing manufacturing economy.

- **A vast frontier:** Early white settlers were able to expand across the continent. Access to a vast frontier encouraged development as thousands of people pushed westward. The frontier also played a role in shaping the American character.

- **Natural resources:** The size and vastly different ecologies of the terrain have also provided Americans with an abundance of natural resources, such as timber, metal ores, coal, oil, and natural gas. Unlimited access to these resources allowed the United States to develop politically and militarily because it did not have to worry about acquiring the natural resources needed to sustain its citizens.

Manifest Destiny

In the nineteenth century, the American frontier loomed large in the public imagination. Many settlers moved west to make their fortunes, escape their unpleasant lives, or seek adventure. Many Americans believed that it was their manifest destiny from God to conquer and settle all the land between the two oceans. Although manifest destiny contributed to the frontier spirit that made America, it frequently resulted in excessive greed and cruelty to the peoples already living there.

The Importance of Immigration

The ethnic, religious, and cultural diversity brought by immigrants in the nineteenth and twentieth centuries has shaped American history and politics.

THREE WAVES OF IMMIGRATION

Political scientists divide immigration to the United States into three major waves:

1. **Early immigration** (1700s–1850): Immigrants from western and northern Europe arrived in great numbers for economic, political, and religious reasons. Germans and Irish, in particular, came to the United States in the 1830s and 1840s. European settlers imported millions of African slaves as well.

2. **Second wave** (1850–1970): Immigrants came primarily from southern and eastern Europe to escape violence and political instability in the late nineteenth and early twentieth centuries. Several million Jews also immigrated to the United States before and after World War II.

3. **Recent immigration** (1970–present): Large numbers of people have come from Mexico, China, Korea, India, and the Philippines, as well as other parts of Latin America and Asia.

> **The New York Melting Pot**
>
> During a 2000 study, the New York State Comptroller discovered that close to 140 languages are spoken in Queens, which probably makes this borough the most diverse area of the United States.

The following chart lists the top ten countries of origin for American immigrants, from 1820 to 2000:

ORIGIN FOR AMERICAN IMMIGRANTS	
Country	**Approximate Number of Immigrants**
Germany	7 million
Mexico	6 million
Italy	5 million
Great Britain	5 million
Ireland	5 million
Canada	5 million
Austria and Hungary	4 million (total)
Russia (former Soviet Union)	4 million
The Philippines	2 million
China and Sweden	1 million (each)

EFFECTS OF IMMIGRATION

Immigration has profoundly shaped American politics and culture. Immigrants not only provided labor for the growing economy but also gave the United States a distinctly unique social and political culture. These effects continue today.

> *EXAMPLE:* The urban political machine is one example of how immigrants helped shape the American political system. Many immigrants in the late nineteenth century were welcomed by political parties and given homes and jobs; in return, the political parties asked for the immigrants' votes and political support. This trading of votes for services is known as **machine politics,** which dominated many cities for decades.

CONTROVERSIES OVER IMMIGRATION

In 2006, immigration became a hot topic as politicians debated about how to handle the large number of illegal immigrants in the United States. But these debates are nothing new. Historically, Americans have frequently scorned new arrivals, despite the fact that their ancestors were also immigrants. In the late nineteenth and early twentieth centuries, for example, Congress passed laws regulating how many immigrants could enter the United States from each country, excluding Asians entirely until the 1960s.

EXAMPLE: The Chinese Exclusion Act of 1882 was the first immigration law aimed at a specific ethnic group. Congress passed the act to keep Chinese laborers out for ten years but renewed the act in 1892 and finally made it permanent in 1902. The act was not repealed until 1965. Many Americans at the time favored the act because they resented the growing number of Chinese laborers working on the railroads in the West.

Prejudice in Language

Some of the prejudices against immigrants have found their way into American slang. The term *paddy wagon,* for example, was originally a jab at Irish Americans. Other terms—most of them racist and inappropriate and thus not listed here—can also be found in the American vernacular.

American Political Ideals

American political culture contains a number of core ideals and values. Not all Americans share the same views, of course, but the vast majority subscribes to these general ideals, including liberty, equality, democracy, individualism, unity, and diversity. Political debates tend to be over how best to achieve these ideals, not over whether these ideals are worth having in the first place.

LIBERTY

Americans today tend to define **liberty** as the freedom for people to do what they want. We also tend to believe liberty is essential to personal fulfillment and happiness. Nevertheless, liberty must be restrained on some level in order to create a stable society. A widely accepted principle of freedom is that we are free to do whatever we want as long as we do not impinge on other people's freedom.

A limited government is a government that places relatively few restrictions on its citizens' freedom. There are some things that the government cannot do, such as limit freedom of speech or impose a single religion on its citizens. A limited government usually has a constitution that defines the limits of governmental power. In the United States, the Constitution outlines the structure of government, whereas the Bill of Rights guarantees some of the citizens' specific liberties.

Economic Liberty

For many Americans, liberty includes economic liberty. People should be free to do as they see fit in the economic sphere without government interference. Throughout most of the nineteenth century, the American economy was based on **laissez-faire capitalism,** an economic system in which the government plays almost no role in producing, distributing, or regulating the production and distribution of goods. Today, people want some governmental intervention in the economy, but most Americans want this intervention to be limited in scope.

EQUALITY

Although no two people are truly equal, they are considered equal under the law. Some Americans may be poorer than others, and some may have cultural backgrounds different from the majority, but all Americans have the same fundamental rights. The term **equality** refers to a number of ways people are treated the same.

Political Equality

Political equality means that everyone is treated in the same way in the political sphere. This means, among other things, that everyone has the same status under the law (everyone is entitled to legal representation, for example, and every citizen gets one vote) and that everyone gets equal treatment under the law. Everybody must obey the laws, regardless of race, creed, religion, gender, or sexual orientation, and in return, everyone enjoys the same rights.

Equal Opportunity Versus Equality of Outcome

In American political culture, political equality also commonly means **equality of opportunity:** All people get the same opportunities to compete and achieve in the world. Some people will succeed and some will fail, but most Americans believe that everyone, no matter what, is entitled to the opportunity to succeed.

Most Americans oppose **equality of outcome.** Under this system, the government ensures all people the same results, regardless of how talented or hardworking they are. Most Americans consider this unfair because this system means that talented and diligent people do not get the success they deserve.

EXAMPLE: In the United States, the government tries to ensure equal opportunity among its citizens by giving everybody access to a solid public education. For example, President George W. Bush and many members of Congress championed the No Child Left Behind Act, passed in 2001, because the law aimed to give all American students a good education. A good education gives people the ability to compete for good jobs, which means that they can achieve success if they so desire.

Equal Opportunity to Succeed

Many liberal social policy advocates argue that Americans do not actually have equal opportunities to succeed. Women, for example, still earn less than men in the same professions, whereas young African Americans from inner-city neighborhoods are much less likely to attend college than young whites. Democratic and Republican political leaders both try to level the playing field so that everyone has equal opportunity, but the two groups have radically different ideas about how to do so.

DEMOCRACY

Most Americans believe that democracy is the best form of government and therefore tend to support policies that protect and expand democracy. The importance placed on democracy in American political culture usually appears in domestic politics, but sometimes a desire to spread democracy to other countries drives American foreign policy.

EXAMPLE: American foreign policy during the Cold War often aimed at supporting and spreading democracy around the world. During the 1980s, members of Ronald Regan's administration illegally sold arms to Iran in order to raise money for the Nicaraguan contras, who were fighting the communist regime in power.

Popular Sovereignty

Popular sovereignty, when the people rule, is an important principle of democracy. Democracy is government by the people, so political leaders in a democratic society are supposed to listen to and heed public opinion. Democracies hold elections to allow the people to exercise their power over government.

Majority Rule

Majority rule, the belief that the power to make decisions about government should reflect the will of most (the majority) of the people, is another important principle of democracy. In fact, American political culture relies on majority rule: The candidate who wins a majority of votes, for example, wins the race. Likewise, a bill that wins the support of a majority of members of Congress passes. Without majority rule, a democracy could not function.

Minority Rights

The flipside of majority rule is that the majority does not have unlimited power. In a democracy, the **rights of the minority** must also be protected, even at the expense of overriding the will of the majority. The minority always has the right to speak out against the majority, for example. Similarly, the minority cannot be arrested or jailed for disagreeing or voting against the majority. Without minority rights, majority rule would easily evolve into **tyranny of the majority,** in which the majority would ignore the basic rights of the minority.

> **Speaking for the Majority**
>
> Because of the power of the majority, political groups often claim to speak for the majority even if they do not actually do so. Making such a claim gives the group some legitimacy. Many authoritarian dictators, for example, hold rigged elections in order to claim popular support and legitimacy even if the election results are fabricated. International elections officials monitor the casting and counting of ballots in elections around the world to make sure democratic elections are really fair.

INDIVIDUALISM

According to the concept of **individualism,** humans are fundamentally individuals who have the freedom to make choices and join (or not join) groups as they wish. An individual's life belongs to no one but that individual, so people should make choices that are right for them regardless of what other people think. A true individual is unlike anyone else. Americans value individualism and respect people who make independent choices.

Individual Rights in American History

The protection of individual rights had been a hallmark of American politics even before the American Revolution. Many colonial governments had bills of rights that, to some extent, granted freedoms of speech, religion, and assembly. At the start of the revolution, states wrote new constitutions for themselves and listed rights that the government could not take away. The first ten amendments to the Constitution, known as the Bill of Rights, were added as soon as the new government took office in 1789.

Rugged Individualism

Rugged individualism is the quintessentially American view that we are responsible for our own lives and ultimately must rely only on ourselves. People who ignore society's wishes and do as they choose are rugged individuals. These people make their own way in the world at the risk of being ostracized by the rest of society.

EXAMPLE: Many American movie heroes are individuals who disdain authority and flout tradition. John Wayne's characters often fit this mold, as do other film heroes such as Bruce Willis's character John McClane in *Die Hard* and Clint Eastwood's "man without a name" in *The Good, the Bad, and the Ugly*.

Conformity

The opposite of individualism is **conformism,** a term used to describe the act of people trying to be the same. Over the centuries, many observers have noted that even in democracies, conformism is common. Americans, for example, frequently watch the same shows on television and read the same books. This seems to conflict with the ideal of individualism but is nevertheless an important component of any civil society.

UNITY AND DIVERSITY

Two interconnected ideals in American political culture are unity and diversity. **Unity** refers to Americans' support of the republic and democracy, even if they disagree with one another about policies. Politicians and other leaders frequently appeal to this sense of unity, especially during times of national crisis. The name of our country—the United States—emphasizes the importance of unity to our national political culture.

> *EXAMPLE:* In the aftermath of September 11th, President George W. Bush rallied the country by appealing to common feelings of patriotism. Leaders made similar appeals after the devastation of Hurricanes Katrina and Rita in 2005.

Diversity refers to the fact that Americans have many different cultural traditions and hold a variety of values. Nearly all Americans descend from immigrants, and many of them take pride in their heritage and cultural history. Americans also hold diverse views and creeds.

> *EXAMPLE:* Many American cities hold parades and celebrations for holidays of different immigrant groups. Irish Americans, as well as others, celebrate St. Patrick's Day every year, whereas Columbus Day parades honor the contributions of Italian and Spanish Americans.

Multiculturalism

Multiculturalism is the view that we should embrace our diversity and learn about one another's cultures. Much of

American culture derives from western European cultures (the British Isles in particular), which makes some other groups feel excluded. Learning about new cultures and respecting diversity have taken on new force in recent years. For many people, being American is about adhering to ideas and principles, not to a particular religious or ethnic identity. So one can be a patriot while still honoring one's ancestral traditions.

The American Dream

Nearly every group that has come to the United States has embraced the idea of the American dream, which, in turn, has different meanings for different people. Some immigrants escaped brutal regimes and therefore pursue an American dream of living in freedom. Others subscribe to an American dream in which hard work leads to economic success.

AMERICAN IDEALS IN PRACTICE

Although Americans have always cherished the ideals of liberty, equality, democracy, individualism, unity, and diversity, the United States has not always lived up to them. Slavery, the mistreatment of Native Americans, and the failure to give women the right to vote for more than a century are the most glaring examples.

American Symbols

Americans have embraced a number of concrete symbols to stand for the abstract American ideals discussed in this chapter. The best example is the American flag, which we honor as a symbol of the United States. The soaring eagle is another significant American symbol that stands for freedom. In popular culture, the trio of mom, baseball, and apple pie encapsulates what many see as the core of American identity.

American Attitudes Toward Government

A skepticism about government and its abilities has always been a key component of American political culture. From the founding of the republic, Americans worried about excessive governmental power, choosing instead to put their faith in individuals and private groups. French writer Alexis de Tocqueville, for example, pointed out that Americans are far more likely than other peoples to join together to solve a problem in his two-volume book *Democracy in America* (1835, 1840).

Many people have seen and continue to see the government as a **necessary evil,** something that is not good in itself but is needed to protect people. James Madison, writing in *Federalist Paper No. 51* (1787), stated that government is only needed because people sometimes mistreat one another and act in their own self-interest to the detriment of others. Since the 1960s, opinion of government has deteriorated even further. Political cynicism has become common, and Americans generally no longer believe in the government's ability to effect change.

OVERARCHING MISTRUST

Recent wars and governmental scandals have heightened American mistrust of government. In the 1960s, many people became disillusioned with the government during the Vietnam War. Likewise, in 1974, President Richard Nixon's resignation in the wake of the Watergate scandal only heightened Americans' suspicion of government. In 1986, the Iran-Contra scandal tarnished President Ronald Reagan's popularity, and some Republicans never forgave President George H. W. Bush for reneging on the "no new taxes" pledge he made in 1988. Likewise, President Bill Clinton's behavior with Monica Lewinsky and subsequent impeachment in 1998 damaged his presidency. As a result of these events, the number of Americans who trust the federal government has steadily declined since the 1960s.

LACK OF POLITICAL EFFICACY

Political efficacy is the belief that one's actions can make a difference in government and that the government listens to normal, everyday people. One sign of American mistrust of government is a decline in feelings of political efficacy over the last few decades. Many Americans feel that the government only listens to special interests, not to average citizens. Some Americans feel such a lack of political efficacy that they do not bother voting or participating in politics in any way.

> **Rallying Young Voters**
>
> MTV stepped into the political arena in 1992 with Rock the Vote, an attempt to get young people to participate in the political process. During presidential elections, MTV runs news about issues that affect young people and explains how to register to vote. In 2004, World Wrestling Entertainment launched a similar effort called Smackdown Your Vote! These and other youth-oriented campaigns have increased voter turnout among young people.

LITTLE KNOWLEDGE ABOUT GOVERNMENT

Many Americans do not know much about their government and are unable to name their representatives in Congress or even key figures in their local governments. For some people, government does not seem to play a major role in their lives, so they do not pay much attention to politics. Others complain about the difficulty involved in learning about the issues and their representatives, particularly state and local representatives. A growing number of people also see the news as biased and thus do not trust what they see on television or read in the newspapers.

Pop Culture and Politics

Polls showing American ignorance of politics are fairly common. Some polls show that Americans usually know more about popular culture than about politics. For example, more people can name a contestant from the television show *American Idol* than a member of the Supreme Court.

According to most theories about democracies, citizens need to be knowledgeable about politics in order to make wise choices. Some argue that because Americans do not know much about politics, they make bad political decisions, which, in turn, leads to political apathy. Others argue that political ignorance does not have such a negative effect because citizens spend their time focusing on issues or hobbies that matter more to them and are thus much happier citizens.

Learning About Government

For those who wish to learn more about their elected leaders, the Internet has all kinds of great resources:

- www.house.gov
The House of Representatives' website

- www.senate.gov
The Senate's website

- www.firstgov.gov
The federal government's web portal, with access to websites for federal agencies, state governments, local governments, and tribal governments

- www.loc.gov/rr/news/stategov/stategov.html
A resource page maintained by the Library of Congress of state and local governments.

American Exceptionalism

American exceptionalism is the idea that the United States differs from the rest of the world. According to this view, the lessons learned by other nations do not necessarily apply to the United States because the United States is exceptional and different. Americans have believed they are different from other peoples in the world because of the following concepts:

- **Divine providence:** Some believe that America has been chosen by God to embody virtue and be a beacon to the world. The back of the one-dollar bill reads, for example, "In God we trust."
- **Just principles:** Unlike most states, the United States was founded on ideas and principles, not by conquest.
- **Geography and resources:** The great wealth of resources and relative isolation of the United States for much of its history has made America unique among most other countries in the world.
- **Diversity:** The American mix of cultures and traditions is the source of American strength.

Exceptionalism in Action

American exceptionalism often influences American foreign policy. During the Cold War, for example, Ronald Reagan felt that America had a duty to be the "shining city on the hill," an example to the world of what a good and blessed country should be.

Sample Test Questions

1. Why was America's isolation from Europe and Asia for much of its history an advantage?

2. Describe the major waves of immigration to the United States.

3. How can diversity and unity fit together?

4. True or false: Americans typically believe that all people should try to be unique.

5. True or false: Many Americans view government as a necessary evil.

6. Which of the following is *not* part of the typical American's view of equality?

A. Equal opportunity
B. Equal result
C. One person, one vote
D. The law treats everyone the same

7. The concept of limited government corresponds to which element of American political culture?

A. Liberty
B. Equality
C. Unity
D. Diversity

8. Which of the following best characterizes Americans' attitudes toward their government?

A. Wholehearted agreement
B. Skepticism
C. Anger
D. Reluctant patriotism

9. Why do some people believe that American political ignorance is a bad thing?

A. It means that Americans are devoting too much time to politics.
B. Voters may make poor decisions because they lack good information.
C. Americans look foolish to people in other countries.
D. Politicians face too much scrutiny.

10. What is American exceptionalism?

A. The belief that America is very much like other countries
B. The view that Americans are smarter than other people
C. The view that people in other countries are better than Americans
D. The belief that America is different than other nations

ANSWERS

1. Isolation meant that the United States did not get drawn into wars and conflicts in Europe or Asia and was free to develop without outside interference.

2. The first major wave came in colonial days. The early republic and was composed of mostly western and northern Europeans. In the late nineteenth and early twentieth centuries, large numbers of southern and eastern Europeans came to the United States. In recent decades, an increasing number of immigrants have come from Latin America and Asia.

3. Americans come from a wide variety of cultural and ethnic backgrounds and, while often valuing the old traditions and customs, fully support the ideals of the American political culture.

4. True

5. True

6. B

7. A

8. B

9. B

10. D

Suggested Reading

• Dahl, Robert. *Democracy and Its Critics.* New Haven, Conn.: Yale University Press, 1989.

This scholarly text addresses criticisms and critics of democracy. Dahl has been a forceful defender of American democracy for decades, and his writings influence many scholars and researchers.

• Dionne, E. J., Jr. *Why Americans Hate Politics: The Death of the Democratic Process.* Reprint, New York: Simon & Schuster, 1992.

A study of American politics and participation in political processes in the mid- to late twentieth century. Dionne concludes that Americans hate politics and therefore should go beyond standard liberal and conservative ideologies.

• Delli Carpini, Michael X., and Scott Keeter. *What Americans Know About Politics and Why It Matters.* New Haven, Conn.: Yale University Press, 1996.

A study of the problems of political ignorance.

• Huntington, Samuel P. *American Politics: The Promise of Disharmony.* Cambridge, Mass.: Harvard University Press, 1981.

Most famous for his theory of the clash of cultures, here Huntington looks at American politics.

• Lipset, Seymour Martin. *American Exceptionalism: A Double-Edged Sword.* New York: Norton, 1996.

Interesting and potentially controversial arguments about how Americans view themselves as blessed and unique in the world.

• Nye, Joseph S., Sr., Philip D. Zelikow, and David C. King, eds. *Why People Don't Trust Government.* Cambridge, Mass.: Harvard University Press, 1997.

A number of scholars examine the problem of political cynicism, reaching different conclusions about its meaning for the American polity.

• Putnam, Robert. *Making Democracy Work: Civic Traditions in Modern Italy.* Princeton, NJ: Princeton University Press, 1993.

Political cultures of other democratic states differ greatly from American political culture. Putnam studies the political culture of Italy and how it affects the Italian version of democracy.

• Schuck, Peter H. *Diversity in America: Keeping Government at a Safe Distance.* Cambridge, Mass.: Belknap Press of Harvard, 2003.

This book examines the ways diversity helps and hurts the national interest.

Useful Websites

- www.conginst.org

The website of the Congressional Institute provides rich survey data on American political culture; has resources for congresspeople, scholars, and students; maintains a blog; and collates other valuable information.

- www.ned.org

The nonpartisan, nongovernmental National Endowment for Democracy seeks to foster democracy around the world through grants, information, conferences, and literature

- www.stateline.org

Sponsored by the University of Richmond and the Pew Charitable Trusts, this site provides up-to-date information about key policies and state politics throughout the United States.

THE FOUNDING AND THE CONSTITUTION

2

Overview

America's Founding Fathers—Thomas Jefferson, Benjamin Franklin, George Washington, Alexander Hamilton, John Adams, James Madison, and the like—created a republican system of government that was, for its time, truly unique. This government reflected the political philosophies of the eighteenth-century Enlightenment. Perhaps more important, the American system of government embodied the conceptions of liberty, equality, and freedom from tyranny held by ordinary Americans.

Both the Declaration of Independence and the Constitution reflect these ideals. The Declaration of Independence cut off all of the colonies' political ties with Great Britain, established the United States as a new nation, and expressed America's political philosophy. The Constitution created a stable federal system of government in which the individual states and a strong national government share political power. The process in which the Constitution was written and later ratified further reflects American ideals and values.

The First Government of the United States

Americans had significant experience with self-government before the writing of the Constitution in 1787, and this experience shaped the political views of the framers who wrote the Constitution and factored into the formation of the first government. A **constitution** is a set of rules that determines how power will be used legitimately in a state. Contrary to popular belief, few governments have been created by written constitutions.

THE COLONIES

Europeans settlers had been living in America for more than 250 years by the time independence from England was declared. Although the colonists were subjects of the British crown, the colonies functioned more or less independently and thus had extensive experience in self-government. Many towns held meetings to discuss public business, for example, and residents had some input into their colonies' governments.

The colonists rebelled, in part, because they felt that the British were increasingly taking away their powers of self-government. Prior to the 1750s, the colonists paid few taxes to Britain. But when the British Parliament passed a number of taxes on the colonists, the colonists decried the measures as **taxation without representation.** In the 1760s, for example, the Stamp Act and the Sugar Act enraged many colonists because the acts levied taxes on certain commodities but gave the colonists no say in how the money would be spent.

Angered by the taxes, representatives from the colonies gathered at the **First Continental Congress** in 1774 and called for a total boycott of British goods. When the British sent troops to enforce the new taxes, many colonists began to agitate for independence. War between the British and the American colonists broke out in 1775.

The table on the next page lists the major events during the early years of the United States.

MAJOR EVENTS IN THE FOUNDING OF THE UNITED STATES	
Date	**Event**
1607	First permanent British colony at Jamestown, Virginia
1620	Pilgrims land in Massachusetts
1620–1732	Founding of the thirteen colonies; colonists govern themselves and develop idea of limited government
1641	Massachusetts Body of Liberties passed; it protects rights of individuals
1764	Sugar Act taxes sugar
1765	Stamp Act taxes a variety of goods
1770	Boston Massacre
1773	Boston Tea Party
1775	Revolutionary War begins
1776	Second Continental Congress convenes; Declaration of Independence is written
1781	Ratification of the Articles of Confederation
1783	Treaty of Paris ends the Revolutionary War
1786	Shays' Rebellion begins in western Massachusetts
1786	Annapolis Convention calls on Congress to convene a meeting to fix the Articles
1787	Constitutional Convention
1787–1789	Battle to ratify the Constitution
1789	Constitution ratified; the new United States government takes power

DECLARING INDEPENDENCE

The first attempt at national government arose during the Revolutionary War (1775–1783). State governments sent representatives to the **Second Continental Congress** in 1776 to organize American efforts immediately before and during the Revolutionary War. Instead of merely demanding better treatment as British subjects, the congress decided to fight for full independence.

The Declaration of Independence

Thomas Jefferson wrote the **Declaration of Independence** in 1776 to formally break away from Great Britain and to justify the Revolutionary War. According to the Declaration, "all men are created equal" and certain rights and liberties cannot be denied to people. Among those rights is self-government: The people must consent to the government for it to be legitimate. Because the British government had repeatedly abused the rights of the colonists and ignored their wishes, the colonists were no longer obligated to obey the government.

> **Jefferson's Wise Words**
>
> The second paragraph of the Declaration of Independence contains perhaps the most famous words in American history: "We hold these truths to be self-evident, that all men are created equal, that they are endowed by their Creator with certain unalienable Rights, that among these are Life, Liberty and the pursuit of Happiness." An **inalienable right** is a right that all people in the world have that no one can take away. Jefferson's argument lays the foundation for American thinking about civil rights and liberties: Any infringement on our rights is an affront to natural law.

The Articles of Confederation

The Second Continental Congress also wrote a constitution to create a new national government. The Continental Congress approved the **Articles of Confederation,** which took effect in 1781 during the war. The national government under the Articles of Confederation consisted of a single legislative body called Congress in which each state received one vote. All congressional decisions required a unanimous vote. The government under the Articles did not have a judicial system (national courts) or an executive (such as a president). As a result, each state had a significant degree of sovereignty and autonomy. The national government under the Articles remained in effect until 1789.

Under the Articles, Congress was empowered to do the following:

- Declare war and make peace
- Establish armed forces
- Make treaties
- Govern western lands owned by the United States
- Borrow money

Congress lacked a number of key powers, though. It could not collect taxes, compel the states to fund the war, contribute troops, or enforce cooperation. Chaos ensued as the various states fought with one another. Nevertheless, Congress achieved two notable successes:

- Negotiating and signing the Treaty of Paris (1783) to end the Revolutionary War
- Passing the Northwest Ordinances (1787) to create a system for admitting new states to the Union

Shays' Rebellion

Facing large debts and heavy taxes, some farmers in western Massachusetts led by Daniel Shays rebelled in 1786 shortly after the end of the Revolutionary War. Compounding their frustrations was the substantial back pay owed to the veterans of the war. The governor of Massachusetts asked Congress to help quell **Shays' Rebellion,** but Congress could not help because it had no army and could not convince the other states to send troops. Even though Massachusetts soldiers managed to defeat Shays and his followers, the rebellion helped convince some Americans that national government was too weak: It could not enforce its authority and could not coerce the individual states to work for the common good of the nation.

The Annapolis Convention

Frustrated by Shays' Rebellion, a conference of delegates from five states convened in Annapolis in fall 1786. The **Annapolis Convention** called on Congress to send officials to Philadelphia to revise the Articles to make Congress stronger.

The Constitutional Convention

Delegates from eleven of the thirteen colonies gathered in Philadelphia in May 1787 to revise the Articles. Instead, however, delegates at the **Constitutional Convention** (sometimes called the **Philadelphia Convention**) quickly decided to scrap the Articles and write a document that created an entirely new, stronger national government.

> **The Cincinnati**
>
> As the delegates gathered to change the government, a group of disgruntled veteran officers also met in Philadelphia. Calling themselves "the Cincinnati" (after a public-minded Roman hero), the veterans hoped that George Washington would join them and take control of the government. Washington's refusal to attend the meeting, let alone lead a rebellion, was an important moment: Washington carried a lot of influence, so his support legitimized the Constitutional Convention and delegitimized splinter groups such as the Cincinnati.

THE FRAMERS OF THE CONSTITUTION

The group that met during the Constitutional Convention included some of the most prominent men of the revolutionary and post-revolutionary era. George Washington attended the convention (and was elected its president), along with Benjamin Franklin, Alexander Hamilton, James Madison, and Roger Sherman, among others. The **framers** of the Constitution were wealthier and better educated than the average American. Nearly all of them had experience in state and national governments, and many of them had fought in the revolution.

> **The Missing Founders**
>
> Although the Constitutional Convention included many luminaries, several famous figures from the revolutionary era did not attend. Patrick Henry and Samuel Adams, for example, were not there, and both expressed serious reservations about the final document. Thomas Jefferson was also absent because he was serving as the American ambassador to France at the time.

The Aims of the Framers

The framers met in Philadelphia to create a stronger national government that would better protect and enhance liberty by preventing tyranny. Shays' Rebellion and the states' inability to cooperate with one another had also demonstrated the weaknesses inherent in the Articles of Confederation, and many worried that Britain would take advantage of American weaknesses. At the same time, however, the framers did not want to abolish the state governments. At this time, most Americans felt more loyalty toward their state governments than to Congress, and strong local government made sense for the operation of a large nation such as the United States.

ISSUES AND COMPROMISES

The delegates to the convention disagreed with one another on three main issues: representation in Congress, slavery, and presidential elections. Failure to reach agreement on any of these issues would likely have led to dissolution of the already tenuous union of the states. Slave states, for example, were not willing to accept a constitution that banned slavery, whereas small states would not accept a document that gave excessive power to large states. Three compromises, summarized in the following table, resolved these disagreements.

SIGNIFICANT ISSUES AND COMPROMISES	
Issue	**Compromise**
Representation in the national legislature	Great Compromise
Slavery	Three-Fifths Compromise
Presidential elections	Electoral College

Representation and the Great Compromise

Delegates debated extensively about how the people and the states would be represented in the national legislature. Most delegates favored one of two representation schemes:

- **The Virginia Plan:** Favored representation based on population. Delegates from the large states supported this plan because it would give them a great deal of power. Representatives from small states, however, rejected the plan because they would have fewer seats than the larger states and consequently less power.

- **The New Jersey Plan:** Proposed giving each state equal representation in the legislature. Delegates from smaller states supported the New Jersey Plan because they believed that all states should have equal power, regardless of population.

> **Supremacy Clause**
>
> The New Jersey Plan also advocated the **supremacy doctrine,** the idea that national law has priority over state law. This doctrine was later included in the Constitution in the **supremacy clause** (Article VI), which states that the Constitution and the laws Congress passes have more weight than state and local laws.

For a time, the delegates' debate over representation threatened to wreck the convention entirely. To save the convention, delegates compromised. The **Great Compromise** created a **bicameral** (composed of two houses) Congress. The upper house, called the Senate, would consist of two delegates from each state, regardless of size or population. Representation in the lower house, called the House of Representatives, would be apportioned according to the population of each state: The larger the state, the more representatives in the House. Both sides got some of what they wanted, and the Congress was created.

Slavery and the Three-Fifths Compromise

Delegates also debated about how slavery should affect representation in the House of Representatives. Roughly 90 percent of slaves in 1787 lived in the South and accounted for about 30 percent of the southern population. Southern delegates wanted slaves to be counted as people only when determining representation in Congress because a larger population meant more representatives and therefore more political power. Northern delegates opposed this view, however, and did not want slaves to be counted as people when determining a state's population. According to the **Three-Fifths Compromise,** which resolved the dispute, slaves would be counted as three-fifths of a person when apportioning seats in the House of Representatives.

Effects of the Three-Fifths Compromise

The Three-Fifths Compromise was probably necessary to keep the states together as a united country. Had slavery been banned outright, southern states would probably have walked out of the convention, possibly leading to the eventual collapse of the United States. But the compromise had severe consequences in that it legitimized slavery and increased the South's power and representation in Congress.

Presidential Elections

Finally, delegates debated about how the president would be elected. Some representatives, for example, favored direct election of the president, whereas others wanted to ensure that only the “best men” could hold the office. They compromised by creating the **Electoral College,** a presidential voting system whereby a special body of electors in each state casts a fixed number of votes for the president according to the combined number of seats the state has in the House and the Senate. For example, if a state had ten seats in the House and two seats in the Senate, it would cast twelve electoral votes in the Electoral College. Electors can chose whether to vote according to the wishes of the people in their state. The framers intended the Electoral College to serve as a safeguard should the people ever elect a president unwisely. According to the Constitution, the House of Representatives chooses the president if no single candidate receives a majority of electoral votes.

The Constitution

Thirty-nine delegates approved the Constitution on September 17, 1787. The final product of the convention is a short document that lays the foundation for a new government.

Constitutional Democracy

The government created by a constitution is best labeled a **constitutional democracy.** The constitution outlines the way power is legitimately used, whereas limitations on government power creates a democratic system.

The American Constitution is divided into seven parts called *articles,* each dealing with a specific issue. The bulk of the document—Articles I, II, and III—describe the structures and powers of the three branches of the federal government. The table on the following page summarizes the structure of the Constitution.

ARTICLES OF THE CONSTITUTION	
Article	**Focus**
I	The Legislative Branch
II	The Executive Branch
III	The Judicial Branch
IV	The States and the People
V	Changing the Constitution
VI	The Supremacy of the Constitution
VII	Ratifying the Constitution

The Father of the Constitution

Although many people contributed to the creation of the Constitution, James Madison played a special role. The **Madisonian model** of government focuses on dispersing power among several branches and establishing constitutional safeguards to prevent any single person or group of people from controlling the government. He outlined this philosophy in an essay now known as *Federalist No. 10* (1787). Madison worked closely with other delegates to shape the final document; for this reason, he is sometimes called the "Father of the Constitution."

LIMITS ON POWER

Even though the framers sought to expand the powers of the national government, they did not want the government to be too powerful. So the framers limited governmental power with the following:

- **Federalism:** The division of power between the federal government and the states allows the different levels of government to check each other.
- **Specificity:** The Constitution grants specific powers to the president, Congress, the states, and the people and explicitly denies them of some other powers.

- **Checks and balances:** The framers balanced the power of the government among three separate and independent branches so that no one branch can dominate the others. Further, each branch of government has some specific power to check or limit the power of the others: The president can **veto** (prevent from becoming law) acts of Congress, Congress can override presidential vetoes, and the Supreme Court has assumed the power of judicial review.

- **The Bill of Rights:** The first ten amendments to the Constitution make up the Bill of Rights, which guarantees some fundamental legal rights to all Americans, including the freedoms of speech, assembly, press, and religion.

- **Rules for elections:** The Constitution ensures that states and the voters have the power to change the government.

Separation of Powers

The Constitution creates a government with three different branches. This **separation of powers** ensures that no branch becomes powerful enough to overwhelm the other two. The legislative branch (Congress) makes the laws, the executive branch (the president) enforces the laws, and the judicial branch (the courts) interprets the law. Each branch functions independently from the others, possessing its own powers and area of influence. No branch can accomplish anything of significance without the cooperation of at least one of the others. By dividing power in this way, the framers sought to prevent tyranny: No one person or group can exercise excessive power.

Checks and Balances

The three separate branches limit one another through a series of **checks and balances.** The framers wanted to make sure that the branches were equally powerful, so they set up rules that enable each branch to stop the others from doing some things. The Constitution contains many examples of checks and balances, as illustrated by the chart on the next page.

CHECKS AND BALANCES AMONG THE BRANCHES	
The Legislative Branch and the Executive Branch	
Congress writes laws and can override a presidential veto, has the power of the purse and control over the budget, has the ability to impeach the president, and approves presidential treaties and appointments.	The president can veto bills passed by Congress, recommend laws for Congress to pass, and calls for Congress to meet. The president also enforces, or executes, bills passed by Congress.
The Judicial Branch and the Legislative Branch	
The courts have assumed the power to declare laws unconstitutional and hear cases relating to disputes arising from laws passed by Congress.	Congress approves the judges appointed by the president, sets judicial salaries, and has some power over the structure and jurisdiction of the courts. Congress also has the power to interpret courts' decisions as legislation.
The Executive Branch and the Judicial Branch	
The president appoints judges, puts court decisions into practice, and has the right to pardon those whom the courts have convicted.	The courts can declare presidential actions unconstitutional.

THE LEGISLATIVE BRANCH

The legislative branch—called Congress—is divided into two parts, which are also called houses: the House of Representatives and the Senate.

The House of Representatives

The House of Representatives is meant to be "the people's house," or the part of government most responsive to public opinion. A state's population determines how many representatives it will have in the House. Every member of the House represents a district within a state, and each district has roughly the same number of people. To make sure that the House accurately mirrors the changing population of the states, the Constitution mandates that a census be taken every ten years. Seats in the House are **reapportioned,** or reassigned, based on new census data to ensure that each House member represents about the same number of people. All 435 seats in the House go up for election every two years.

> **Representation in the House**
>
> With fifty-four seats since the last census, California has the most representatives in the House. Several states, including Delaware, Vermont, Montana, Wyoming, and Alaska, have just one member each.

The Senate

The framers envisioned the Senate as a body of rational deliberation and statesmanship, not subject to the changing moods of the general population, which is why senators are elected every six years instead of every two years. Because the Senate was also intended to serve as a check on excessive democracy, only one-third of the Senate is elected at a time. Every state has two seats in the Senate, regardless of population.

Selection of Senators

Prior to the passage of the Seventeenth Amendment in 1913, senators were appointed by the governors and legislatures of their home states and were not directly elected by their constituents.

The Powers of Congress

Article I, Section 8, of the Constitution outlines the powers of Congress. These specified powers are sometimes called the **enumerated powers.** The **necessary and proper clause**—commonly referred to as the **elastic clause**—also gives Congress the power to do whatever it deems "necessary and proper" to meet its constitutional mandate.

EXAMPLE: The federal government spends billions of dollars each year on highway construction, which is not specifically mentioned in the Constitution. Congress justifies funding federal highways through the necessary and proper clause: Federal roads improve transportation, which, in turn, facilitates interstate commerce, a power the Constitution does specifically grant to Congress. In other words, funding federal roads is "necessary and proper" to regulate interstate commerce.

The Constitution gives Congress two important powers:

1. **The power to make laws:** Only Congress can make laws. For a bill to become a law, it must first be approved by both the House and the Senate. The bill then goes to the president, who either signs it or vetoes it. Congress can override the president's veto with a two-thirds vote in both houses.

2. **The power of the purse:** Only Congress can tax citizens and spend money raised by taxes.

The Senate has some additional powers: It confirms presidential appointments to key federal offices, including federal judgeships. The Senate also ratifies all treaties.

The Constitution also lists **prohibited powers,** or things Congress may not do, including:

- **Passing an ex post facto law,** which makes something illegal after it has already been done
- **Passing a bill of attainder,** which declares a person guilty of a crime
- **Suspending the writ of habeas corpus,** which requires police to charge everyone they arrest. Congress can only suspended this writ during times of national emergency.

Impeachment

Congress also has the power to expel elected officials within the government for committing crimes. First, the House must impeach the official by listing the specific charges. The Constitution states that a person can be impeached for "high crimes and misdemeanors," which is not very precise. As a result, scholars and politicians have debated what constitutes "high crimes and misdemeanors." The Senate, presided by the chief justice of the Supreme Court, then tries the official. Two-thirds of senators must vote in favor of conviction for the official to be removed from office. Although the House has impeached a number of federal officials and judges, it has only impeached two presidents: Andrew Johnson in 1867 and Bill Clinton in 1998. The Senate acquitted both presidents (in Johnson's case, by a single vote).

THE EXECUTIVE BRANCH

The president heads the executive branch. According to the Constitution, the president has five powers:

1. Conduct foreign policy
2. Command the armed forces
3. Appoint federal judges and other government officials
4. Veto congressional bills
5. Grant clemency

The Vice President

The other elected official within the executive branch is the vice president. The vice president has to following responsibilities:

- Preside over the Senate and casts the deciding vote in case of a tie
- Become president if the president dies, relinquishes the office, or is otherwise unable to perform the duties

The role of the vice president has evolved over time. Most vice presidents in the past were excluded from policymaking. After World War II, however, most presidents saw the value of including the vice president in discussions on foreign and domestic policy. Recent vice presidents, including Al Gore (1993–2001) and Dick Cheney (2001–2009), have been heavily involved in policymaking.

A Stepping Stone to the Presidency

A fair number of vice presidents have later been elected president, including John Adams, Thomas Jefferson, Richard Nixon, and George H. W. Bush, to name just a few. In the second half of the twentieth century, however, few sitting vice presidents had electoral success.

THE JUDICIAL BRANCH

The Constitution says little about the judicial branch. It names the Supreme Court as the highest court in the land and declares that the head of the court should be the chief justice. But Congress, and not the Constitution, determines the size and structure of the rest of the federal court system.

Appointment to the Bench

To become a federal judge, a person must be appointed by the president and approved by the Senate. Once in office, a judge can only be forced to leave if impeached and convicted. Otherwise, federal judges serve life terms.

Judicial Review

The courts' power of **judicial review**—the power to declare laws and presidential actions unconstitutional—is not actually specified in the Constitution. The Supreme Court gave itself this power in the landmark case *Marbury v. Madison* (1803).

EXAMPLE: The courts have exercised their power of judicial review throughout American history. The Supreme Court decision *Brown v. Board of Education of Topeka, Kansas* (1954), for example, ended segregation in public schools. The Supreme Court made use of judicial review by declaring racial segregation in public facilities unconstitutional.

KEY POWERS GRANTED BY THE CONSTITUTION

Legislative Branch	Executive Branch	Judicial Branch
The power to make laws The power of the purse	The power to conduct foreign policy The power to command the armed forces The power to appoint federal judges and government officials The power to veto bills from Congress The power to grant pardons and clemency	The Supreme Court is the most powerful court in the United States

FEDERALISM

Federalism is a system of government in which the national and state governments share power. The Constitution recognizes state governments and grants them certain powers, making federalism an implicit part of the Constitution.

EXAMPLE: The national, or federal, government and the state governments share power in a variety of ways. The federal government, for example, has little power in the formation of education policy, leaving each individual state government to set its own education standards. State governments also reflect the political ideologies of their constituents, which is why different states have different laws regarding smoking, capital punishment, euthanasia, gun control, and so on.

CHANGING THE CONSTITUTION

Article V of the Constitution explains how Americans can change the Constitution. A change in the Constitution is called an **amendment.** The framers intentionally made the process of changing the Constitution difficult because they wanted the Constitution to be stable. Although more than 11,000 amendments have been proposed since 1789, only twenty-seven have been approved, or ratified.

Changing the Constitution is a two-step process:

1. An amendment must be proposed by either a two-thirds vote in both houses of Congress or by conventions called in two-thirds of the states.

2. The amendment must then be ratified by either the approval of three-fourths of the state legislatures or by special ratifying conventions held in three-fourths of the states.

Informal Methods of Changing the Constitution

Even though only twenty-seven amendments have been ratified, the Constitution has changed in other ways. For example, Congress has given the president the responsibility of submitting a budget. The president has also entered into executive agreements with foreign leaders without getting prior approval or treaty ratification from the Senate. By far the biggest informal change to the Constitution has been the Supreme Court's assertion of the power of judicial review.

THE BILL OF RIGHTS

Many states ratified the Constitution in 1788 and 1789 on the condition that Congress amend it to guarantee certain civil liberties. James Madison drafted these first ten amendments himself, which collectively became known as the **Bill of Rights.** The Bill of Rights safeguards some specific rights of both the American people and the states. The table on the next page summarizes the twenty-seven amendments to the Constitution.

CHAPTER 2

AMENDMENTS TO THE CONSTITUTION

Amendment	Date of Ratification	Content
1st	1791	Grants freedoms of religion, speech, press, petition, and assembly
2nd	1791	Grants the right to bear arms
3rd	1791	Forbids the quartering of soldiers in citizens' houses
4th	1791	Grants freedom from unreasonable searches and seizures
5th	1791	Grants the right against self-incrimination, of trial by jury, and of protection of private property
6th	1791	Grants the right to an attorney in any criminal case
7th	1791	Grants the right to a trial by jury in civil cases
8th	1791	Bans excessive bail and cruel and unusual punishment
9th	1791	States that the people's rights are not limited to those explicitly listed in the Constitution
10th	1791	States that the states' rights are not limited to those explicitly listed in the Constitution
11th	1798	Limits the jurisdiction of federal courts
12th	1804	Changes the rules for electing the vice president
13th	1865	Abolishes slavery
14th	1868	Defines American citizenship
15th	1870	Extends the right to vote to all male citizens
16th	1913	Allows Congress to levy income taxes

AMENDMENTS TO THE CONSTITUTION

Amendment	Date of Ratification	Content
17th	1913	Allows people to elect their senators directly
18th	1919	Prohibits the manufacture, sale, and transport of liquor
19th	1920	Extends the right to vote to all female citizens
20th	1933	Changes the start date of presidential and congressional terms; outlines presidential succession
21st	1933	Repeals Prohibition
22nd	1951	Sets a two-term limit on presidents
23rd	1961	Gives Washington, D.C., electoral votes
24th	1964	Outlaws poll taxes
25th	1967	Changes the order of succession to the presidency
26th	1971	Extends the right to vote to all eighteen-year-old citizens
27th	1992	Limits congressional pay raises

The Lost Amendments

Congress originally proposed twelve amendments as the Bill of Rights, but the states only ratified ten. One of the two that failed—an amendment that specified how many people each member of the House represented—never passed. But the other—which stated that pay raises voted to Congress only take effect after the next election—was finally passed as the Twenty-seventh Amendment in 1992.

The Amendment Process in the Real World

There are four possible routes to creating a new amendment: two options for proposing, plus two options for ratifying. But in practice, all but one of the twenty-seven amendments have been proposed by Congress and ratified by the state legislatures. The one exception was the Twenty-first Amendment, which repealed Prohibition. It was proposed by Congress and ratified by conventions held in three-fourths of the states. No successful amendment has ever been proposed by special conventions in two-thirds of the states.

The Struggle for Ratification

Article VII specifies that at least nine of the thirteen states had to ratify the Constitution in order for it to become law. The framers of the Constitution, however, knew that the Constitution would only have real power if all thirteen states ratified it. The debate over ratification from 1787 to 1789 was extremely bitter and divided Americans into two factions, the Federalists who supported the new Constitution and the Antifederalists who did not.

Federalists and Antifederalists disagreed on a number of issues, as indicated by the table on the next page.

FEDERALISTS VERSUS ANTIFEDERALISTS

Issue	Federalists	Antifederalists
Constitution	In favor of the Constitution	Against the Constitution
Popular Sovereignty	Feared too much democracy, so advocated limited popular election of federal officials	Feared that the Constitution took too much power away from the people
Federal Power	Wanted a strong federal government to hold the nation together	Thought the Constitution gave too much power to the federal government
State Power	Believed that states are ultimately subordinate to the federal government	Believed that states should be more powerful than the federal government because states are closer to the people
Bill of Rights	Considered unnecessary because state governments already had such bills	Considered necessary because the absence of such a bill raises the threat of tyranny

SUPPORTERS: THE FEDERALISTS

Supporters of the new Constitution, known as the **Federalists,** included such prominent figures as George Washington, Alexander Hamilton, and James Madison. Their chief concern was strengthening the national government in order to promote unity and stability.

The Federalist Papers

James Madison, Alexander Hamilton, and John Jay wrote a series of newspaper articles to convince New Yorkers to ratify the Constitution. These articles collectively are known as the *Federalist Papers* and are among the most important writings in American history. First published in 1787–1788, the papers explained the new federal system and probably helped convince many Americans in New York and in other states to approve the Constitution.

Federalist No. 10 and No. 51

Federalist No. 10 and *No. 51* are the most commonly read essays of the *Federalist Papers* because they articulate the political philosophy behind the Constitution. James Madison wrote *Federalist No. 10,* and most scholars believe he also wrote *Federalist No. 51,* which argues that we must assume government officials will be ambitious and try to expand their power. We can prevent tyranny and bad government by setting people's desires against one another. In the words of the author, "Ambition must be made to counteract ambition."

OPPONENTS: THE ANTIFEDERALISTS

The Antifederalists were a diverse group that included small farmers and shopkeepers, as well as prominent men such as Patrick Henry, George Mason, and Elbridge Gerry. Their chief complaint about the Constitution was that it took power away from the states, thereby taking power away from the people.

RATIFICATION

The debates between the two sides raged fiercely. The Federalists agreed to add a bill of rights to the Constitution as soon as possible after ratification, which convinced some in the middle to back the new document. By 1788, enough states had ratified the Constitution so that it went into effect in early 1789. The few holdouts all ratified the document by 1790.

Sample Test Questions

1. Describe Shays' Rebellion and its significance to American history.

2. Why did the Antifederalists oppose the Constitution?

3. What was the Great Compromise?

4. True or false: Senators were originally chosen by state legislatures.

5. True or false: The Bill of Rights was a part of the Constitution before it was ratified.

6. Which of the following is *not* a power held by the president?

   A. Conduct foreign policy
   B. Tax citizens
   C. Grant clemency
   D. Command the armed forces

7. Who or what determines the size of the judiciary branch?

   A. Congress
   B. The Constitution
   C. The president
   D. The Chief Justice

8. What was the Three-Fifths Compromise?

   A. A compromise over federal judges
   B. A compromise over election of senators

C. A compromise over slavery
D. A compromise over presidential power

9. Which three authors wrote the *Federalist Papers?*

A. John Adams, John Jay, and Alexander Hamilton
B. John Jay, Alexander Hamilton, and James Madison
C. James Madison, George Washington, and Alexander Hamilton
D. James Madison, Patrick Henry, and Alexander Hamilton

10. What is one way that a constitutional amendment can be ratified?

A. Approval by two-thirds of conventions called in each state
B. Approval of three-fourths of state legislatures
C. Approval by popular vote
D. Approval by Congress

ANSWERS

1. Shays' Rebellion was an uprising by farmers in western Massachusetts against high taxes and heavy debt. It was significant because it highlighted the weakness of the national government under the Articles of Confederation.

2. Antifederalists believed that the Constitution gave too much power to the national government and took too much power away from the states.

3. The Great Compromise was a compromise between delegates favoring the Virginia Plan, which called for representation by population, and the New Jersey Plan, which called for equal representation for each state. The Compromise created a bicameral legislature in which the upper house—the Senate—has equal representation for each state, whereas seats in the lower house—the House of Representatives—are apportioned according to the population of each state.

4. True

5. False

6. B

7. A

8. C

9. B

10. B

Suggested Reading

- Beard, Charles. *An Economic Interpretation of the Constitution of the United States.* New York: Macmillan, 1913.

The most famous critic of the framers, Beard argues that the Constitution was written to protect landed elites.

- Dahl, Robert. *How Democratic is the American Constitution?* 2nd ed. New Haven, Conn.: Yale University Press, 2002.

Dahl raises provocative questions about the government created by the American Constitution.

Ellis, Joseph J. *Founding Brothers: The Revolutionary Generation.* New York: Vintage, 2002.A popular and fascinating portrayal of the founders.

- Jensen, Merrill. *The Articles of Confederation.* Madison: University of Wisconsin Press, 1963.

An account of the first government of the United States.

- Storing, Herbert, ed. *The Complete Anti-Federalist.* Seven vols. Chicago: University of Chicago Press, 1981.

A comprehensive collection of Antifederalist writings.

• Wills, Gary. *Explaining America.* New York: Penguin, 1982.

A leading public intellectual explores and explains the founding of the United States.

• Wood, Gordon S. *The Creation of the American Republic.* New York: Norton, 1982.

One of the most influential and controversial accounts of the American founding.

Useful Websites

• www.constitutioncenter.org

Home website of the National Constitution Center, which has a great deal of history, news, and analyses of current debates about the Constitution.

• www.law.ou.edu/hist

The University of Oklahoma Law Center's site has many historical documents.

• www.nara.gov

The National Archives website has in-depth information on the Declaration of Independence and the Constitution.

• www.yale.edu/lawweb/avalon/constpap.htm

This website contains a through archive of documents relating to the American Revolution and the Constitution.

• www.yale.edu/lawweb/avalon/presiden/jeffpap.htm

This website has electronic versions of the papers of Thomas Jefferson, a founder perhaps best known as the author of the Declaration of Independence.

FEDERALISM

3

Overview

Federalism in the United States is a complex and ever-changing network of relations between national, state, and local governments. Federalism requires that state and local governments play a role in nearly every policy area. To fight the War on Terror, for example, the FBI, a federal organization, seeks to cooperate with state and local police forces. Worries about an impending avian flu epidemic have state health agencies and local hospitals working with the Centers for Disease Control and Prevention and the federal Department of Health. Even federal tax cuts affect state governments because states rely on the federal government for financial help. As a result, it is sometimes difficult to figure out where one level of government ends and the others begin.

There are three ways to organize power among national (or central) and state (regional or local) governments: unitary, federal, and confederal. Unitary governments concentrate almost all government power into a single national government, whereas confederal system disperse government power to regional or local governments. The federal system, also known as **federalism,** divides power between national and state governments. Under federalism, each level of government is independent and has its own powers and responsibilities. Because it is often not clear whether a state or national government has jurisdiction on a particular matter, the national and state governments alternate between cooperating and competing with each other.

THREE GOVERNMENT SYSTEMS		
System	Description	Examples
Unitary	Concentrates all power in the hands of the national government; state governments (if they exist at all) merely follow the orders of the national government	Japan, France, Sweden, Saudi Arabia
Federal	Regional and national governments both have real power, but the national government is usually supreme over the regional governments	United States, Canada, Australia, Nigeria, India, Germany
Confederal	Diffuses nearly all the power to the state governments; the national government merely keeps the states loosely bound together	The Confederate States of America, the United Nations, the European Union

The Constitutional Basis of Federalism

The U.S. Constitution does not use the term *federalism,* nor does it provide extensive details about the federal system. Nevertheless, the framers helped created a federalist system in thc United States, particularly in the ways the Constitution allocates power.

THE NATIONAL GOVERNMENT

Article VI of the Constitution declares that the Constitution and any laws passed under it form the "supreme Law of the Land" in a passage called the **supremacy clause.** This clause implies that the national government has authority over the state governments.

The Constitution grants the national government several different kinds of powers and prohibits it from taking certain actions. The Constitution outlines four major types of power: enumerated, implied, inherent, and prohibited.

THE NATIONAL GOVERNMENT'S POWERS

Type	Key Clause	Explanation	Examples
Enumerated (expressed)	Article I, Section 8	Powers explicitly granted to Congress	Declare war, coin money, levy taxes, regulate interstate commerce
Implied	Necessary and proper (Article I, Section 8)	Powers that Congress has assumed in order to better do its job	Regulate telecommunications, build interstate highways
Inherent	Preamble	Powers inherent to a sovereign nation	Defend itself from foreign and domestic enemies
Prohibited	Article I, Section 9	Powers prohibited to the national government	Suspend the writ of habeas corpus, tax exports

Enumerated Powers

In Article I, Section 8, the Constitution specifically grants Congress a number of different powers, now known as the **enumerated powers.** The enumerated powers include the power to declare war, coin money, and regulate interstate commerce. Because these powers are expressly stated in the Constitution, political scientists sometimes also refer to them as **expressed powers.**

Implied Powers

The national government is not limited to the enumerated powers. At the end of Article I, Section 8, the Constitution also grants Congress the power to do anything "necessary and proper" to carry out its duties. This clause is known as the **necessary and proper clause** or the **elastic clause** because of its mutability. Because the powers bestowed by this clause are implied rather than stated, they also are known as **implied powers.**

EXAMPLE: The Constitution does not specifically grant Congress the power to regulate telecommunications because such technology did not exist at the time of the founding. But according to the Constitution, Congress has the power to regulate interstate commerce. Regulating telecommunications is considered necessary for Congress to properly regulate interstate commerce, and so Congress has since assumed this power.

McCulloch v. Maryland

This landmark Supreme Court case from 1819 concerned a state government's ability to tax a national bank. The Court, relying on the necessary and proper clause, ruled that the national government has far more powers than the Constitution enumerates in Article I, Section 8. The necessary and proper clause has allowed the national government to regulate air travel, combat industrial pollution, and foster the creation and growth of the Internet.

Inherent Powers

The preamble to the Constitution lays out the basic purposes of the United States government: to provide for the welfare of its citizens and to defend against external enemies. Because the federal government is sovereign, it also has certain powers called **inherent powers,** which are necessary to protect its citizens and defend its right to exist. The primary inherent power is self-preservation: A state has the right to defend itself from foreign and domestic enemies.

Prohibited Powers

The Constitution also explicitly denies the national government certain powers. For example, Congress cannot tax exports or tell states how to choose electors for the Electoral College. The powers denied to the national government are called the **prohibited powers.**

The Commerce Clause

The Supreme Court's decision in the 1824 case *Gibbons v. Ogden* reasserted the federal government's authority over the states. Aaron Ogden had a monopoly on steamship navigation from the state of New York. When Thomas Gibbons began operating his steamship in New York waterways, Ogden sued. The Court found that New York State did not have the right to issue a monopoly to Ogden because only the national government has the power to regulate interstate commerce. Chief Justice John Marshall referred to the **commerce clause** (which gives Congress the authority to regulate interstate commerce) of the Constitution as justification for his decision.

THE STATE GOVERNMENTS

The Constitution also grants state governments some key powers, including the right to determine how to choose delegates to the Electoral College. States also have a great deal of latitude to write their own constitutions and pass their own laws. All state governments have three branches (paralleling the national government), although the powers granted to the branches differ in each state. In some states, for example, the governor has a great deal of power, whereas in others, his or her power is severely limited. States also use a variety of methods to choose judges.

The vast expanse of the national government has led some to conclude that state governments are of secondary importance. In 1941, for example, Supreme Court justice Harlan Stone remarked that the Tenth Amendment (which reserves powers to the states) had no real meaning. State governments, however, are still vital political actors, and they have adapted to new roles and new circumstances. At the start of the twenty-first century, many states have reasserted their strength and taken a larger role in homeland security, economics, and environmental policy.

Professional and Nonprofessional Legislatures

All states have a legislative body that makes laws, and all but one of the legislatures are bicameral. (Nebraska is the lone state with a unicameral legislature.) In some states, being a legislator is a full-time job. These legislators are paid well, have large staffs, and meet in session for much of the year. Political scientists call this type of legislature a **professional legislature.** In other states, the legislators are in session for short periods, receive very little pay, and have almost no staff. These states pride themselves on having nonprofessional citizen legislators rather than professional politicians.

Reserved Powers

The Tenth Amendment states that the powers not granted to the national government, and not prohibited to state governments, are "reserved to the States." Political scientists call this the **reservation clause,** and the powers that states derive from this clause are known as the **reserved powers.**

Concurrent Powers

Powers held by both states and the national government are known as **concurrent powers.** The power to tax is an example of a concurrent power: People pay taxes at the local, state, and federal levels.

The Full Faith and Credit Clause

The **full faith and credit clause** (found in Article IV of the Constitution) both establishes and limits state powers. It declares that state governments must respect the laws and decisions of other state governments, such as driver licenses and marriage certificates issued by other states. To some extent, then, the clause expands state power: A state's decision is binding on other states. At the same time, the clause limits state power by forcing the states to honor one another's laws.

LOCAL GOVERNMENTS

Although the Constitution mentions state governments and grants them some specific powers, it does not mention local governments at all. Courts have interpreted this omission to mean that local governments are entirely under the authority of state governments and that a state can create and abolish local governments as it sees fit.

> **State Power**
>
> The most obvious example of state supremacy over local government is that state governments take over local institutions somewhat regularly. State governments also have the power to redefine local governments, stripping their powers and changing the laws. In 1995, for example, the state of Illinois gave the mayor of Chicago almost complete control of the Chicago school system because the previous board of education had failed to improve schools.

Types of Local Government

States have created a multitude of types of local government. In fact, there are approximately 84,000 local governments in the United States. Each state has the power to define local government in any way it wants, allocating different types and degrees of power and responsibility. For a local government to have power, it must be granted a **charter** by the state, specifying its powers and responsibilities.

Most states grant some degree of autonomy to local governments. This autonomy is known as **home rule:** a promise by the state government to refrain from interfering in local issues. State governments give up this power because local governments with substantial autonomy can often manage local affairs better than the state government could. Ultimately, however, the state can still take power away from local governments, even those with home rule.

Some states have a complicated patchwork of town governments, with villages, townships, counties, and cities all having different powers. The most common—and probably the least known—type of local government is called a **special district,** a local government created to deal with a single issue or problem. Special districts frequently overlap with other types of local government, and the range of powers they possess varies greatly. Control of special districts also varies greatly: Some have elected leadership, whereas others have leaders appointed by the governor or legislature.

EXAMPLE: Special districts are the most numerous type of government in the United States—totaling more than 39,000 across the country. They are also the most diverse. In some states, boards of education are special districts. Most states also have very specialized districts, such as water reclamation districts, boards to oversee public universities, and economic development districts. In some states, many of these districts have elected leaders. In Illinois, for example, citizens vote for dozens of local governments. Some special districts have the power to borrow money and oversee major construction projects (such as bridges, landfills, and treatment plants).

History of Federalism

Federalism has evolved over the course of American history. At different points in time, the balance and boundaries between the national and state government have changed substantially. In the twentieth century, the role of the national government expanded dramatically, and it continues to expand in the twenty-first century.

DUAL FEDERALISM (1789–1945)

Dual federalism describes the nature of federalism for the first 150 years of the American republic, roughly 1789 through World War II. The Constitution outlined provisions for two types of government in the United States, national and state. For the most part, the national government dealt with national defense, foreign policy, and fostering commerce, whereas the states dealt with local matters, economic regulation, and criminal law. This type of federalism is also called **layer-cake federalism** because, like a layer cake, the states' and the national governments each had their own distinct areas of responsibility, and the different levels rarely overlapped.

Layer-Cake Federalism

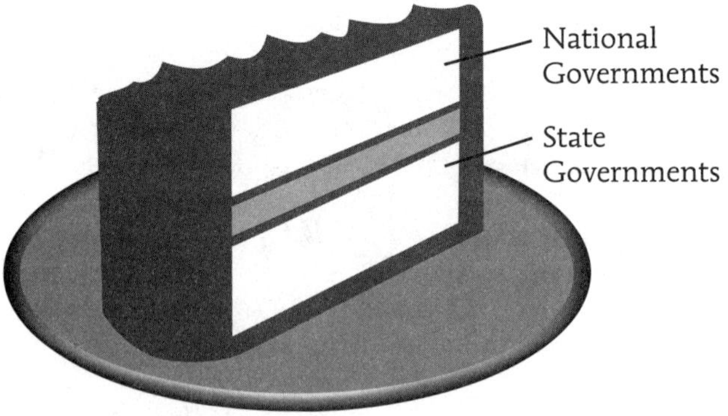

The Civil War and the Fourteenth Amendment (1861–1868)

Part of the disputes that led to the Civil War (1861–1865) concerned federalism. Many Southerners felt that state governments alone had the right to make important decisions, such as whether slavery should be legal. Advocates of **states' rights** believed that the individual state governments had power over the federal government because the states had ratified the Constitution to create the federal government in the first place. Most Southern states eventually seceded from the Union because they felt that secession was the only way to protect their rights. But Abraham Lincoln and many Northerners held that the Union could not be dissolved. The Union victory solidified the federal government's power over the states and ended the debate over states' rights.

The Fourteenth Amendment, ratified a few years after the Civil War in 1868, includes three key clauses, which limit state power and protect the basic rights of citizens:

1. The **privileges and immunities clause** declares that no state can deny any citizen the privileges and immunities of American citizenship.

2. The **due process clause** limits states' abilities to deprive citizens of their legal rights.

3. The **equal protection clause** declares that all people get the equal protection of the laws

Industrialization and Globalization (1865–1945)

The nature of government and politics in the United States changed dramatically in the late nineteenth and early twentieth centuries. The national government assumed a larger role as a result of two major events:

1. **Industrialization:** The economy became a national, industrial economy, and the federal government was much better equipped than the states to deal with this change. For much of the nineteenth century, the government pursued a hands-off, laissez-faire economic policy, but it began to take a stronger regulatory role in the early twentieth century.

2. **Globalization:** Because of its vast economy and its extensive trading networks, the United States emerged as a global economic power. The federal government assumed a greater economic role as American businesses and states began trading abroad heavily.

Although these events played out over many decades, they reached their high points during the presidency of Franklin Roosevelt (1933–1945). The Great Depression, brought about by the crash of the stock market in 1929, was one of the most severe economic downturns in American history. Many businesses failed, roughly one-third of the population was out of work, and poverty was widespread. In response, Roosevelt implemented the New Deal, a series of programs and policies that attempted to revive the economy and prevent further depression. The New Deal included increased regulation of banking and commerce and programs to alleviate poverty, including the formation of the Works Progress Administration and a social security plan. In order to implement these programs, the national government had to grow dramatically, which consequently took power away from the states.

COOPERATIVE FEDERALISM (1945–1969)

Federalism over much of the last century has more closely resembled a marble cake rather than a layer cake as federal authority and state authority have become intertwined. The national government has become integrated with the state and local governments, making it difficult to tell where one type of government begins and the other types end. State and local governments administer many federal programs, for example, and states depend heavily on federal funds to support their own programs. This type of federalism is called **cooperative federalism,** or **marble-cake federalism.**

Marble-Cake Federalism

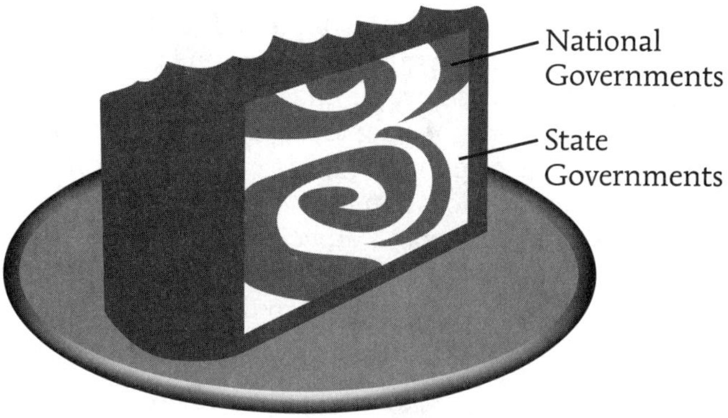

NEW FEDERALISM (1969–PRESENT)

Since the 1970s, political leaders and scholars of the **New Federalism** school have argued that the national government has grown too powerful and that power should be given back to the states. Although the national government remains extremely important, state governments have regained some power. Richard Nixon began supporting New Federalism during his presidency (1969–1974), and every president since Nixon has continued to support the return of some powers to state and local governments. Although political leaders disagree on the details, most support the general principle of giving power to the states.

New Federalism has taken concrete form in a variety of policies. New Federalists have argued for specific limits on federal power, as well as **devolution,** a policy of giving states power and responsibility for some programs. For example, the 1996 welfare reforms gave states the ability to spend federal dollars as they saw fit. Supporters claim that local and state governments can be more effective because they understand the circumstances of the issue in their state. They argue that a one-size-fits-all program imposed by Washington cannot function as effectively.

Advantages and Disadvantages of New Federalism

New Federalism appeals to many people because of its emphasis on local and state governments. Many Americans feel that the national government has become too intrusive and unaccountable. These people champion state and local government as closer to the people and thus more accountable. However, Americans often want a single seat of power for some tasks. Competing local and state governments can cause more problems than they solve, especially during emergencies. For example, the terrible hurricanes of 2005 led residents of Louisiana, Mississippi, and Alabama to demand a better, more unified national response.

The Supreme Court and New Federalism

The Supreme Court has played a New Federalist role by siding with state governments in a number of cases. Perhaps the most well known of these cases is *United States v. Lopez* (1995), in which the Court ruled that Congress had overstepped its authority in creating gun-free school zones. More controversially, in 2000, the Court struck down parts of the Violence Against Women Act (1994) for much the same reason in *United States v. Morrison.* In other cases, the court has ruled that state governments cannot be sued for violating rights established by federal law. Overall, the Supreme Court in the 1990s reduced the power of the federal government in important ways, particularly in relation to the commerce clause.

Federalism in Practice

Money plays a key role in the federal government's relationship with the states. Congress gives money to the states, for example, but stipulates how this money should be used in order to force the states to cooperate with federal policies.

FEDERAL AID TO THE STATES

Since World War II, states have come to rely heavily on federal money. Likewise, the national government has also relied on the states to administer some federal policies, a practice called **fiscal federalism.** The term **grants-in-aid** refers to the federal government giving money to the states for a particular purpose. There are two general types of grants-in-aid:

1. **Block grants:** Money given for a fairly broad purpose with few strings attached.
2. **Categorical grants:** Money given for a specific purpose that comes with restrictions concerning how the money should be spent. There are two types of categorical grants:
   - **Project grants:** Money states apply for by submitting specific project proposals
   - **Formula grants:** Money given to states according to a mathematical formula

EXAMPLE: When the Republicans retook Congress in 1994, they changed many federal grants into block grants. Instead of giving money to states to buy textbooks or repair schools, for example, Congress gave states blocks of money to spend on education in any way the states saw fit.

Revenue Sharing

In 1972, the Nixon Administration initiated a practice called *revenue sharing*, in which the federal government gave money to the states with no restrictions attached whatsoever. Presidents Gerald Ford and Jimmy Carter relied less on revenue sharing, which disappeared completely in the 1980s during the Reagan Administration.

FEDERAL PRESSURE ON THE STATES

The federal government uses a number of tactics to compel states to follow its policies and guidelines. Congress can order states to comply but usually applies pressure more subtly by threatening to withhold funds from disobedient states.

EXAMPLE: When the federal government decided to raise the drinking age to twenty-one, it denied certain highway funds to states that opted not to comply.

Mandates

Sometimes the federal government orders states to do certain things, such as obeying housing laws or environmental regulations. These demands are called **mandates.** An **unfunded mandate** is one for which the federal government provides no money. For example, the federal government has required state and local governments to live up to the Americans with Disabilities Act without providing money to make buildings accessible to handicapped people. State governments resent unfunded mandates because they drain state coffers.

One way for Congress to pass mandates is to impose regulations and standards on state and local governments. In the past, Congress has forced state governments to meet certain environmental standards, for example. Scholars call this practice **regulated federalism.**

PREEMPTION

Because of the supremacy clause, all laws passed by the national government take priority over state and local laws. The national government, then, can override state laws if it can demonstrate a compelling national interest; this practice is called **preemption.**

HORIZONTAL FEDERALISM

Horizontal federalism refers to the ways state governments relate to one another. States often compete or cooperate on many different issues, from environmental policy to economic development. One state, for example, may lower its tax rate in order to attract businesses away from other states. States have a great deal of leeway in how they behave toward one another.

Advantages and Disadvantages of Federalism

The pros and cons of federalism have been the subject of debate since the creation of the republic.

FEDERALISM'S ADVANTAGES

Proponents argue that federalism does the following:

- **Fosters state loyalties:** Many Americans feel close ties to their home state, and federalism maintains that connection by giving power to the states.
- **Practices pragmatism:** Running a country the size of the United States, with such a diverse population, is much easier to do if power is given to local officials. Likewise, state and local officials are closer to the problems of their areas, so it makes sense for them to choose policies to solve those problems.
- **Creates laboratories of democracy:** State governments can experiment with policies, and other states (and the federal government) can learn from their successes and failures.

EXAMPLE: California has frequently led the nation in environmental regulations: Many measures adopted by California are subsequently adopted by other states. And during the 1990s, Wisconsin governor Tommy Thompson experimented with welfare policy, and those experiments influenced federal welfare reform.

- **Leads to political stability:** By removing the national government from some contentious issue areas, federalism allowed the early U.S. government to achieve and maintain stability.
- **Encourages pluralism:** Federal systems expand government on national, state, and local levels, giving people more access to leaders and opportunities to get involved in their government.
- **Ensures the separation of powers and prevents tyranny:** Even if one person or group took control of all three branches of the federal government, federalism ensures that state governments would still function independently. Federalism, therefore, fulfills the framers' vision of a governmental structure that ensures liberty.

FEDERALISM'S DISADVANTAGES

Critics argue that federalism falls short in two ways:

- **Prevents the creation of a national policy:** The United States does not have a single policy on issues; instead, it has fifty-one policies, which often leads to confusion.
- **Leads to a lack of accountability:** The overlap of the boundaries among national and state governments makes it tricky to assign blame for failed policies.

Citizen Ignorance

Critics argue that federalism cannot function well due to ignorance. Most Americans know little about their state and local governments, and turnout in state and local elections is often less than 25 percent. Citizens consequently often ignore state and local governments, even though these governments have a lot of power to affect people's lives.

Sample Test Questions

1. How does federalism differ from unitary and confederal systems?

2. Describe the difference between layer-cake and marble-cake federalism.

3. What two historical events prompted the rise in power of the federal government?

4. True or false: *McCulloch v. Maryland* formed the constitutional basis for the restriction of federal power.

5. True or false: Since the 1980s, the Supreme Court has increasingly sided with the states in disputes with the federal government.

6. Which of the following is not a type of federal aid given to state governments?

A. Revenue-sharing
B. Dual federalism
C. Categorical grants
D. Block grants

7. What does an unfunded mandate do?

A. It requires states to do certain things.
B. It gives states money with no strings attached.
C. It requires states to do certain things without providing any money.
D. It clarifies how state governments relate to one another.

8. Which Supreme Court case gave the federal government extensive power through the commerce clause?

A. *McCulloch v. Maryland*
B. *Ogden v. Maryland*
C. *Marbury v. Madison*
D. *Gibbons v. Ogden*

9. What kind of powers are held by both the states and the federal government?

A. Concurrent powers
B. Enumerated powers
C. Explicit powers
D. Implied powers

10. Which of the following is an argument in favor of federalism?

A. It protects prejudice and inequality.
B. The United States lacks a coherent national policy.
C. It is impractical.
D. It allows states to experiment with different policies.

ANSWERS

1. In a federal system, a national government and the state governments share power. In a unitary system, all power lies with the national government, whereas in a confederation, the vast majority of power rests with the states.

2. In dual federalism, which existed through most of the nineteenth century, the powers and issue areas of state and federal governments rarely overlapped, much like a layer cake. Cooperative federalism describes federalism in much of the twentieth century, where the powers and responsibilities of the states and federal government overlap a great deal, resembling a marble cake.

3. The two key events that occurred in the late nineteenth and early twentieth centuries were the development of a national industrial economy and the emergence of the United States as a world power.

4. False

5. True

6. B

7. C

8. D

9. A

10. D

Suggested Reading

• Bensel, Richard. *Sectionalism and American Political Development: 1880-1980.* Madison: University of Wisconsin Press, 1984.

A look at the effects of sectionalism on American history.

• Dye, Thomas R. *American Federalism: Competition Among Governments.* Lexington, Mass.: Lexington Books, 1990.

A prominent political scientist studies how different governments compete on many matters.

• Farber, Daniel A. *Lincoln's Constitution.* Chicago: University of Chicago Press, 2003.

States' rights and the extent of federal power were key issues in the events that led to the Civil War. Farber looks at the Constitution as it existed in Lincoln's time and thinks through the arguments used by the contending sides in their disputes.

• Kelley, E. Wood. *Policy and Politics in the United States: The Limits of Localism.* Philadelphia: Temple University Press, 1987.

What effect do local and state politics have on American policy? Kelley answers this question—and others—in this work.

• Nagel, Robert. *The Implosion of American Federalism.* New York: Oxford University Press, 2002.

Nagel laments the loss of state power despite court rulings in favor of states in recent years. He warns that centralized power is dangerous to a democratic society.

• Peterson, Paul E. *The Price of Federalism.* Washington, D.C.: Brookings, 1995

Peterson looks at the costs of America's federal system.

- Walker, David B. *The Rebirth of Federalism.* 2nd ed. Chatham, NJ: Chatham, 2000.

Walker takes a look at the current state of federalism in a positive light.

- Yarbrough, Tinsley. *The Rehnquist Court and the Constitution.* New York: Oxford University Press, 2000.

The Rehnquist Court limited federal power by striking down a number of laws. This book examines all of the Rehnquist Court's decisions, including those on federalism.

Useful Websites

- http://urban.org/center/anf/index.cfm

The Urban Institute's program, known as "Assessing the New Federalism," examines the effects of recent laws and court decisions on federalism.

- www.cog.org

The homepage for the Washington Metropolitan Council of Governments, a fairly successful collaboration among state and local governments around Washington, D.C.

- www.csg.org

The Council of State Governments helps coordinate state policies and practices.

- www.nga.org

The National Governors' Association also helps coordinate state policies and practices.

- www.temple.edu/federalism

The Center for the Study of Federalism at Temple University offers information on American federalism.

CONGRESS

4

Overview

An old adage about American life states that when you have a problem, you should call your representative in Congress. Although Congress primarily passes laws, its members also do many other things, from helping a constituent navigate the social security system to impeaching federal officials to attending the groundbreaking of civic buildings. Congress is the branch of the federal government closest to the people, and the framers of the Constitution intended Congress to be the most powerful of the three branches of government. In the nineteenth and twentieth centuries, however, Congress decreased in importance as the powers of the presidency expanded. Nevertheless, Congress remains a vital component of American politics and government.

The Structure of Congress

Article I of the Constitution describes the legislative branch, called **Congress.** After hashing out the terms of the Great Compromise, the framers created a **bicameral** legislature, with a lower chamber called the House of Representatives and an upper chamber called the Senate.

THE HOUSE OF REPRESENTATIVES

The House of Representatives is meant to be "the people's house," or the part of government most responsive to public opinion. Each state's representation in the House is based on population, with each state getting at least one member. California has the most members (54), while several states, including Delaware, Vermont, Montana, and Alaska, each have only one member. Every member of the House represents a district within a state, and each district has roughly the same population (roughly 660,000 in 2006). Membership in the House is capped at 435.

To keep them responsive to the people, House members face reelection every two years, and the entire body is elected at the same time. A person must be twenty-five years old and a resident of the state he or she represents in order to run for a seat in the House.

THE SENATE

The framers envisioned the Senate as a body of statesmen who make decisions based on experience and wisdom, not on the unpredictable whims of the people. As a check on excessive democracy, only one-third of the Senate is elected every two years. The framers hoped that staggered elections of only portions of the Senate would prevent a single popular faction from taking control of the whole Senate in a single election. The framers of the Constitution were often wary of public opinion, so they attempted to structure the national government such that the public could never take control of it at one time. Also, because both the Senate and House must pass identical versions of a **bill**, the Senate can check any democratic excesses in the House.

Representation in the Senate is equal for every state: Each state has two senators. Senators serve six-year terms. The length of the term is supposed to insulate senators from public opinion and allow them to act independently. For nearly a hundred years, senators were appointed by the legislatures of the states they represented. The Seventeenth Amendment, ratified in 1913, gave the people the power to elect their senators directly. To serve in the Senate, a person must be at least thirty years old and live in the state he or she represents.

The Effect of Equal Representation

The representation system in the Senate benefits small states because all states have equal representation regardless of their population. As of the 2000 census, for example, California's population was roughly 36 million, whereas Wyoming's was roughly 509,000, but each state still has two senators. This causes issues important to small states to get a lot of attention and money. Agriculture is a good example: Most Americans do not work in the agricultural sector, yet the federal government spends huge amounts of money on agriculture every year.

POLITICAL PARTIES AND LEADERSHIP

Political parties play an important role in Congress because the houses are organized around parties. Although the Constitution does not mention political parties, they have developed into essential institutions of American politics. Although there were (and are) dozens of political parties, the American political system quickly evolved into a two-party system, which means that two parties have almost always dominated American politics. Since the 1850s, the dominant political parties in the United States have been the Democrats and the Republicans. Each chamber of Congress has a **majority party,** which holds more than half of the seats, and a **minority party,** which holds less than half. The parties elect their own leadership, organize for votes, and formulate strategy.

At the start of every congressional session, the parties meet in a **caucus,** an informal meeting of people with common interests. Caucuses consist of all members interested in a particular issue, and examples include the congressional Black Caucus, the Travel and Tourism Caucus, and Concerned Senators for the Arts. Although caucuses have no formal power, they can be important in formulating bills and rallying support.

House Leadership

The leader of the House of Representatives is the **Speaker of the House.** The Speaker is elected by the majority party (the Democratic Party Caucus or the Republican Party Caucus, depending on which party controls the House) and sets the schedule for debates and votes on the House floor. The majority party also elects a **majority leader,** who works closely with the Speaker and the caucus leadership, and several **whips,** who count votes and connect the leadership to the rank-and-file members. The minority party in the House, meanwhile, elects a **minority leader** and several whips of its own.

The leadership in the House has a great deal of power over its party because the leaders have the ability to reward and punish members. Members who cooperate with the leadership may be given good committee assignments or even leadership of a committee. Conversely, members who defy leadership may be ostracized by other party members. Party discipline is usually very strong in the House.

Senate Leadership

According to the Constitution, the vice president of the United States presides over the Senate. In reality, however, the most senior member of the senate—also called the **president pro tempore** (informally called the president pro tem)—usually presides over the Senate in the vice president's absence. The president pro tem position is mostly a ceremonial position.

The majority party of the Senate elects a majority leader, who performs some of the same tasks as the Speaker of the House of Representatives. The minority party also elects a minority leader. Leaders in the Senate have much less ability to punish and reward members than their counterparts do in the House. Senators are expected to be independent, and party leaders give members wide latitude in how they behave.

FLOOR DEBATE RULES

A major difference between the House and Senate concerns the rules governing floor debate. In both houses, a majority of members must vote in favor of a bill for it to pass, but the rules for the debating and voting process differ greatly.

Debate in the House

Due to its large size, the House does not permit unlimited debate. Before a bill goes to the floor for debate, it must go through the **House Rules Committee,** which passes a rule to accompany each bill. This rule determines how much debate is permitted, as well as how many amendments to the bill can be proposed. A **closed rule** strongly limits or forbids any amendments, whereas an **open rule** allows for anyone to propose amendments.

Debate in the Senate

Because senators are supposed to be experienced and independent legislators, the Senate offers few rules for floor debate. In general, there are no rules: Senators can speak for as long as they wish and offer as many amendments as they want. This leads to the **filibuster,** a tactic in which a senator in the minority on a bill holds the floor indefinitely with the aim of blocking all Senate business until the majority backs down. A filibuster can be stopped by a vote of **cloture,** which requires sixty votes. Filibusters are uncommon, but even the threat of one can cause consternation among senators.

Because senators are allowed to offer as many amendments as they wish, they sometimes propose amendments that have nothing to do with the bill. These amendments are called **riders** and can serve a number of purposes. One rider may be added to attract votes—by adding funding for a popular cause, for example—whereas others can discourage votes by adding a controversial provision to a bill.

The Longest Filibuster

Filibusters are the stuff of legend, in part because of the movie *Mr. Smith Goes to Washington* (1939), in which actor Jimmy Stewart plays the part of a senator who filibusters against corrupt senators. Former senator Strom Thurmond of South Carolina holds the record for the longest filibuster: twenty-four hours and eighteen minutes against a civil rights bill in 1957.

COMMITTEES: LITTLE LEGISLATURES

Members of Congress serve on a number of committees and subcommittees. Committees are sometimes called *little legislatures* because of the influence they wield. These committees do most of the legislative work in Congress and therefore have great power in determining which bills get reviewed and in shaping the laws that are passed. Only after a committee has reviewed a bill does the whole body deliberate and vote on it. The committee system allows Congress to operate more efficiently through division of labor and specialization.

Types of Committees

There are four major types of congressional committees:

1. **Standing committees:** The most common type of committee, standing committees deal with issues of permanent legislative concern. Standing committees also handle the vast majority of legislation. Most standing committees have subcommittees covering more specific areas of an issue.

2. **Conference committees:** A very common kind of joint committee with members from both the House and the Senate. For a bill to become law, both houses must approve identical versions. When different versions are passed, the leaders create a conference committee to reconcile the differences between the two bills. Conference committees issue a single bill for both houses to vote on.

3. **Select committees:** Select committees are created for a limited period and for a specific purpose.

4. **Joint committees:** Joint committees consist of members of both houses, usually created to deal with a specific issue.

The table on the next page lists some of the current standing committees in Congress.

CONGRESSIONAL STANDING COMMITTEES	
House	**Senate**
Agriculture	Agriculture, Nutrition, and Forestry
Appropriations	Appropriations
Armed Services	Armed Services
Budget, Education, and Workforce	Banking, Housing, and Urban Affairs
Energy and Commerce	Budget
Financial Services	Commerce, Science, and Transportation
Government Reform	Energy and Natural Resources
Homeland Security	Environment and Public Works
House Administration	Finance
International Relations	Foreign Relations
Judiciary	Health, Education, Labor, and Pensions
Resources	Homeland Security and Governmental Affairs
Rules	Judiciary
Science	Rules and Administration
Small Business	Small Business and Entrepreneurship
Standards of Official Conduct	Veterans' Affairs
Transportation and Infrastructure	
Veterans' Affairs	
Ways and Means	

Committee Powers

Committees have a great deal of power over bills. Thousands of bills are introduced in Congress during each congressional session, but only a small fraction of those bills are actually put to a vote on the floor. Most bills, particularly controversial ones, die in committees. Committees review bills, hold hearings, rewrite the bill in open session (called **markup**), and choose whether to refer a bill to the whole house.

Committees are not all-powerful, especially in the House. Although most bills die in committee, the whole House can override the committee's decision to kill a bill by passing a **discharge petition,** which brings the bill out of the committee and to a vote. Discharge petitions are not that common because they anger the members of the committee that initially killed the bill.

Composition of Committees

Party leaders determine which members serve on each committee. The majority party always has a majority of members on each committee. The majority party names the chair of each committee based on seniority, power, loyalty, and other criteria. Committee chairs have substantial power: They schedule hearings and votes and can easily kill a bill if they choose. The senior committee member from the minority party is called the **ranking member.**

Members of Congress try to get good committee assignments. Most members want to be on powerful committees, such as the Ways and Means Committee (which deals with taxes and revenue), or on a committee that covers issues important to their constituents. Getting a good committee assignment can make reelection easier for members.

THE STAFF SYSTEM

Congress employs a significant number of people, called **staffers,** who assist members in a variety of ways. There are several types of staff:

- **Members' staff:** Each member has staffers who provide clerical support, help with constituent relations, and conduct research on issues important to the member. The members divide their staffers between their home offices and their offices in Washington, D.C.

- **Committee staff:** Each committee employs a number of staffers who organize and administer the committee's work. Staffers also conduct research, offer legal advice, and draft legislation.

- **Staff agencies:** Organizations created by Congress to offer policy analysis, including the Congressional Research Service and the Government Accountability Office, employ staffers.

The Powers of Congress

The framers of the Constitution intended Congress to be the preeminent branch of government, sitting at the center of national power. As a result, Congress wields significant but limited power.

POWERS GRANTED BY THE CONSTITUTION

The Constitution enumerates some powers that Congress has but also specifies some powers that Congress does not have.

Enumerated

Enumerated powers, or the **expressed powers,** are powers the Constitution explicitly grants to Congress, including the power to declare war and levy taxes.

Implied Powers

Article I, Section 8, of the Constitution also contains the **necessary and proper clause,** or the **elastic clause,** which gives Congress extra powers. As interpreted by the Supreme Court in *McCulloch v. Maryland* (1819), this clause means that Congress can assume other powers and pass laws in order to fulfill its duties. The powers granted by the necessary and proper clause are called **implied powers.**

Limits on Congress

Article I, Section 9, of the Constitution places three important limits on Congress and its powers. Congress cannot

- pass **ex post facto laws,** which outlaw acts after they have already been committed.
- pass **bills of attainder,** which punish individuals outside of the court system.
- suspend the **writ of habeas corpus,** a court order requiring the federal government to charge individuals arrested for crimes. Congress can only suspend the writ of habeas corpus during times of national emergency.

POWER IN A BICAMERAL LEGISLATURE

The House of Representatives and the Senate must jointly decide to exercise most of the powers granted to Congress. When Congress declares war, for example, both houses must pass the exact same declaration. Similarly, both houses must pass identical versions of the same law before the law can take effect. There are some exceptions, however, in which the House and the Senate wield power alone.

Unique Powers of the House

The Constitution gives the House of Representatives a few unique powers, including the power to do the following:

- Propose all tax bills.
- Impeach a federal official. **Impeachment** is the process of formally charging a government official with an offense serious enough to warrant removal from office.

Unique Powers of the Senate

The Constitution also grants the Senate a few unique powers, including the power to do the following:

- Approve presidential appointments to key federal offices
- Confirm all federal judicial appointments
- Ratify treaties
- Try impeached officials

EXAMPLE: The Senate acquitted both Andrew Johnson and Bill Clinton during their respective impeachment trials (in 1868 and 1999, respectively), so the presidents remained in office.

The Functions of Congress

Congress has five main functions: lawmaking, representing the people, performing oversight, helping constituents, and educating the public.

LAWMAKING

The primary function of Congress is to pass rules that all Americans must obey, a function called **lawmaking.** Congress deals in a huge range of matters, from regulating television to passing a federal budget to voting on gun control. Many of the bills considered by Congress originate with the executive branch, but only Congress can create laws. Parties, interest groups, and constituents all influence members of Congress in their vote choices, and members also compromise and negotiate with one another to reach agreements. A common practice is **logrolling,** in which members agree to vote for one another's bills. For more on lawmaking, see "The Legislative Process" section later in this chapter.

REPRESENTING THE PEOPLE

Congress represents the people of the United States. Members serve their **constituents,** the people who live in the district from which they are elected. The old adage that "all politics is local" applies to Congress: Members must please their constituents if they want to stay in office, and every issue must therefore be considered from the perspectives of those constituents. There are three theories of representation, or how people choose their representatives: trustee representation, sociological representation, and agency representation.

Trustee Representation

According to the theory of **trustee representation,** the people choose a representative whose judgment and experience they trust. The representative votes for what he or she thinks is right, regardless of the opinions of the constituents. Because the constituents trust their representative's judgment, they will not be angry every time they disagree with the representative. A constituent who views his or her representative as a trustee need not pay close attention to political events. For key issues, the constituent likely monitors the representative's votes, but for other matters, the constituent likely trusts the representative and does not monitor votes too closely.

Sociological Representation

According to the theory of **sociological representation,** the people choose a representative whose ethnic, religious, racial, social, or educational background resembles their own. Because the views of people with similar backgrounds tend to be similar, the representative will act in ways that suit his or her constituents. Thus, constituents do not need to monitor their representatives too closely.

Agency Representation

According to the theory of **agency representation,** the people choose a representative to carry out their wishes in Congress. If the representative does not do what the constituents want, then the constituents "fire" the member by electing someone else in the next election. Those who view their representatives as agents tend to closely monitor their representatives because they must know what the representative does in order to keep him or her accountable. This theory is also known as the **instructed-delegate representation.**

The Representativeness of Representatives

On average, members of Congress do not resemble their constituents. The typical congressperson is a white Protestant male, a lawyer by profession, and wealthier than the average citizen. The number of women, African Americans, and Hispanics has increased substantially since 1990, but women and minorities are still proportionally underrepresented. The following chart compares the population of the United States to the members of Congress (data taken from the 2000 census and the 108th Congress).

Characteristic	U.S. Population	House	Senate
Median Age	35.3	54	59.5
Percentage of Minorities	24.9	15.4	3
Percentage of Women	50.9	14.3	14
Percentage of Population with Assets Worth $1 Million or More	0.7	16	33

PERFORMING OVERSIGHT

Congress oversees the bureaucracy and ensures that laws go into effect properly through a process known as **oversight.** Committees regularly hold hearings and launch investigations to check for abuse and waste.

EXAMPLE: Some of the most memorable moments in political history have come as a result of oversight. In the early and mid-1970s, both houses had committees investigating the Watergate scandal, which eventually pushed President Richard Nixon out of office. Americans closely followed similar hearings about the Iran-Contra scandal in the 1980s.

Political Uses of Oversight

Sometimes members of Congress will use oversight for political gain. In the 1990s, for example, Congress held hearings about IRS abuse of taxpayers. Although the stories told there were true, they accounted for a minuscule percentage of cases. Nevertheless, members were happy to publicize the hearings in order to look like they were cracking down on the IRS, a federal agency citizens love to hate. Sometimes fear of oversight is used as a political tool. Leading up to the 2006 elections, for example, Republicans charged that a Democratic takeover of either house of Congress would lead to punitive oversight investigations.

The Government Accountability Office

The **Government Accountability Office (GAO)** is the main investigative agency of Congress. The GAO regularly examines federal expenditures and activities on request from Congress. GAO reports are usually nonpartisan and well researched. These reports often form the basis of new legislation and at times spark public outcry.

HELPING CONSTITUENTS

Members do a variety of things to please and aid their constituents. Sometimes they support legislation that will help the district. Members also have their staff engage in **casework,** which helps constituents with individual problems from recommendations for military academies to signing up for Medicare. Part of casework involves acting as an **ombudsperson,** a person who investigates complaints against government agencies or employees. To stay in touch with their constituents, members spend as much time in their districts as possible, performing community service, attending the openings of new businesses, and meeting with local leaders to discuss key issues. The way members of Congress behave at home is known collectively as their **home style.**

Pork

Members of Congress help their constituents by getting money for their districts through legislation. The federal government, for example, may fund a highway project or a research project at a local university. The term **pork** refers to federal money that is funneled into a specific legislative district. A member of Congress will often insert pork into a bill in order to gain another member's support or to win votes back home.

EXAMPLE: An infamous example of pork in 2006 was the so-called bridge to nowhere, a bridge in a remote part of Alaska (to be built with federal money) that would be used by very few people. The bridge was inserted into the budget by Alaska senator Ted Stevens.

> **Defining Pork**
>
> To some degree, one's person's pork is another person's worthy way to spend money. People often label money as "pork" when the money goes to someone else's district.

EDUCATING THE PUBLIC

Congress also engages in **public education,** informing the public about issues and what Congress intends to do or has done about them. Members of Congress keep in touch with their constituents and educate them on the issues through mailings and websites. Congresspeople present various opinions on such issues as gun control and abortion, which allows the public to become better informed.

Congress picks the issues about which to debate and act on through a process known as **agenda setting.** Agenda setting informs people about which issues are most pressing to members of Congress and lets them know what Congress wants to do about those issues.

The Legislative Process

Congress's primary duty is to pass laws. The legislative process is often slow, just as the framers of the Constitution intended. The framers believed that a slow-moving legislature would be less able to infringe on citizens' rights and liberties.

BILLS AND LAWS

Most bills that Congress considers are public bills, meaning that they affect the public as a whole. A **private bill** grants some relief or benefit to a single person, named in the bill. Many private bills help foreign nationals obtain visas, but they can cover a variety of other matters.

The process through which a bill becomes law occurs in several stages in both houses:

1. **Introduction:** Only a member of Congress may introduce a bill. After a bill is introduced, it is assigned a designation number. Only members of the House of Representatives may introduce bills concerning taxes.

2. **Referral to committee:** The leader of the house in which the bill was introduced then refers the bill to an appropriate committee or committees.

3. **Committee action:** The committees can refer the bill to subcommittees for action, hearings, markup sessions, and votes. The committee can also kill the bill by doing nothing at all, a process known as **pigeonholing.**

4. **Referral to the full body:** If a committee approves a bill, the bill is sent on to the full House or Senate.

5. **Floor debate and vote:** The full body debates the bill and then votes. The two houses differ significantly in how they handle debate:

    - In the House, the Rules Committee has the power to limit debate and the number of amendments offered during debate. A vote in which every member's vote is recorded is called a **roll-call vote.**

    - In the Senate, members are allowed to speak as much as they wish and to propose as many amendments as they wish. There is no Senate Rules Committee.

6. **Conference committee:** Often, the two houses produce different versions of a single bill. When this happens, both houses appoint members to a conference committee, which works to combine the versions. After the conference committee's report, both houses must vote on the new bill.

7. **The President:** The president's only official legislative duty is to sign or veto bills passed by Congress. If the president signs the bill, it becomes law. If the bill is vetoed, it goes back to Congress, which can override the veto with a two-thirds vote in both houses. Veto overrides are rare—it is extremely difficult to get two-thirds of each house of Congress to agree to override. Instead, presidential vetoes usually kill bills.

Sometimes the president chooses to do nothing with bills that Congress sends. If the president still has not signed or vetoed the bill after ten days, the bill becomes law if Congress is in session. If Congress has since adjourned, the bill does not become law. This is called a **pocket veto.**

How a Bill Becomes a Law

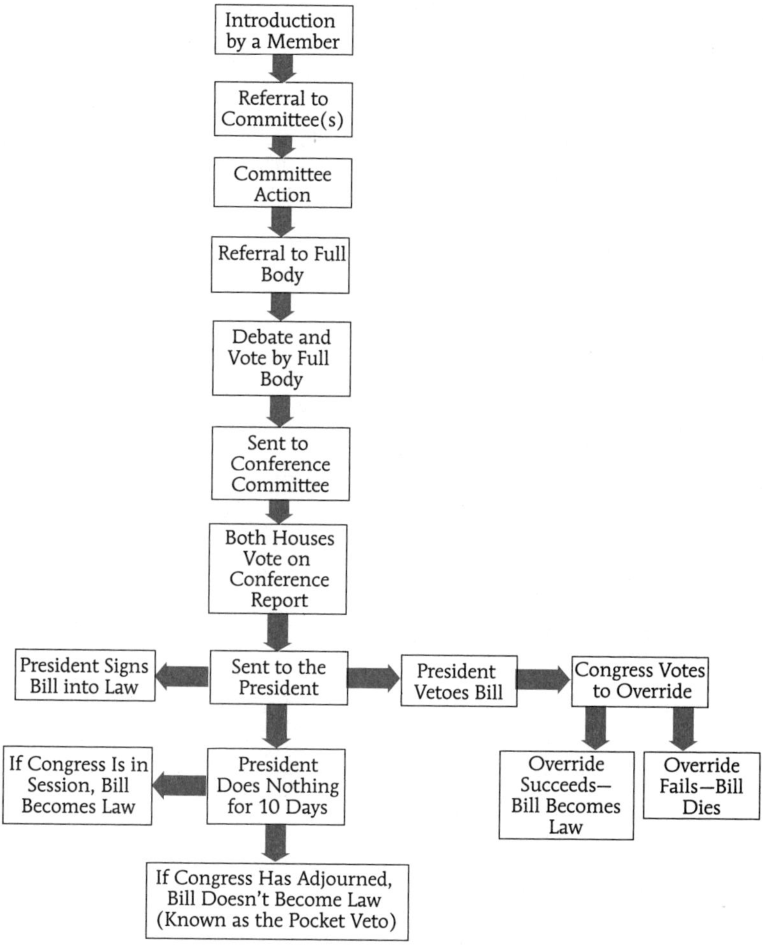

THE BUDGET

Congress must also pass the federal budget. According to the Constitution, Congress must approve all government spending. In other words, Congress has the **power of the purse.** Many congressional activities are related to spending and generating revenue. The U.S. government runs on a **fiscal year,** a twelve-month period used for accounting purposes. Currently, the fiscal years starts on the first day of October, but Congress has the power to change the start date. Congress must pass a budget for every fiscal year.

Because the budget is so complex, the president and Congress begin work on it as much as eighteen months before the start of a fiscal year. The president submits a budget proposal to Congress every January for the upcoming fiscal year. Congress then acts on the proposal, usually granting much of what the president wants. To prevent a government shutdown, Congress must pass the budget by the end of the fiscal year.

Authorization and Appropriation

Spending money is a two-step process:

1. Congress must **authorize** the money being spent. Authorization is a declaration by a committee that a specific amount of money will be made available to an agency or department.

2. After authorizing expenditures, Congress must **appropriate** the money by declaring how much of the authorized money an agency or department will spend. Sometimes **appropriation bills** come with strict guidelines for spending the money.

Congress usually ends up creating an appropriation bill for each government department, although sometimes departments are combined into a single bill. Each bill must be passed for that department to receive funding. Some appropriation bills are easily passed, but others are very controversial.

Continuing Resolutions

Congress must pass a budget every year by the start of the new fiscal year, which means that appropriation bills must be passed for every part of the government. If an appropriation bill does not pass, then the department whose budget is being discussed will shut down, and all nonessential employees will be temporarily out of work. Sometimes Congress passes a **continuing resolution,** which provides funding for a limited period (usually a week or two). Congress then uses the extra time to reach an agreement on the budget.

> **The Politics of Government Shutdowns**
>
> The federal government last shut down in 1995. The Republican-controlled Congress could not agree with President Bill Clinton on the budget, and Congress allowed the government to shut down to make the Democratic president look bad. Clinton, however, managed to convince most Americans that the shutdown was Congress's fault, which damaged the Republicans' reputations. Clinton gained a great deal of leverage over Congress via his comments in the press.

Congressional Elections

Every two years, voters elect all of the members of the House and one-third of the Senate. Although the Constitution lays out certain rules about how members of Congress should be elected, the states determine the details of elections, such as who can vote, how the votes will be counted, and the appearance of the ballots. There are three types of congressional elections: **primary elections, general elections,** and **special elections.**

TYPES OF ELECTIONS	
Type of Election	Explanation
Primary Election	Contest between candidates within a party to choose the party's nominee
General Election	Contest between all party nominees and independent candidates; the winner becomes a member of Congress
Special Election	Contest to replace a member of Congress who leaves office in between regular elections

Midterm elections are general elections that fall between presidential elections (or in the middle of the president's term). The general election of 2002, for example, was a midterm election because it fell between the general elections of 2000 and 2004 in which George W. Bush was elected and then reelected president.

Election by Governor

Special elections are called to replace a member of Congress who has died, become ill, or otherwise left office. Not all states have special elections; in some states, the governor can appoint someone who will serve out the remainder of the member's term.

CANDIDATES AND CAMPAIGNS

Who runs for Congress? Congress consists of a self-selecting group of people who choose to run on their own initiative. Sometimes the party organizations will ask a particular person to run. The table on the next page summarizes the requirements for holding office in the House and Senate.

ELIGIBILITY FOR CONGRESS		
	House of Representatives	**Senate**
Minimum Age	25	30
Minimum Length of Citizenship	7 years	9 years
State Residency	Yes	Yes

Age in the House

According to the Congressional Research Service, the youngest member of the 108th Congress was Adam Putnam, a Republican representative from Florida, age 30, and the oldest member was Ralph Hall, a Republican representative from Texas, age 81.

In the past few decades, congressional elections have become very expensive. In the early 2000s, the average winning House race cost roughly $750,000, whereas a winning Senate campaign cost about $5 million. The money comes from a variety of sources: individual donors, political action committees (PACs), and party organizations (some of which is soft money—unregulated money given to political parties and advocacy groups). Federal law regulates donations, limiting how much an individual and a PAC can donate in a given election cycle. In 2002, Congress passed the Bipartisan Campaign Reform Act (commonly known as McCain-Feingold), which banned soft money.

Incumbent Advantage

An **incumbent** is a person who currently holds an office. Incumbents running for reelection have an **incumbent advantage,** which makes them extremely difficult to defeat. Incumbency gives a candidate significant benefits: better name recognition, a track record of pork and casework, and privileges of congressional membership, such as **franking,** which is the ability to mail letters to constituents for free. More than 90 percent of all incumbents win reelection in House races, although that number is a bit lower in the Senate. Challenging an incumbent, particularly one who has been in office for a while, is an uphill fight.

The High Cost of Campaigning

To win, candidates must raise large amounts of money, which takes considerable time and energy. Incumbents have a far easier time raising money than challengers, and sometimes incumbents out-fundraise their opponents by astonishing amounts. In the 2003–2004 election cycle, for example, incumbent Colorado congressman Mark Udall raised approximately $1.1 million, whereas his challenger, Stephen Michael Hackman, raised only $8,000. Not surprisingly, Udall was reelected.

TERM LIMITS

Members of Congress can be reelected as many times as the people will reelect them, and some members have served many, many years in office. In May 2006, for example, Senator Robert Byrd of West Virginia became the longest-serving senator after having served eight six-year terms. Some people argue that the number of terms members serve should be limited in order to maintain democracy. **Term limits** exist for many state and local offices, as well as for the office of the president, but establishing them for members of Congress would require a constitutional amendment.

REAPPORTIONMENT AND REDISTRICTING

In order to keep representation in the House in line with population shifts, the Constitution mandates that a **census** be taken every ten years. Representation is then adjusted after the census: Some states lose members, whereas others gain members. Political scientists call districts that have become unfairly populous or empty because of population shifts **malapportioned districts.** The process of correcting malapportionment is called **reapportionment.**

If a state gains or loses seats, the state government must redraw its district boundaries, a process known as **redistricting.** Sometimes the party that controls the state government uses redistricting to its own political advantage, a process known as **gerrymandering.** By combining areas that usually vote for one party, politicians can all but ensure their party will win that seat.

The courts have gotten involved in reapportionment and redistricting, declaring that such matters are **justiciable questions** (matters that the courts can review). Drawing on the Fourteenth Amendment's equal protection clause, the courts have forced states to treat voters equally. In *Baker v. Carr* (1962), for example, the Supreme Court ruled that districts within a state must have the same population.

Redistricting and Competition

Both parties have become so skilled at drawing district maps for political advantage that most districts are not competitive. In the 2006 elections, for example, election analysts estimated that only twenty to forty seats would be competitive—less than 10 percent of the House.

Minority-Majority Districts

Following the passage of the Voting Rights Act of 1965, some states began to draw district boundaries to maximize minority representation in Congress. To accomplish this, states created **minority-majority districts,** districts specifically created to have more than 50 percent minority voters. These districts might combine neighborhoods that are far apart, a process sometimes called racial gerrymandering. The Supreme Court has overturned racial gerrymandering, but because racial gerrymandering is as difficult to prove as ordinary gerrymandering, the process continues.

Sample Test Questions

1. The framers intended the two houses of Congress to be different. Describe the differences.

2. What roles do the two houses of Congress play in impeachment?

3. What are sociological and agency representation?

4. True or false: Parties play a key role in structuring Congress.

5. True or false: A committee that reconciles different versions of a bill passed by the Senate and the House, and issues a single bill for the two houses to vote on, is referred to as a select committee.

6. What is a caucus?

   A. A formal meeting of members of one political party
   B. A committee with members of both houses of Congress
   C. An informal meeting of members of Congress with shared interests
   D. Part of a congressional committee

7. Which of the following committee types is a permanent one formed to deal with an issue of ongoing importance?

A. Select
B. Joint
C. Standing
D. Conference

8. What does GAO stand for?

A. General Admissions Office
B. Government Accounting Office
C. General Acquisitions Office
D. Government Accountability Office

9. What is incumbency advantage?

A. Committee members tend to support the committee chair.
B. Incumbent members of Congress overwhelmingly win reelection bids.
C. Incumbent members of Congress have a hard time winning reelection.
D. Incumbent members of Congress usually do not run for reelection.

10. Which of the following constitutes a pocket veto?

A. Congress fails to pass a bill.
B. The president gives no reason for vetoing a bill.
C. The president fails to sign a bill for ten days, and Congress is in session.
D. The president fails to sign a bill for ten days, and Congress is not in session because it adjourned.

ANSWERS

1. The Senate was intended to be a body of statesmen who make choices based on wisdom and deliberation. The House of Representatives is the people's house and is supposed to be attentive to public opinion.

2. The House impeaches an official. The Senate holds the trial and votes on conviction or acquittal.

3. Sociological representation occurs when the representative resembles his or her constituents in terms of race, religion, ethnicity, and education. Agency representation occurs when the representative acts as an agent of his or her constituents and is thrown out of office if the people do not like what he or she does.

4. True

5. False

6. C

7. C

8. D

9. B

10. D

Suggested Reading

- Barone, Michael, and Grant Ujifusa. *The Almanac of American Politics 2006*. Washington, D.C.: National Journal, 2005.

An essential reference for American politics that includes information on all members of Congress. The almanac is updated every two years.

• Burrell, Barbara C. *A Woman's Place Is in the House: Campaigning for Congress in the Feminist Era.* Ann Arbor: University of Michigan Press, 1994.

A study of female candidates for Congress, coming in the wake of 1992's "Year of the Woman."

• Davidson, Roger H., and Walter J. Oleszek. *Congress and Its Members.* 8th ed. Washington, D.C.: Congressional Quarterly Press, 2002.

Davidson and Oleszek examine who gets elected to Congress and how they behave.

• Fenno, Richard F. *Homestyle: House Members in their Districts.* Boston: Little, Brown, 1978.

A classic study of how members of Congress build support in their home districts.

• Fowler, Linda, and Robert McClure. *Political Ambition: Who Decides to Run for Congress?* New Haven, Conn.: Yale University Press, 1989.

This book examines candidate recruitment.

• Thomas, Sue. *How Women Legislate.* New York: Oxford University Press, 1994.

Do female members of Congress behave differently than their male counterparts? Thomas argues that the number of women legislators involved affects the results of legislation.

Useful Websites

• http://thomas.loc.gov

The website of the Library of Congress, which has a wealth of information on current proceedings in Congress.

- www.cbo.gov

Homepage of the Congressional Budget Office, which assists Congress in budgetary matters. The site also provides budget estimates.

- www.hillnews.com
  www.rollcall.com
  www.cq.com

Three top sources for news on Congress: *The Hill, Roll Call,* and *Congressional Quarterly.* All three are nonpartisan newspapers that provide a wealth of information about Congress.

- www.house.gov
  www.senate.gov

The official websites for the United States Senate and House of Representatives. These sites give information about congress-people, bills, committees, and upcoming debates and hearings.

THE PRESIDENCY

5

Overview

In popular culture, the president of the United States has been an action hero (*Air Force One, Independence Day*), a romantic leading man (*The American President*), a dastardly villain (*Absolute Power*), a lovable ordinary guy (*Dave*), a buffoon (*Wag the Dog*), and a well-meaning do-gooder (*The West Wing*). Other movies explore the lives of actual presidents, including *George Washington, Young Mr. Lincoln, Wilson, JFK,* and *Nixon.*

In reality, being president of the United States is one of the most difficult jobs in the world. The president is under constant pressure to please many people, including members of his or her political party and the American people. Every move is examined under a critical microscope, and every gaffe is widely reported. For better or worse, the president becomes the face of the United States for the four-year term spent in office.

The History of the Presidency

The nature of the presidency has evolved considerably over the course of American history, from the limited role the framers of the Constitution had in mind to the rise of the president-centered government of the twentieth century.

THE FRAMERS' VIEWS OF THE PRESIDENCY (1789)

The framers of the Constitution were wary of executive power because they saw it as the most likely source of tyranny. King George III of Britain was, for many, the villain of the Revolutionary War; he was an example of executive power run amok. At the same time, the framers knew that the first president would almost certainly be George Washington, whom they all admired greatly.

As they wrote the Constitution, the framers decided not to provide great detail about the president. Instead, the framers gave the office only a few specific powers. They wanted a strong executive who could deal with emergencies, particularly those involving other nations, but who would not dominate the U.S.

government. The framers expected that Congress would be the focal point of the national government, and they structured the Constitution accordingly. They made the president powerful enough to check and balance Congress but not so powerful as to overrun Congress.

KING CAUCUS (1789–1830s)

For the first few decades of the republic, congressional delegations chose their party's presidential candidate in a **caucus,** a meeting of political leaders to select candidates or plot strategy. As a result, the president was, to some extent, dependent on the representatives of his party in Congress. Critics derided this system as undemocratic, labeling it "King Caucus." Starting in the 1830s, however, parties began using conventions to choose their presidential nominees. This change gave more power to party members outside of Congress, opening up the nomination process to increased public participation, a trend that has continued into the present day. The end of King Caucus gave more power to the president because he was no longer beholden to his party's members of Congress and could act more independently.

CLERK IN CHIEF (1840s–1900)

Even though the end of King Caucus opened up the possibility of greater presidential power, presidents refrained from seizing that power because of long-standing attitudes toward the presidency. For most of the nineteenth century, political leaders believed that political power should center on Congress and that the president's job should be to execute decisions made by Congress. Some scholars have referred to the presidency during this era as a "clerk in chief" because the president was not expected to initiate or guide national policy. Many nineteenth-century presidents acted more like clerks in chief, exercising little initiative or independent power.

Assertive Early Presidents

Despite the general trend of weak presidents, several early presidents stand out for their assertiveness and importance.

George Washington (president from 1775 to 1783) established the character of the office that nearly all his successors would emulate. Washington carried himself in a statesmanlike manner and set the standard of serving no more than two terms. He also created an indelible image of what a president should be: strong, capable, honorable, and above partisanship. Thomas Jefferson (president from 1801 to 1809), in contrast, acted without congressional approval a number of times, such as when he made the Louisiana Purchase in 1803. Andrew Jackson (president from 1829 to 1837) was another assertive president and was the first to appeal directly to the average voter as a means of building support.

Abraham Lincoln (president from 1861 to 1865) took substantial control of the federal government in order to conduct the Civil War effectively. Lincoln suspended the writ of habeas corpus and other civil liberties, for example, and also spent money without congressional authorization. After the war, however, Congress reasserted itself as the dominant branch of the federal government.

THE RISE OF PRESIDENT-CENTERED GOVERNMENT (1901–1950s)

At the start of the twentieth century, the president began to emerge as the key political actor in the federal government. Both Theodore Roosevelt (president from 1901 to 1909) and Woodrow Wilson (president from 1913 to 1921) believed in a strong presidency, one in which the president would be assertive and initiate federal policy. After Wilson left office, however, presidents returned to acting as clerks in chief until Franklin Delano Roosevelt was elected in 1933 during the Great Depression.

Congress and the Strong Presidency

Congress played a role in the expanding power of the presidency by granting the president certain powers. For example, according to the Constitution, the president has no role in drafting the federal budget. But in the early 1920s, Congress included the president in the budget process, so that now the president submits a budget proposal, which Congress then uses as the foundation for its legislation.

Franklin D. Roosevelt

Franklin Roosevelt (president from 1933 to 1945) permanently changed the nature of the American presidency. Elected during the Great Depression, Roosevelt expanded the size and scope of the federal government. As a result, the government became involved in many aspects of its citizens' lives. FDR's New Deal policies included social security, the Tennessee Valley Authority, the Works Progress Administration, and several other programs designed to give jobs to the unemployed.

World War II furthered the scope of the president's power as commander in chief: Many people thought that because the president was the person best positioned to lead the war effort, power should be concentrated in the president's hands. During the war, for example, FDR curtailed civil liberties, nationalized industries to aid the war effort, and decided how the war would be waged. When the Cold War began shortly after the end of World War II, the next president, Harry S Truman (president from 1945 to 1953) continued FDR's policies.

Fireside Chats

FDR also revolutionized the way presidents communicate with the public. Roosevelt began the practice of delivering frequent addresses to the American people over the radio (a practice continued to this day). His manner of speaking as if his listeners were his friends gathered around a fireplace led to the name *fireside chats.* FDR used radio and other media to speak to the people directly.

THE IMPERIAL PRESIDENCY (1960s–PRESENT)

Presidents have assumed extraordinary powers in the areas of foreign and domestic policy since the 1930s. In the 1960s and 1970s, a number of people decried the "imperial presidency," which they felt threatened democracy by giving too much power to one person. The imperial presidency may have peaked with Richard Nixon (president from 1969 to 1974). In the aftermath of the Watergate scandal, Congress took a more assertive role in government, and the power of the president receded. In particular, Congress began an active campaign of oversight, investigating the president's actions and demanding more information from the executive branch.

Since September 11th, the War on Terror has created new concerns about the power of the presidency. Many people feel that President George W. Bush (president from 2001 to 2009) has taken too much power as well. Others feel that Bush is doing what is necessary to win the War on Terror. It remains to be seen whether the office of the president will decrease in strength.

Becoming President

In order to be elected president, a person must meet the eligibility requirements laid out in the Constitution. After that, the person must secure his or her party's nomination. Finally, he or she must face a demanding campaign and election process.

ELIGIBILITY

According to the Constitution anyone who wishes to become president must be:

- At least thirty-five years old
- A resident of the United States for at least fourteen years
- A natural-born citizen

The last requirement has caused some confusion and controversy. According to U.S. law, a child born abroad to parents who are American citizens is also a citizen, but it is not clear from the Constitution whether such a person could be president. As of 2006, the courts have not ruled on whether an American citizen born outside of the United States may be president. A variety of people have tried to amend the Constitution to allow citizens born abroad to be president, but so far they have had no success.

America's Youngest President

Even though the Constitution allows anyone at least thirty-five years old to be president, every American president thus far has been much older: The average age of presidents at inauguration is fifty-four. Most people think that John F. Kennedy was the nation's youngest president—he was forty-three when elected in 1960—but that's not accurate. In reality, Kennedy was the youngest person to be *elected* president. The youngest person to *be* president, however, was Theodore Roosevelt, who was forty-two when he became president following the assassination of William McKinley in 1901.

Demographics of the Presidents

Technically, the Constitution allows women and members of any ethnic, racial, or religious group to be president, but so far all of the presidents have been white men, and all but one have been Protestant (John F. Kennedy was a Catholic).

Firsts in Presidential Nominations

In 1984, Geraldine Ferraro became the first woman nominated for the vice presidency by a major political party. She and presidential nominee Walter Mondale were soundly defeated by Ronald Reagan. In 2000, Joseph Lieberman became the first Jew nominated by a major party; Lieberman and presidential nominee Albert Gore lost one of the tightest races in American history.

CAMPAIGNING

The major parties select their presidential nominee at their national conventions, held every four years. At the conventions, delegates from each state vote and whichever candidate wins a majority of delegates becomes the party's nominee. To win delegates, candidates compete in primary elections, held in each state prior to the convention. Primary races are usually hotly contested.

Because citizens get to vote in the primaries, they have a large role in the election. Prior to the 1972 election, voters played little role in selecting the party nominees, but that is not the case anymore. Before acquiring the party nomination, a presidential candidate must prove that he or she can attract voters by winning primaries.

Choosing a Running Mate

When a candidate decides to run, he or she must choose a running mate, the person who will be the party's nominee for vice president. Many factors go into the choice of running mates: age, geographical location, ideological platforms, and personality. Abraham Lincoln, for example, chose slaveholding senator Andrew Johnson from Tennessee to be his running mate during his reelection campaign, hoping to convince the slaveholding states that had not seceded to remain in the Union. Ronald Reagan, in contrast, asked his former rival, George H. W. Bush, to be his running mate because Reagan knew that Bush would appeal to moderates and fiscal conservatives.

The general election pits each party's nominees against each other. Candidates can usually rely on the support of voters from their own party, so the campaign is frequently a competition for independent voters. The candidates travel to battleground states to hold rallies, aimed at both turning out their own base and persuading undecided voters to support them. The candidates usually debate each other on television. Following a blitz of last-minute campaigning, the voters go to the polls on election day.

The Electoral College

The Constitution only states that the candidate who receives a majority of votes in the **Electoral College** becomes president. It says nothing about the popular vote. The intent of the framers was to filter public opinion through a body composed of wiser, more experienced people; the framers did not want the president to be chosen directly by the people.

Each state gets a number of **electors** equal to its total number of members of Congress (all states get at least three). State governments determine how electors are chosen. No federal officeholders can serve as electors.

Voters think that when they cast their vote, they are voting for a presidential candidate. But in all but two states (Nevada and Maine are the exceptions), voters actually vote for electors, who have pledged to vote for their party's candidate during the Electoral College. Some states have laws that require every elector to vote for the candidate who received the most popular votes in the state, a **winner-take-all system.** Many of the states with a winner-take-all system have laws to punish **faithless electors,** those who vote for someone other than the winner of the state's popular vote.

Keeping the Faith

Al Gore received more of the popular vote than George W. Bush in 2000, and court challenges in Florida stretched the conflict out for thirty-six days. Given the closeness of the race, some pundits speculated that several faithless electors would throw the race to Gore. But perhaps due to the penalties, this did not happen. Florida's electoral college elected Bush by a very thin margin.

Sometimes a candidate loses the popular vote but still becomes the president. In fact, this has happened four times in American history: John Quincy Adams in 1824, Rutherford B. Hayes in 1876, Benjamin Harrison in 1888, and George W. Bush in 2000. These men all became president despite having lost the popular vote. In races with a significant third-party candidate, the winner frequently gets less than 50 percent of the popular vote, such as when Woodrow Wilson defeated opponents Theodore Roosevelt and William Howard Taft in 1912 or when Bill Clinton defeated George H. W. Bush and Ross Perot in 1992.

The Role of the House in History

If no candidate receives a majority of electoral votes, the House of Representatives votes to determine which candidate becomes president. This has happened only once, when Andrew Jackson won the popular vote and more electoral votes than any other candidate in 1824, but he didn't win a majority of electoral votes. The House chose Jackson's rival, John Quincy Adams, to be the next president.

Choosing the Vice President

Originally, the presidential candidate who received the second-greatest number of electoral votes became the vice president, but this created problems between presidents and vice presidents who were from different political parties. The Twelfth Amendment, ratified in 1804, made it so that the Electoral College chooses the president and the vice president separately.

Presidential Term Limits

George Washington set a key precedent when he stepped down from office after serving only two terms. For more than 100 years after Washington, presidents refused to run for office more than twice, until Franklin Roosevelt was elected to four consecutive terms during the Great Depression and World War II. The Twenty-second Amendment was ratified in 1951, making it illegal for presidents to be elected more than twice.

PRESIDENTIAL SUCCESSION

According to the Constitution, the vice president's main job is to assume the office of the president if the president dies, leaves office, or can no longer perform presidential duties. Congress has the power to determine succession if both the president and vice president die, leave office, or cannot perform their jobs. The chart on the next page shows how the Succession Act of 1947 sets the order of presidential succession.

ORDER OF PRESIDENTIAL SUCCESSION	
1	Vice President
2	Speaker of the House
3	President Pro Tempore of the Senate
4	Secretary of State
5	Secretary of the Treasury
6	Secretary of Defense
7	Attorney General
8	Secretary of the Interior
9	Secretary of Agriculture
10	Secretary of Commerce
11	Secretary of Labor
12	Secretary of Health and Human Services
13	Secretary of Housing and Urban Development
14	Secretary of Transportation
15	Secretary of Energy
16	Secretary of Education
17	Secretary of Veterans' Affairs
18	Secretary of Homeland Security

Vice Presidential Succession

Until the Twenty-fifth Amendment was ratified in 1967, there was no law about what to do when the office of the vice president was vacant. When a vice president succeeded a president who had died, for example, he had no vice president. The Twenty-fifth Amendment specified that a new vice president would be nominated by the president and approved by both houses of Congress.

The Special Case of Gerald Ford

The Twenty-fifth Amendment's provision for filling a vice-presidential vacancy has been used twice—and both times involved Gerald Ford. Nixon's first vice president, Spiro Agnew, resigned in 1973 after pleading guilty to tax evasion charges. Nixon and Congress appointed Ford, who was then serving as a member of the House of Representatives. When Nixon resigned in 1974, Ford became president. He then chose Nelson Rockefeller as his vice president. Ford thus has the honor of being the only unelected president in American history because he was never elected to the vice presidency or the presidency.

The President's Roles

The president must serve in a number of capacities to fulfill a number of duties. Some of these roles are specified in the Constitution, but most of them have evolved over time; the following chart summarizes some of the president's roles.

THE PRESIDENT'S ROLES

Role	Summary
Chief of State	Acts as the symbolic leader of the country
Chief Executive	Executes the laws, appoints key federal officials, grants pardons and reprieves
Commander in Chief	Runs the armed forces
Chief Diplomat	Negotiates with other countries
Chief Legislator	Signs or vetoes legislation, introduces legislation, works with Congress on the budget
Superpolitician	Helps his or her party raise money and elect candidates

CHIEF OF STATE

Every nation has a **chief of state,** a person who serves as the symbolic leader of the country and represents the nation. In the United States, the president both leads the government and acts as the chief of state, although this is not the case in many countries. As chief of state, the president presides over commemorations of war heroes, throws out the first pitch at baseball games, and attends funerals of world leaders, among other duties.

> **The Other Chiefs of State**
>
> Obviously, the president cannot attend all ceremonies in his or her role as chief of state. Therefore, sometimes the first lady or the vice president stands in for the president as a symbolic chief of state.

CHIEF EXECUTIVE

The president is the head of the executive branch and is responsible for running the federal **bureaucracy** and enforcing the laws passed by Congress. To do this, the president is allowed to appoint people to key offices, a power called **appointment power.** The president nominates members of the **cabinet,** which consists of appointees who are in charge of the major executive departments and advise the president on policy matters. The president also chooses heads of agencies, federal judges, and about 2,000 lesser jobs. The Senate must approve these nominations. The president also has the power to fire these officials.

The President's Staff

To do the job effectively, the president needs a large staff. The president sits atop a vast bureaucracy, including the White House staff, the president's closest advisers. Not surprisingly, as the president relies more heavily on his staff, he often loses the ability to control it.

The president works with the White House staff every day. They help organize the president's schedule, set priorities, and work with Congress. The president frequently chooses close friends and trusted advisers to the White House staff, and the staff plays a crucial role in shaping the presidency. The head of the White House staff is the White House Chief of Staff. Each president runs the staff differently: Some create rigid hierarchies, whereas others encourage competition among the staffers. The president's closest advisers are sometimes informally called the **kitchen cabinet.**

The Executive Office of the Presidency

The executive office of the presidency (EOP) consists of agencies designed to help the president set policy and respond to key issues. These groups work closely with the president, supplying advice and help. Because they are closer to the president than cabinet members, officials from the EOP frequently have more influence than cabinet members.

As of 2007, the EOP includes the following agencies and councils:

- The Cabinet
- Council of Economic Advisers
- Council on Environmental Quality
- Domestic Policy Council
- National Economic Council
- National Security Council
- Office of Administration
- Office of Faith-Based and Community Initiatives
- Office of Global Communications
- Office of Management and Budget
- Office of National AIDS Policy
- Office of National Drug Control Policy
- Office of Science and Technology Policy
- Office of the United States Trade Representative
- President's Foreign Intelligence Advisory Board
- USA Freedom Corps Volunteer Network
- White House Military Office

Pardons and Reprieves

As part of the power to enforce the law, the Constitution grants the president the power to **pardon,** or release from punishment, people convicted of crimes. In theory, this power allows the president to prevent a miscarriage of justice. Presidential pardons are absolute, and they cannot be overturned. The president can also grant **reprieves,** which are formal postponements of the execution of a sentence.

> **The Most Notorious Pardon**
>
> Probably the most notorious presidential pardon was Gerald Ford's pardon of Richard Nixon for any crimes Nixon may have committed as part of the Watergate scandal in 1974. Ford hoped to bring the tumultuous scandal to a close, but many people felt that Ford actually made the situation worse by ensuring that Nixon would never face charges.

COMMANDER IN CHIEF

The Constitution states that the president is commander in chief of the armed forces. This means that the president—a civilian—controls the entire American military. Civilian control of the military has been a cornerstone of the United States since its founding.

As commander in chief, the president can send troops into battle without a formal declaration of war from Congress and has final authority over military operations. During wartime, the president's powers expand dramatically: Most Americans willingly grant the president a great deal of freedom in order to win the war. During World War I, for example, the Wilson Administration rationed food and important materials and, with the media's cooperation, controlled the news.

> **The President's Controversial Power**
>
> Even though only Congress can declare war, the president is the commander in chief. Most of the time, Congress and the president cooperate, but sometimes problems do arise. During the Vietnam War in 1973, for example, Congress passed the **War Powers Resolution,** which requires the president to consult with Congress when sending troops into combat. The resolution also gave Congress the power to force the president to withdraw troops, but this power has never been used.

CHIEF DIPLOMAT

The president is the main face and voice of American foreign policy, negotiating treaties and other sorts of agreements with foreign leaders (although the Senate must approve all treaties). The president uses two key tools to conduct foreign policy:

1. **Executive agreement:** An agreement made with foreign leaders that does not require Senate approval (although Congress may refuse to fund the agreement); executive agreements are not necessarily binding on future presidents

2. **Diplomatic recognition:** Formal acknowledgment of a government as legitimate; this recognition allows the exchange of ambassadors

CHIEF LEGISLATOR

The president does not have any formal legislative power but has acquired a great deal of informal power as relations between the president and Congress have evolved. People expect the president to have a **legislative agenda,** a series of laws he or she wishes to pass, which is presented each year during the

State of the Union address to Congress and the American people. The president can also play a key role in getting legislation passed by persuading members of Congress to vote for certain bills. The president's popularity and the partisan makeup of Congress influence how effective a president can be in getting legislation passed.

> **The Evolution of the State of the Union Address**
>
> The president is obligated by the Constitution to deliver a state of the union message to Congress each year. However, the manner in which the message is given and the importance of the message have changed dramatically. Prior to the early twentieth century, presidents generally sent the message to Congress in written form, and the message was mostly a description of the status of the country. By the end of the twentieth century, the state of the union address had become a crucial political event, far more important than the framers of the Constitution had originally foreseen.

For a bill to become law, the president must sign it. Often, the signing of a bill is turned into a ceremony, with the president using many pens to sign the bill into law and then distributing those pens to everyone who helped pass the law. If the bill is an unpopular one, the signing is usually done in private. The president sometimes includes a **signing message** that explains his support and understanding of the new law.

The Veto

The president's most powerful tool in dealing with Congress is the veto, through which the president can reject a bill passed by Congress. Congress can override a veto with a two-thirds vote in both houses, but overrides are extremely rare. The president attaches a **veto message** to a bill that is sent back to Congress, explaining the reasoning for the veto.

The president can also make use of the **pocket veto.** If the president neither signs nor vetoes a bill while Congress is not in session, the bill dies at the end of ten days. If Congress is in session and the president does not sign the bill within ten days, then the bill becomes law anyway. The president might make use of the pocket veto for political reasons: He or she may not want the bill to become law but fears political damage if he or she actually vetoes it.

The presidential veto is all or nothing: The bill dies, or it does not. The **line-item veto** is a special type of veto that the president can use to strike the specific parts of the bill he or she dislikes without rejecting the entire bill. Many state governors have line-item veto power, but the president does not. Congress has passed laws giving the president this power, but the Supreme Court has rejected these laws as unconstitutional.

The Budget

The major part of the president's legislative agenda is the **federal budget,** which explains how federal money will be spent during the next year. The federal government operates on **fiscal years,** a twelve-month period (that does not coincide with the calendar year) used for accounting purposes. Every year, the president proposes a budget. Congress can reject or approve the budget, but the president's budget usually lays out the contours of debate on fiscal matters.

SUPERPOLITICIAN

In addition to formal roles, the president also serves as the leader of his or her party. The president, for example, chooses the chairperson of the national party organization and campaigns on behalf of fellow party members. As the most visible party member, the president can play a huge role in raising money and generating support for candidates from this party, especially if the president is popular. Sometimes, however, party members seek to distance themselves from an unpopular president.

Presidential Power

There are three categories of presidential power:

1. **Constitutional powers:** powers explicitly granted by the Constitution

2. **Delegated powers:** powers granted by Congress to help the president fulfill his duties

3. **Inherent powers:** powers inherent in the president's power as chief of the executive branch

Constitutional and delegated powers make up the **expressed powers** because these powers are clearly outlined in the Constitution. Presidents have interpreted inherent powers differently, sometimes in ways that grant the president great power.

EMERGENCY POWERS

The most common inherent powers are **emergency powers,** exercised only in times of great need. Some emergency powers are limited in scope. The president can declare a place devastated by a storm a federal disaster area, making it eligible for federal aid. Other emergency powers are much vaster in scope. During the Civil War, for example, President Abraham Lincoln spent money without congressional approval, and he also suspended a number of civil liberties, including the writ of habeas corpus.

EXECUTIVE ORDERS

Another type of inherent power is the **executive order,** which is a rule or regulation issued by the president that has the force of law. The president can issue executive orders for three reasons:

1. To enforce statutes

2. To enforce the Constitution or treaties

3. To establish or modify how executive agencies operate

All executive orders must be published in the ***Federal Register,*** the daily publication of federal rules and regulations.

EXECUTIVE PRIVILEGE

Executive privilege is the right of officials of the executive branch to refuse to disclose some information to other branches of government or to the public. It includes refusing to appear before congressional committees. Executive privilege is an inherent power that is not clearly defined, and the courts have had to set limitations on the use of the privilege. In 1974, for example, the Supreme Court ruled that executive privilege could not be invoked to prevent evidence from being used in criminal proceedings against the president.

ABUSE OF POWER AND IMPEACHMENT

If the president abuses power, the House of Representatives can **impeach** him, or formally charge him of committing crimes severe enough to call for removal from office. The Senate then tries the impeached president to determine whether he is innocent or guilty of the charges. If convicted, the president is removed from office. Two presidents have been impeached—Andrew Johnson in 1867 and Bill Clinton in 1998—but no president has been convicted by the Senate and removed from office. Richard Nixon would probably have been convicted for his involvement in the Watergate scandal, which is why he resigned in 1974 before the House began impeachment proceedings.

PRESIDENTIAL LEADERSHIP

To be successful, a president must be a strong leader, someone who successfully engages in **statecraft,** the combination of power and wisdom in service of the public good. Scholars have long studied the art of statecraft and have debated what it takes for a president to be successful. Stagecraft always includes the following traits:

- **Political skill:** the ability to persuade, cajole, or coerce people

- **Prudence:** the ability to apply general principles to specific situations in a successful manner
- **Opportunity:** the ability to behave in decisive and meaningful ways

> **The Illusion of Presidential Government**
>
> Presidents wish to convey an image of strength and effectiveness to the public, but in reality, the president's power is often constrained and limited. In 1981, presidential scholar Hugh Heclo labeled the perception that the president is in charge of the government the "illusion of presidential government." Portraying strength and confidence can be a successful strategy, but it can also backfire because a president who appears too successful may get blamed later for anything that goes wrong.

The President and the Public

Theodore Roosevelt changed the public's perception of the presidency by asserting the centrality of the office in American government. The president is chosen by the whole nation, not just a district or state, and therefore the office of the president is the most important office in the federal government. Roosevelt's **stewardship theory** of the presidency claimed that the president has the right to do whatever the nation needs, within the limits of the law.

THE PRESIDENT'S CONSTITUENTS

The president has a number of different constituencies. The most obvious constituency is the citizens of the United States: He or she is the president of all people in the United States, not just those who voted for him or her. But the president also has constituents in the political party, members of the opposing party whose cooperation the president needs, as well as interest groups. The **Washington community**—a term used to describe the government officials, pundits, and columnists in Washington, D.C.—is an often unwanted constituency but one that has influence because of its impact on public opinion.

PRESIDENTIAL APPROVAL

A **presidential approval** poll measures the degree to which Americans approve of the president's job. The president's popularity affects presidential power because a popular president is much more likely to persuade reluctant members of Congress or the public than an unpopular one. A high approval rating—60 percent or above—makes a president very strong, whereas a weak rating—below 50 percent—weakens a presidency. Presidential approval sometimes changes dramatically during the president's term.

EXAMPLE: George H. W. Bush's approval rating hit extremes that few other presidents have reached within a single term in office (1989–1993). Bush's approval rating peaked at 89 percent after the Persian Gulf War in 1991. He was defeated in his bid for reelection only eighteen months later, however, after his approval rating dropped to 29 percent at the end of July 1992. He left office with an approval rating of 56 percent.

When a president first takes office, he is often given what is called a **honeymoon period:** For a few months, the public, the media, and members of Congress tend to give the president the benefit of the doubt and treat him well. However, this honeymoon period is usually fairly short and often gives way to opposition and hostility.

The Permanent Campaign

Recent presidents have sometimes been accused of running a permanent campaign, meaning that the president and his staff always operate as if they are running an election campaign. This includes the use of campaign tactics—such as immediate response, staying on message, and photo opportunities—to govern.

THE PRESIDENT AND THE MEDIA

Presidents often use the media to speak to the American people directly in order to generate public support for their policies. Since World War II, presidents have increasingly used the media to gain popularity and leverage in their relationship with Congress. This strategy has been dubbed *going public.*

EXAMPLE: At the end of 2002 and the beginning of 2003, President George W. Bush and his aides decided to "go public." Bush made many speeches in support of going to war in Iraq, and he convinced many, many people to support the war. Perhaps as a result, support for Bush surged in the spring of 2003.

Changes in Media Coverage

Reporters covering the president today are very different from their counterparts a few decades ago. Journalists today are much more likely to report anything that the president does, including things that could hurt the president's image. Many White House correspondents knew, for example, that FDR needed a wheelchair and that John Kennedy cheated on his wife, yet no one reported those facts. It's hard to imagine something like that happening today because media scrutiny is much more intense.

Understanding and Evaluating Presidents

Understanding and evaluating presidents poses problems for political scientists because only one president serves at time and since each president faces very different challenges. Political scientists call this the *one-n problem.* Because the circumstances of a presidency have a tremendous impact on the success and failure of that presidency, determining whether a president was good or bad is difficult, particularly when we start comparing presidents. Only Franklin Roosevelt was president at the time of the attack on Pearl Harbor, for example, and only Abraham Lincoln was president during the Civil War. How can one judge, then, how Lincoln would have handled Pearl Harbor or FDR the Civil War?

FACTORS CONTRIBUTING TO SUCCESS AND FAILURE

Many factors affect how successful a president will be:

- **Strong leadership:** The ability to rally people behind him
- **Congress:** The ability to control or persuade members of Congress
- **Popularity:** The ability to convince others to do as he wishes

DECISION-MAKING ANALYSIS

Decision-making analysis explores the methods and circumstances under which key decisions are made. Graham T. Allison's *Essence of Decision: Explaining the Cuban Missile Crisis* (1971) is a famous example. Allison sought to understand the decisions made by the inner circle of the Kennedy Administration (and to a lesser extent, by the Soviets) during the crisis in 1962. He devised three models, all of which explain parts of the decision-making process:

- **The rational actor model:** Decision makers act in a rational manner: They gather all the evidence, weigh their options, and make an informed choice.
- **The organizational process model:** The structure of organizations shapes how decisions are made.
- **The bureaucratic politics model:** Leaders of different organizations are in competition with one another, and that affects how decisions are made.

Another decision-making model—known as the *groupthink approach*—examines how group dynamics can affect decision outcomes. According to this model, under some circumstances, group members reinforce one another's faulty reasoning, leading to disastrous decisions.

PSYCHOLOGICAL ANALYSIS

Psychological approaches seek to understand the inner workings of the president's mind and how they affect decision-making. Some psychological accounts are simplistic, but others are serious studies of presidential character. James Barber's bivariate typology is a prominent example. Barber argues that presidents should be evaluated based on how active a role they should play in initiating policies (active or passive) and how they view themselves and their status as president (positive or negative). Combining these two variables, we get four categories of presidents: passive-positive, passive-negative, active-positive, and active-negative. Barber claims that active-positive presidents are likely the best, whereas active-negative can be disastrous.

BARBER'S CATEGORIZATIONS OF PRESIDENTS

	Active	**Passive**
Positive	Franklin Roosevelt, Harry S Truman, John F. Kennedy	Ronald Reagan, William Howard Taft, James Madison
Negative	Lyndon Johnson, Richard Nixon, Herbert Hoover, Woodrow Wilson	George Washington, Dwight Eisenhower, George H. W. Bush

HISTORICAL COMPARISON

Some scholars compare presidents by the role they play in history. For example, some see FDR as particularly significant because he framed the terms of debate in the United States for decades to come. Other studies examine the lasting impact a president had by studying how much of what he did survived their presidencies. Again FDR is significant under this criteria because his New Deal still exists.

> **The Best and Worst**
>
> Scholars and historians debate about the best and worst presidents in American history. Although there is no consensus, there is a general agreement as to who should be considered great. This list includes Presidents Abraham Lincoln, Franklin D. Roosevelt, George Washington, Thomas Jefferson, and Theodore Roosevelt.

Sample Test Questions

1. Describe the general trend of the development of presidential power.

2. Why is the veto such a strong tool?

3. What does the term *imperial presidency* mean?

4. True or false: Executive agreements must be ratified by the Senate.

5. True or false: Inherent powers are those listed in the Constitution.

6. Which of the following is a constitutional duty of the vice president?

A. Breaking tie votes in the House of Representatives
B. Attending funerals of foreign leaders
C. Breaking tie votes in the Senate
D. Serving as a goodwill ambassador

7. Which of the following presidents was impeached during his term of office?

A. Andrew Jackson
B. Andrew Johnson
C. Richard Nixon
D. Ulysses S. Grant

8. What happens when no presidential candidate wins a majority of electoral votes?

A. The House of Representatives chooses the next president.
B. The Senate chooses the next president.
C. The Supreme Court chooses the next president.
D. The candidate with the most popular votes wins.

9. What does the president lay out in the State of the Union address?

A. His defense against impeachment
B. His legislative agenda for the coming year
C. His strategy for reelection
D. His criticisms of the opposition party

10. What is executive privilege?

A. The privilege of getting the best seats in a restaurant
B. The privilege of submitting a budget proposal to Congress
C. The right of members of the executive branch to withhold information from Congress and the public
D. The right to veto bills passed by Congress

ANSWERS

1. The general trend is that the president has gained more power over time. In the early republic, most presidents thought their main job was to carry out Congress's wishes. Starting in the early twentieth century, presidents saw themselves as leading actors in American politics. During the Great Depression and World War II, FDR dramatically expanded the power of the presidency. Presidents in recent years have continued to be very powerful.
2. The veto is a powerful tool because few vetoes are overridden. The president can stop Congress from enacting a law.
3. The "imperial presidency" is the view that the president has become too strong and is a threat to democracy.
4. False
5. False
6. C
7. B
8. A
9. B
10. C

Suggested Reading

• Allison, Graham T., and Philip Zelikow. *Essence of Decision: Explaining the Cuban Missile Crisis.* 2nd ed. New York: Longman, 1999.

A classic text in decision-making theory. Allison and Zelikow present three models of decision-making, each of which accounts for some of the decisions made during the Cuban Missile Crisis.

• Barber, James David. *Presidential Character: Predicting Performance in the White House.* 4th ed. Englewood Cliffs, NJ: Prentice Hall, 1992.

Barber's classic of psychological studies of the presidents has influenced many scholars, who use his conclusions to study candidates.

• Eisinger, Robert M. *The Evolution of Presidential Polling.* New York: Cambridge University Press, 2003.

All modern presidents consult polls, but the way they use them has changed. Eisinger chronicles the use of polls since Franklin Roosevelt's presidency.

• Frum, David. *The Right Man: The Surprise Presidency of George Bush.* New York: Random House, 2003.

Frum served as a speechwriter in George W. Bush's White House, and he recounts his experiences during the eventful first year of Bush's presidency.

• Janis, Irving J. *Groupthink: Psychological Studies of Policy Decisions and Fiascoes.* 2nd ed. New York: Houghton Mifflin, 1982.

Janis's description of how groupthink can lead to policy disasters has influenced many decision-making studies of the presidents.

• Kernell, Samuel. *Going Public: New Strategies of Presidential Leadership.* Washington, D.C.: Congressional Quarterly Press, 2006.

Kernell examines the power of going public and how it can help the president in his relations with Congress.

• Neustadt, Richard E. *Presidential Power and the Modern Presidents: The Politics of Leadership from Roosevelt to Reagan.* New York: Free Press, 1990.

Neustadt's account of the limits of presidential power is a classic. He argues that the key to presidential power is persuasion.

• Walcott, Charles E., and Karen M. Hult. *Governing the White House: From Hoover Through LBJ.* Lawrence: University Press of Kansas, 1995.

A clever study of how the structure of the White House affects a president's success and failure.

• Woodward, Bob and Carl Bernstein. *All the President's Men.* 2nd ed. New York: Simon & Schuster, 1994.

A classic of investigative journalism, Woodward and Bernstein broke open the Watergate scandal through their relentless reporting.

Useful Websites

• http://uselectionatlas.org

An excellent source for information about presidential elections.

• www.bartleby.com/124

This site publishes the texts of every presidential inaugural address.

• www.vote-smart.org/index.htm

This nonpartisan website provides information about American elections, including presidential races.

• www.whitehouse.gov

The website for the White House. It includes the latest executive orders, text of key speeches, and information on the president's policy priorities.

THE BUREAUCRACY

6

Overview

In everyday language, we use the word *bureaucracy* as an insult. For most people, the term conjures long lines of angry people, piles of papers just about to tip over, and workers asleep at their desks. The truth is that every government needs a bureaucracy in order to function properly. In fact, the federal government of the United States employs roughly 1 percent of the American population, or approximately 2.6 million people, within its bureaucracy.

The Department of Motor Vehicles, the Central Intelligence Agency, the Peace Corps, the Office of Government Ethics, the U.S. Capitol Police, and the Small Business Administration are all part of the American bureaucracy, but so are religious groups, businesses, and educational institutions. For better or worse, a bureaucracy is the best way to organize large numbers of people working toward the same goal.

What Is a Bureaucracy?

A **bureaucracy** is a way of administratively organizing large numbers of people who need to work together. Organizations in the public and private sector, including universities and governments, rely on bureaucracies to function. The term *bureaucracy* literally means "rule by desks or offices," a definition that highlights the often impersonal character of bureaucracies. Even though bureaucracies sometimes seem inefficient or wasteful, setting up a bureaucracy helps ensure that thousands of people work together in compatible ways by defining everyone's roles within a hierarchy.

WHAT BUREAUCRATS DO

Government bureaucrats perform a wide variety of tasks. We often think of bureaucrats as paper-pushing desk clerks, but bureaucrats fight fires, teach, and monitor how federal candidates raise money, among other activities.

The job of a bureaucrat is to **implement** government policy, to take the laws and decisions made by elected officials and put them into practice. Some bureaucrats implement policy by writing rules and regulations, whereas others administer policies directly to people (such as distributing small business loans or treating patients at a veterans' hospital). The task of running the government, and providing services through policy implementation, is called **public administration.**

Bureaucratic Functions

One useful approach to understanding what bureaucrats do is to examine the actions of different governmental agencies. The following table summarizes the government's major functions and provides examples of agencies that perform those tasks.

FUNCTIONS OF BUREAUCRACIES

Function	Bureaucratic Agencies
Promote the public good	National Institutes of Health, Environmental Protection Agency, Federal Bureau of Investigation
Protect the nation	Armed forces, Coast Guard, Central Intelligence Agency
Sustain a strong economy	Federal Reserve Bank, Export-Import Bank, Securities and Exchange Commission

BUREAUCRATIC MODELS

Scholars have proposed three different models to explain how bureaucracies function, summarized in the following chart.

THREE MODELS OF BUREAUCRACY

Model	Important Trait	Problematic Behavior
Weberian Model	Hierarchy	Lethargy
Acquisitive Model	Expansionism	Competition
Monopolistic Model	Lack of competition	Inefficiency

Weberian Model

According to the **Weberian model,** created by German sociologist Max Weber, a bureaucracy always displays the following characteristics:

- **Hierarchy:** A bureaucracy is set up with clear chains of command so that everyone has a boss. At the top of the organization is a chief who oversees the entire bureaucracy. Power flows downward.

- **Specialization:** Bureaucrats specialize in one area of the issue their agency covers. This allows efficiency because the specialist does what he or she knows best, then passes the matter along to another specialist.

- **Division of labor:** Each task is broken down into smaller tasks, and different people work on different parts of the task.

- **Standard operating procedure (SOP):** Also called **formalized rules,** SOP informs workers about how to handle tasks and situations. Everybody always follows the same procedures to increase efficiency and predictability so that the organization will produce similar results in similar circumstances. SOP can sometimes make bureaucracy move slowly because new procedures must be developed as circumstances change.

Acquisitive Model

The **acquisitive model** can be distinguished by the following characteristics:

- **Expansion:** Leaders of bureaucracies always seek to expand the size and budget of their agency.

- **Turf wars:** Bureaucrats defend their responsibilities, resources, and jurisdiction from potential competitors. Even though government bureaucracies do not work for profit, agency heads still jockey for power and try to outdo one another.

Turf Wars

Federal bureaucracies often engage in turf wars, fights over which agency has the power to perform certain tasks. For example, the Central Intelligence Agency is the leading intelligence organization, but it faces competition from the National Security Agency, the Defense Intelligence Agency, and intelligence agencies within each of the armed forces, as well as an intelligence operation at the State Department. At times, the fighting between agencies hampers policy implementation and wastes money.

Monopolistic Model

Proponents of the **monopolistic model** believe that bureaucracies can be distinguished by two characteristics:

1. **Monopoly:** Federal bureaucracies face no real competition and therefore act like any other monopolies.
2. **Inefficiency:** Bureaucracies use their resources inefficiently because they do not have to compete.

The Federal Bureaucracy

The federal bureaucracy is huge: roughly 2.6 million employees, plus many freelance contractors. Everybody in the bureaucracy works to administer the law. For the most part, the executive branch manages the federal bureaucracy. Although the executive branch controls the majority of the federal bureaucracy, the legislative and judiciary branches also have some influence. Congress, for example, controls the Library of Congress, the Congressional Research Service, and the Government Accountability Office, among other bureaucracies. Through its power of oversight, Congress also monitors the federal bureaucracy to make sure that it acts properly. The courts sometimes get involved in the bureaucracy when issues of law and constitutionality arise, such as when a civil service regulation is violated or if an agency oversteps its jurisdiction.

There are five types of organizations in the federal bureaucracy:

1. Cabinet departments
2. Independent executive agencies
3. Independent regulatory agencies
4. Government corporations
5. Presidential commissions

> **Bureaucratic Growth**
>
> The federal bureaucracy was small throughout much of American history. But the Great Depression, World War II, the Cold War, and President Lyndon Johnson's Great Society programs greatly expanded the role of the federal government. George W. Bush's War on Terror has also expanded and redefined the role of the federal government and has necessitated the creation of new organizations, such as the Department of Homeland Security.

CABINET DEPARTMENTS

The executive office consists of fifteen departments, as shown by the table on the next page. Each department is headed by a secretary.

CABINET DEPARTMENTS	
Department	**Date Established**
State	1789
Treasury	1789
Interior	1849
Justice	1870
Agriculture	1889
Commerce	1913
Labor	1913
Defense	1947
Housing and Urban Development	1965
Transportation	1967
Energy	1977
Health and Human Services	1979
Education	1979
Veterans' Affairs	1988
Homeland Security	2002

Line Organizations and Managerial Presidents

The president must oversee the executive bureaucracy, which includes what are known as **line organizations,** or the federal agencies that report directly to the president. The fifteen cabinet departments are line organizations. Political scientists sometimes refer to modern presidents as *managerial presidents* because they spend so much time overseeing and managing the bureaucracy.

INDEPENDENT EXECUTIVE AGENCIES

Independent executive agencies are line organizations that do not fall under the control of any one department. Presidents often like new agencies to be independent so that they have more direct control over them. Congress decides how to fit new independent executive agencies within the existing bureaucracy.

> **Very Important Agencies**
>
> The government needs money to function, so generating revenue is crucial. A number of different federal agencies are **revenue agencies:** They raise money by collecting taxes and fees. The most notorious revenue agency is the Internal Revenue Service, but it is not the only one. The Department of the Interior, for example, collects fees from people who use national parks.

INDEPENDENT REGULATORY AGENCIES

An **independent regulatory agency** is an agency outside of the cabinet departments that makes and enforces rules and regulations. The president nominates people to regulatory boards and agencies, and the Senate confirms them. Generally, these bureaucrats serve set terms in office and can only be removed for illegal behavior. Regulatory agencies tend to function independently from the elected parts of government, which gives them the freedom to make policy without any political interference.

> *EXAMPLE:* The Securities and Exchange Commission, the Federal Election Commission, and the Federal Reserve Board are all powerful independent regulatory agencies.

Agency Capture

Scholars argue that some agencies have been taken over by the very industries they are supposed to regulate. The industries then dictate terms and policies to the agency rather than the other way around. Scholars use the term **agency capture** to describe this process. Agency capture causes decreased competition and higher prices.

GOVERNMENT CORPORATIONS

Some federal agencies resemble corporations in that they function in a businesslike manner and charge clients for their services. **Government corporations** differ in some important ways from private corporations. For example, government corporations do not have stockholders and do not pay dividends if they make a profit; instead, the government corporation retains all profits.

EXAMPLES: The Federal Deposit Insurance Corporation, which guarantees deposits up to $100,000, and the Post Office are government corporations.

PRESIDENTIAL COMMISSIONS

Presidents regularly appoint **presidential commissions** to investigate problems and make recommendations. Although most of these commissions are temporary—such as President George W. Bush's Commission to Strengthen Social Security or the September 11th Commission—some are permanent, such as the Commission on Civil Rights. Presidents are not bound to follow the recommendations of commissions, even though they often do.

Becoming a Bureaucrat

There are two types of bureaucrats in the federal bureaucracy: political appointees and civil servants.

POLITICAL APPOINTEES

The president can appoint approximately 2,000 people to top positions within the federal bureaucracy. These people are known as **political appointees.**

Choosing Political Appointees

The president usually receives nominations and suggestions from party officials, political allies, close advisers, academics, and business leaders on whom to appoint to bureaucratic offices. Sometimes the president appoints loyal political allies to key positions, particularly ambassadorships. This tradition is referred to as the **spoils system** or simply **patronage.**

> **Garfield's Assassination**
>
> Charles Julius Guiteau, a strong supporter of the spoils system, grew angry when President James Garfield repeatedly denied him a diplomatic posting in Paris. On July 2, 1881, Guiteau shot Garfield, who later died of complications from the wound. Garfield's assassination prompted Congress to change rules governing the selection of bureaucratic officials.

THE CIVIL SERVANTS

In the late nineteenth century, members of the Progressive Party argued that most government jobs should be filled with skilled experts, not unskilled political appointees. In other words, they argued that competence rather than political loyalty should determine who holds these jobs. The **civil service** consists of the federal employees hired for their knowledge and experience, and it constitutes most of the federal bureaucracy.

The Emergence of the Federal Civil Service

For much of the nineteenth century, presidents routinely hired political supporters to work in the bureaucracy. Over time, the federal bureaucracy became corrupt and inept, leading to calls for reform. In 1883, Congress passed the **Pendleton Act** (also called the **Civil Service Reform Act**), which put limits on the spoils system for the first time. The act also created the **Civil Service Commission,** the first central personnel agency for the federal government. At first, civil service rules applied to only about 10 percent of federal employees, but since then Congress has expanded the civil service, so that it now encompasses about 90 percent of the bureaucracy.

President Jimmy Carter's **Civil Service Reform Act of 1978** reformed and clarified the rules of the civil service. The law created the **Office of Personnel Management** to replace the Civil Service Commission, and it also established the **Merit Systems Protection Board** to hear complaints from employees about violations of the rules.

Civil Servants

All civil servant applicants must pass an exam that measures skills related to the particular civil service position they hope to fill. Some civil service exams are general and apply to a wide range of jobs, whereas others are focused on a particular type of job. The civil service uses the **merit system,** meaning that it hires and promotes civil servants based on their technical skills. Most civil servants are also protected from political pressure. The best example of this protection is the fact that it is extremely difficult to fire civil servants. In theory, this job security prevents politicians from firing those who disagree with them. In practice, however, it makes it hard to fire incompetent employees.

A Bureaucratic Democracy

The power of the bureaucracy raises important questions about accountability. In a democratic system, the government is accountable to the people, yet bureaucrats are unelected, hard to fire, and wield important power. Therefore, some people view the bureaucracy as undemocratic. Others argue that Congress and the president may make the bureaucracy accountable. The president, for example, might appoint reform-minded people to head agencies or threaten to slash the budgets of recalcitrant agencies. Congress might change the laws affecting agencies or hold hearings to air grievances, which can force an agency to change its behavior.

The Bureaucracy and Policymaking

Bureaucrats put government policy into practice, and therefore the federal bureaucracy has a large impact on policymaking. In order to get their policies passed, the president and Congress must work with the bureaucracy. Controlling the bureaucracy can be difficult for the following reasons:

- **Size:** The president cannot monitor everyone or even every group within the bureaucracy, so much of what bureaucrats do goes unmonitored.
- **Expertise of bureaucrats:** The people who administer policy often know much more about those issues than the president or members of Congress. This expertise gives the bureaucrats power.
- **Civil service laws:** Firing bureaucrats, even for incompetence, is very difficult.

- **Clientele groups:** Many federal agencies provide services to thousands of people, and those people sometimes rally to defend the agency.

- **Policy implementation:** When Congress creates a new program, it does not establish all the details on how the policy will be implemented. Instead, Congress passes **enabling legislation,** which grants power to an agency to work out the specifics. Although the agency must stay within some bounds, it has a great deal of latitude in determining how to carry out the wishes of Congress.

> **Power of Persuasion**
>
> Presidential scholar Richard Neustadt has argued that the president's primary power is that of persuasion. The president must lobby or persuade bureaucrats. But trying to convince members of the bureaucracy that their goals fit with the president's goals is a time-consuming and often frustrating process. For this reason, many presidents have seen the bureaucracy as an obstacle to getting their agendas approved.

RULE-MAKING

The federal bureaucracy makes rules that affect how programs operate, and these rules must be obeyed, just as if they were laws. The **rule-making** process for government agencies occurs in stages. After Congress passes new regulatory laws, the agency charged with implementing the law proposes a series of rules, which are published in the *Federal Register.* Interested parties can comment on the rules, either at public hearings or by submitting documents to the agency. After the agency publishes the final regulations, it must wait sixty days before enforcing those rules. During that time, Congress can review and change the rules if it desires. If Congress makes no changes, the rules go into effect at the end of sixty days.

Federal regulations affect many groups of people, who have often challenged those regulations in court. Because litigation is a slow and expensive way to change regulations, Congress passed the Negotiated Rulemaking Act of 1990 to limit the need for litigation by opening the rulemaking process to those affected by it. The act encouraged federal agencies to engage in **negotiated rule-making.** If an agency agrees to the proposed regulations, for example, it publishes the proposals in the *Federal Register* and then participates in a negotiating committee overseen by a third party. Agreements reached by the committee are then open to the normal public review process. Parties to negotiated rule-making agree not to sue over the rules.

Administrative Adjudication

In some cases, executive agencies function like courts: They hold hearings in which each party presents arguments and evidence for or against certain rules. The executive agencies then make a decision that settles the argument between the agencies. This power is called **administrative adjudication,** and it involves applying rules and precedents to specific cases.

Deregulation and Reregulation

Since the Carter Administration in the late 1970s, the federal government has frequently sought to remove regulations established by earlier administrations, a practice called **deregulation.** The federal bureaucracy usually carries out deregulation, often with encouragement from the president. In the late 1970s and early 1980s, for example, the government deregulated the airline industry, significantly increasing competition and lowering prices. Sometimes the federal government changes its regulations significantly, a process known as **reregulation.**

BUREAUCRATS AS POLICYMAKERS

In theory, federal bureaucracies merely carry out the policies enacted by Congress and the president. In practice, however, many scholars argue that the bureaucracy plays a significant role in federal policymaking via iron triangles and issue networks.

Iron Triangles

An **iron triangle** is an alliance of people from three groups: a congressional subcommittee that deals with an issue, the executive agency that enforces laws on that issue, and private interest groups. Often, the members of the triangle know each other well, and people frequently move from one corner of the triangle to another. The members of the iron triangle work together to create policy that serves their interests.

EXAMPLE: An iron triangle might form around a particular weapons system. The Defense Department may want a new weapons system, members of congressional Armed Services Committees may want to look tough on defense by voting for a new system, and military suppliers want to make money by selling weapons systems. Therefore, it is in the interests of all three parties to push Congress to authorize the new weapons system.

Issue Networks

An **issue network** is a group of individuals who support a specific policy, not a broader issue. The three parts of the iron triangle are often parts of a single issue network, but other people may also be a part of the network, including experts, scholars, and the media. The influence of issue networks is similar to that of iron triangles: By working together, members of an issue network can shape and determine policy.

Reforming the Bureaucracy

Nearly every modern president has attempted to reform the bureaucracy. Some recent successful attempts at bureaucratic reform include the following:

- Sunshine laws
- Sunset provisions
- Privatization
- Increased incentives for efficiency
- Protection of whistleblowers

SUNSHINE LAWS

In 1976, Congress passed the Government in the Sunshine Act, which required that the public have access to the proceedings and actions of the bureaucracies. Such openness is meant to encourage the public to complain about hostile or inefficient bureaucrats. **Sunshine laws** require government agencies to hold public meetings on a regular basis. Some proceedings, such as court meetings, top secret matters, and personnel matters that could be embarrassing can remain secret.

SUNSET PROVISIONS

Sometimes Congress passes laws with an expiration date, known as **sunset provisions,** because the laws will end at a specified time. For a program to continue past its expiration date, the agency must demonstrate that the program achieves its goals in an efficient manner. Sunset provisions make bureaucrats accountable for their performance: Only successful programs get renewed.

PRIVATIZATION

Privatization occurs when private companies perform services that were formerly handled by a government agency. For example, the government may abolish public housing and instead give rental vouchers to residents to use in privately owned apartments. Supporters of privatization argue that private profit-driven organizations are more efficient than government bureaucracies because companies have strong incentives to be as efficient as possible. Privatization has been somewhat successful, particularly for services provided by local governments (such as trash collection). Some services do not translate well from public to private, however, and some—such as national defense—cannot be transferred to private firms at all.

INCREASED INCENTIVES FOR EFFICIENCY

Critics complain that government bureaucrats lack incentives to perform efficiently. To overcome inefficiency, some state governments have started offering more incentives to employees, such as financial rewards tied to job performance. The president and Congress have also required government agencies to list specific goals, and the agencies then receive feedback about how well those goals have been met. President George W. Bush's performance-based budgeting carries this idea a step further by tying funding directly to performance.

TQM and Reinventing Government

During the Clinton Administration (1993–2001), Vice President Al Gore decided to revamp the bureaucracy. His effort, known as "Reinventing Government," relied on Total Quality Management, a set of principles that create a culture of quality in an organization, in which everyone constantly thinks about improving performance. Gore's efforts achieved some successes: Every year the government gave out the "Hammer Award" (named for the scandalous prices the Pentagon paid for hammers) to those who did the most to improve quality in government.

PROTECTING WHISTLEBLOWERS

A **whistleblower** is a person who exposes corruption or inefficiency. As a result of blowing the whistle, some people have been demoted or fired. Congress has sought to protect whistleblowers because whistleblowers increase accountability by exposing problems. Despite the laws passed by Congress, many whistleblowers still suffer because of their actions.

Sample Test Questions

1. According to Max Weber, what are the basic characteristics of bureaucracy?

2. Critics assert that bureaucracies act in an acquisitive manner and behave like monopolies. What do these criticisms mean?

3. Why does the president so often have difficulty controlling the bureaucracy?

4. True or false: The merit system replaced the spoils system in most of the federal bureaucracy.

5. True or false: Whistleblower protection is a source of bureaucratic power.

6. What is agency capture?

A. When one government agency takes over another agency's functions
B. When government services are provided by private companies
C. When an industry regulated by an agency gains substantial power over the agency
D. When the Congress takes power over an agency away from the president

7. What is a line organization?

A. An agency that reports directly to the president
B. An agency that is part of a larger department
C. An independent commission that does not answer to the president
D. An agency that is part of the legislative branch

8. What do sunshine laws require agencies to do?

A. Save energy by using solar power
B. Only operate during the day
C. Hold regular public sessions
D. Ignore daylight savings time

9. What is an iron triangle?

A. A term to describe the three branches of the federal government
B. A term to describe the organization of the White House staff
C. A collection of three executive agencies that work together regularly
D. An alliance of legislators, bureaucrats, and interest groups concerned with an issue

10. What is the civil service?

A. Rules that require government workers to be polite to the public
B. The part of the bureaucracy governed by the merit system
C. Rules that force government agencies to hold public meetings
D. Government officials appointed by the president

ANSWERS

1. Weber says the basic traits of bureaucracy are hierarchy, division of labor, specialization, and standard operating procedure.

2. The acquisitive model of bureaucracy states that agency chiefs seek to expand their agency's power, size, and budget. The monopolistic model argues that because bureaucracies face no competition, they have no real incentive to improve efficiency.

3. The bureaucracy has substantial independence, stemming from its civil service laws, size, expertise, clientele groups, and role in implementing policy. All of these sources of power make it hard for the president to control the bureaucracy.

4. True

5. False

6. C

7. A

8. C

9. D

10. B

Suggested Reading

• Arnold, Peri E. *Making the Managerial Presidency: Comprehensive Organization Planning.* Princeton, NJ: Princeton University Press, 1986.

Managing the federal bureaucracy is a monumental task. Arnold studies how effectively it can be done and argues for the importance of large-scale planning.

• Brehm, John, and Scott Gates. *Working, Shirking, and Sabotage: Bureaucratic Response to a Democratic Public.* Ann Arbor: University of Michigan Press, 1996.

Brehm and Gates argue that, in general, bureaucracies do a good job of responding to the public.

• Fesler, James W., and Donald F. Kettl. *The Politics of the Administration Process.* Chatham, NJ: Chatham House, 1991.

Fesler and Kettl study how politics affects the bureaucracy and how bureaucratic politics shape policy.

• Kerwin, Cornelius M. *Rulemaking: How Government Agencies Write Law and Make Policy.* Washington, D.C.: Congressional Quarterly Press, 2003.

An in-depth study of the rule-making process.

• Wilson, James Q. *Bureaucracy: What Government Agencies Do and Why They Do It.* New York: Basic Books, 1989.

Wilson, a prominent scholar, provides a thorough account of the nuts and bolts of the bureaucracy: how bureaucracies provide services, and how they are managed.

• Wood, Dan B. *Bureaucratic Dynamics: The Role of Bureaucracy in a Democracy.* Boulder, Col.: Westview, 1994.

Democratic governments are supposed to be accountable to the people, but bureaucracies are unelected and powerful. Wood explores how bureaucracy can function—and be held accountable—in a democratic society.

Useful Websites

• www.census.gov

The U.S. Census Bureau provides extensive statistical information on government agencies, not just on the public.

- www.gpoaccess.gov/fr/index.html

The *Federal Register* lists all proposed rule changes issued by government agencies.

- www.icma.org

The website for the International City/County Management Association, a professional organization of city managers. The city manager system of local government was a key component of the Progressive movement, which also spawned the civil service.

- www.opm.gov

The Office of Personnel Management is the central personnel agency for the federal government. The site contains information about civil service exams and rules.

- www.whistleblower.org

The site of the Government Accountability Project, which offers support and encouragement to whistleblowers.

- www.whitehouse.gov/omb

The Office of Management and Budget is one of the most important parts of the Executive Office of the president. The site contains extensive budget information.

THE JUDICIARY

7

Overview

The United States has more lawyers per capita than any other country: two and a half times as many as Great Britain, five times as many as Germany, and twenty-five times as many as Japan. There's even an entire television network devoted to covering trials (Court TV) and three versions of NBC's popular show *Law and Order.*

Courts—and lawyers—have played crucial roles throughout American history. In the twentieth century, for example, court cases such as *Brown v. Board of Education* (1954) and *Miranda v. Arizona* (1966) have shaped the political landscape and caused tremendous controversy. In today's political environment, we hear complaints from some who say that the courts are overstepping their bounds and undermining democracy, whereas others see the courts as the last protection against tyranny of the majority. The judicial branch of government is an integral, albeit complicated, part of American democracy.

The Foundations of American Law

There are three bases of American law:

1. **Case law:** Court decisions that inform judicial rulings

2. **Constitutions:** Agreements, such the U.S. Constitution and the state constitutions, that outline the structure of government

3. **Statutes:** Laws made by governments

CASE LAW

The American legal system has its roots in the British system, which is based on **common law.** In this system, judges shape the law through their decisions, interpretations, and rulings, which are then collected into a body of law known as *case law* that other judges can use as reference. When judges make decisions, they look to similar cases for **precedent,** a court ruling from the past similar to the current case. The Latin phrase ***stare decisis*** denotes the legal doctrine of relying on precedent.

EXAMPLE: The Fourth Amendment states that citizens are protected from "unreasonable searches and seizures" and that search warrants can only be issued based on "probable cause." Many cases have laid down rules about how the courts should handle such matters. In the case *Mapp v. Ohio* (1961), the Supreme Court applied the **exclusionary rule**—which states that any evidence obtained through an illegal search is excluded from trial—to state courts. Since then, judges have referred to the precedent set in *Mapp v. Ohio* to keep illegally obtained evidence out of the courtroom.

Overturning Precedent

Judges rely on precedents when deciding their cases, but the Supreme Court also has the power to overturn precedents. Some of the most famous cases in American legal history have overturned precedents. For example, the civil rights case *Brown v. Board of Education* (1954), which outlawed segregation in public schools, overturned the 1896 case *Plessy v. Ferguson.* State and federal courts are reluctant to overturn precedent because the law needs to be stable for the courts to have legitimacy. It would be impossible for anyone to obey a law that kept changing. At the same time, judges recognize that the law must change to stay relevant. The courts need to strike a balance between stability and change.

CONSTITUTIONS

The U.S. Constitution is the supreme law of the land. No law or act of government—at the local, state, or federal level—can violate its principles. Similarly, a state's constitution is the supreme law within the state's borders, so long as the state constitution does not conflict with the national Constitution.

Marbury v. Madison

Federal courts have assumed the power of **judicial review,** the right to determine the constitutional legality of state and federal laws, congressional and presidential acts, and lower-court rulings. Likewise, each state court has assumed the power to determine the legality of legislative and gubernatorial decisions within its own borders.

The power of judicial review is not codified in the Constitution, however. Many state supreme courts had already assumed this power by the time the Constitution was ratified in 1789, and Chief Justice John Marshall set a precedent for federal judicial review in the 1803 case *Marbury v. Madison.* Federal courts use their power of judicial review sparingly, primarily because they have no means of enforcing their decisions. Nevertheless, judicial review is the most significant power of the judiciary branch.

STATUTES

Statutes are laws passed by Congress and states legislatures. Congress passed an unprecedented number of statutes in the twentieth century, covering such issues as environmental regulation, criminal law, and contracts. State governments can also pass statues according to the rules of their own constitutions. Some government agencies can issue administrative regulations, which have the force of law.

Types of Law

American courts handle three types of law:

1. **Criminal law:** Forbids people from acting in certain ways. In criminal cases, a government prosecutor brings charges against a defendant. The outcome is either acquittal or punishment.
2. **Civil law:** Governs how people relate to one another. It can involve disputes about contracts, suits over responsibility for injury, and the like. Both parties in a civil suit are private citizens; the government does not bring civil charges against people.
3. **Constitutional law:** Covers the fundamentals of the political system, including cases that test the constitutionality of a law or government action.

TYPES OF COURTS AND JURISDICTION

There are two types of courts in the United States: federal and state. Each type of court has a certain **jurisdiction,** the unique power to hear and decide on certain types of cases. Federal courts, for example, have jurisdiction over cases that involve the national government or parties from more than one state or from another country. Only federal courts can hear these cases, not state courts. Each state court has jurisdiction over cases that involve disputing parties from within its own borders. There are four types of jurisdiction:

1. **Original jurisdiction:** The authority to be the first court to hear a case

2. **Appellate jurisdiction:** The power to review cases already decided in lower courts

3. **General jurisdiction:** The power to hear any type of case

4. **Limited jurisdiction:** The power to hear only certain kinds of cases (such as tax cases)

These types of jurisdiction are not mutually exclusive, which means that a court might have both original and limited jurisdiction or appellate and general jurisdiction.

The Federal Courts

There are three layers of authority in the federal court system:

1. The Supreme Court is the highest federal court in the country.

2. The twelve Courts of Appeals and the Court of Appeals for the Federal Circuit have moderate jurisdiction.

3. Several district and specialized courts have the most restricted jurisdiction in the federal court system.

The Structure of the Federal Courts

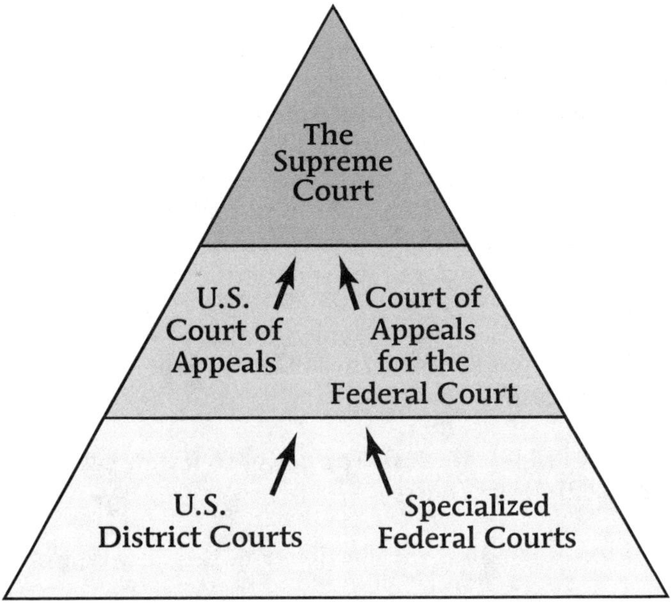

THE SUPREME COURT

The Supreme Court is the highest court in the land. Sometimes it hears cases as a trial court, but most of the time the Court functions as an appellate court. The Court has traditionally consisted of nine justices: one chief justice and eight associate justices. Although Congress has the power to change the number of justices, the number has held steady at nine justices since 1869. Supreme Court justices serve for life.

Selecting Cases

The Supreme Court receives thousands of appeals every year but hears only a small percentage of them. The Court meets in closed session to decide which cases to hear. The Court generally follows the **rule of four** in choosing cases: If four justices want to hear a case, the Court will accept it. When the Court decides to hear a case, it issues a **writ of certiorari,** a legal document ordering a lower court to send a case to the Supreme Court for review. The writ of certiorari signals that the Supreme Court will hear the case. The Court tends to hear only cases of great importance, such as cases involving a constitutional matter or a possible overturning of precedent.

The Court is more likely to grant a writ of certiorari if one of the appellants is the U.S. government. The solicitor general, a high-ranking official in the Justice Department, submits the requests for certiorari and argues cases in front of the Court as the lawyer for the federal government.

Briefs and Oral Arguments

Both parties in a case must submit **briefs** to the Court, documents that present the party's position and argument. Sometimes, other groups submit **amicus curiae briefs** (friend of the court briefs), which present further arguments in favor of one party or the other. The justices read the briefs and then may hear **oral arguments,** in which both parties have thirty minutes to make their case before the full Court. During oral arguments, the justices frequently interrupt the attorneys to ask questions.

Deciding Cases

After oral arguments, the justices meet in **judicial conference** to discuss the case. Sometimes the Court issues a **per curiam rejection,** an unsigned decision that reaffirms lower court's ruling. This rejection means that the Supreme Court has decided not to hear the case. Only the justices and their clerks attend the conference, and the proceedings are kept secret. After debating the case, the justices vote. The Court then issues a **decision,** which states the Court's ruling, and an **opinion,** which explains the Court's legal reasoning behind its decision.

There are several types of opinions:

- **Majority opinions** are issued when at least five justices agree with the legal reasoning behind the decision. These opinions form new precedents that lower courts must follow.

- **Plurality opinions** are issued when several justices agree with the decision but not the legal reasoning behind it. A plurality opinion represents the views of a majority of the justices on the winning side.

- **Concurring opinions** are issued by justices who agree with the winning side but disagrees with the legal reasoning.

- **Dissenting opinions** are issued by justices who opposed the ruling decision and favored the losing party in a case. Dissenting opinions explain why the dissenting justices find the ruling decision wrong.

The decision can **affirm** the lower court's ruling, in which case that ruling stands. If the Supreme Court finds error in the lower court's ruling, it can **reverse** the ruling. Sometimes when a case is reversed, it gets **remanded,** or sent back to a lower court for a new trial or proceeding.

The following table summarizes some of the most important court cases in American history.

LANDMARK SUPREME COURT CASES		
Case	Date	Significance
Marbury v. Madison	1803	Courts assumed the power of judicial review (the power to declare laws unconstitutional)
McCulloch v. Maryland	1819	Granted the federal government broad powers through the necessary and proper clause
Dred Scott v. Sanford	1857	Forcibly returned a slave to his owner in the South and thus increased tensions over slavery
Plessy v. Ferguson	1896	Ruled that "separate but equal" was constitutional; legalized segregation and Jim Crow laws
Brown v. Board of Education	1954	Overturned *Plessy;* declared segregation unconstitutional
Mapp v. Ohio	1961	Expanded the exclusionary rule to cover state courts
Gideon v. Wainwright	1963	Ruled that the government must supply a lawyer to those who cannot afford one
Miranda v. Arizona	1966	Ruled that police must inform people they are about to question of their right against self-incrimination
Roe v. Wade	1973	Legalized abortions in the first trimester of pregnancy
Bush v. Gore	2000	Decided the 2000 presidential election by ruling that the Florida Supreme Court was wrong in ordering a recount

COURTS OF APPEALS

The U.S. Courts of Appeals hear cases from federal district courts that have been appealed. The United States has twelve Courts of Appeals, each of which covers a **circuit,** a geographic area containing several district courts. For this reason, the Courts of Appeals are also known as *circuit courts*. When a party appeals a decision made in a district court, a circuit court reviews the details of the case. The Courts of Appeals do not hold trials; if a new trial is warranted, the Courts of Appeals send the case back to the district court. Courts of Appeals will not review all cases that have been appealed. Cases only get reviewed for a good reason, such as if the ruling discarded precedent.

The Court of Appeals for the Federal Circuit

The U.S. court system also has a thirteenth Court of Appeals, called the Court of Appeals for the Federal Circuit. This court has national jurisdiction over certain cases, such as those in which the U.S. government is a defendant.

SPECIALIZED FEDERAL COURTS

The federal court system includes a number of specialty courts that fall outside the primary system that have similar authority to the district courts. These courts include the U.S. Claims Court (which covers cases in which the federal government is being sued for damages), the U.S. Court of International Trade, the U.S. Tax Court, and the U.S. Court of Military Appeals. These courts are all inferior to the Supreme Court, and the losing party in a case heard in one of these courts can appeal directly to the Supreme Court.

DISTRICT COURTS

The lowest level of the federal judicial system is the U.S. District Courts, which hear most federal trials. Each district court hears cases within a particular district, or geographical area. There are more than ninety districts. Every state has at least one district court, but some have as many as four. District courts are courts of original jurisdiction. Because they are the lowest federal courts, district courts must follow Supreme Court precedent as much as possible. Most federal cases begin and end at the district court level.

SELECTION OF FEDERAL JUDGES

All federal judges are appointed by the president and approved by the Senate. **Senatorial courtesy,** a tradition since the 1840s, allows senators of the president's party to have a say in the appointment of judges to their states. Once on the bench, a federal judge keeps the position for a term of "good behavior," which is tantamount to life, barring criminal acts. As Alexander Hamilton argued in *Federalist Papers No. 78* (1787), keeping judges in office for life gives them the independence they need to serve as a proper check on the executive and legislative branches.

Qualifications

The Constitution does not list any specific requirements an individual must meet in order to become a federal judge. A person does not, in theory, even have to be a lawyer in order to be a judge, although the vast majority of judges are lawyers. In recent years, more nominees have had prior experience as judges (either on a lower court or on a state court). The American Bar Association (ABA), the professional association of lawyers, issues ratings of nominees based on their qualifications.

Supreme Court Nominees

The president nominates someone to be a Supreme Court justice only when there is a vacancy on the Court. Most presidents choose nominees based on judicial philosophy, hoping to appoint someone who will most likely decide cases in accordance with the political views of the president and members of his political party. Other factors that influence the president's choice include the nominee's qualifications, input from any outside groups, and the likelihood that the Senate will confirm the nominee.

Supreme Ghosts

Sometimes a nomination to the Supreme Court will come back to haunt the president because the justice behaves differently than expected. When President Dwight Eisenhower appointed Earl Warren as chief justice in 1953, he expected Warren to be a conservative. Instead, Warren led the Court through some of its most liberal decisions, including *Brown v. Board of Education* and *Miranda v. Arizona.*

Senate confirmation is often brutal process. Because federal justices serve for life, senators take great care to thoroughly question and investigate nominees. A failed nomination can be devastating to an administration and can make the president look foolish and politically weak.

EXAMPLE: In July 2005, President George W. Bush nominated White House Counsel Harriet Miers to the Supreme Court. Republicans and conservatives of all stripes immediately criticized the choice, partly because they felt that Miers lacked the experience to be an effective justice. The media portrayed the president as out of touch with the Republican Party, and many critics argued that Bush had placed loyalty above experience in choosing Miers. Miers consequently withdrew her nomination.

The State Courts

More than 95 percent of court cases in the United States take place in state courts. Most crimes fall under state law, and violations of those laws are tried in state courts. Under the Tenth Amendment, the states have great latitude in how they structure their courts. Most states have a system similar to the federal system: a set of courts with original jurisdiction, appellate courts to hear appeals from these courts, and a state supreme court with final say on state law. States use different terms to describe their courts, so a court with the same (or similar) name might serve very different functions in two different states.

STATE JUDGES

Each state determines how to select its state judges. The most popular ways of selecting state judges include the following:

- **Election:** This is the most common way in which states select judges.
- **Political appointment:** In some states, the governor appoints state judges.
- **The merit plan:** The governor appoints judges from a list of qualified candidates provided by a judicial selection committee. This method of selection (also known as the *Missouri Plan*) tries to put qualifications ahead of partisanship. Judges then must face **retention elections,** which let voters decide whether the judge should stay in office.

APPEALS TO THE SUPREME COURT

When a state supreme court has made a decision, losing parties have no higher state court to which they can appeal, but they can appeal the decision to the U.S. Supreme Court. The Supreme Court will only hear these cases if there is a federal or constitutional issue at stake. The Supreme Court has ultimate judicial power in the United States, but it does not settle matters of state law and instead defers to the state courts.

Judicial Philosophy, Politics, and Policy

Although judges do not run on a platform, as do elected officials, they nevertheless hold political beliefs that influence their decisions. People strongly debate the role of the courts in politics and the role that personal beliefs and political philosophy should play.

JUDICIAL PHILOSOPHY

Judicial philosophy is the way in which a judge understands and interprets the law. Laws are universal, but they must be applied to particular cases with unique circumstances. To do this, judges interpret the law, determining its meaning and sometimes the intent of those who wrote it.

The main types of contrasting judicial philosophies include judicial activism versus judicial restraint, loose constructionism versus strict constructionism, and living document versus original intent.

Some judges develop a philosophy of activism, using the bench to enact social and political change. Other judges practice a philosophy of restraint, believing that judges must interpret the law strictly rather than seek to make new laws. And all judges, regardless of their philosophies, develop their own methods of reading the Constitution. Some judicial philosophies tend to coincide with certain political views. Most strict constructionists, for example, are also advocates of judicial restraint, but not all. Similarly, many advocates of judicial restraint also follow the doctrine of original intent. These views, however, do not always overlap. As a result, judicial philosophies are not the same as political ideologies.

We explore these philosophies in more detail in the following tables.

JUDICIAL ACTIVISM VERSUS JUDICIAL RESTRAINT		
	Judicial Activism	**Judicial Restraint**
Beliefs	Courts should overturn bad laws and create new policies	Courts must interpret the law, not legislate new policies
Example	Warren Court (1953–1969)	Rehnquist Court (1986–2005)
Key Decisions	Advanced civil rights and the rights of the accused	Limits on expansion of federal power
Politics	Tend to be liberal	Tend to be conservative

LOOSE CONSTRUCTIONISM VERSUS STRICT CONSTRUCTIONISM

	Loose Constructionism	Strict Constructionism
Beliefs	Courts should read the Constitution expansively and should not limit themselves to what is explicitly stated	Courts should not reinterpret the Constitution
Example	Warren Court (1953–1969)	Rehnquist Court (1986–2005)
Key Decisions	Exclusionary rule, right to a government-funded attorney for the poor	Restrictions on abortion, eliminating federal rules for state governments
Politics	Tend to be liberal	Tend to be conservative

LIVING DOCUMENT VERSUS ORIGINAL INTENT

	Living Document	Original Intent
Beliefs	The Constitution must grow and adapt to new circumstances.	Courts should interpret the Constitution as the framers intended.
Example	Warren Court (1953–1969)	Rehnquist Court (1986–2005)
Key Decisions	Expansion of use of interstate commerce clause	Restrictions on privacy rights
Politics	Tend to be liberal	Tend to be conservative

Constructionism in Action

Privacy is not explicitly mentioned in the Constitution, so strict constructionists of the Constitution believe that the only privacy rights Americans have are those specifically outlined in the Constitution, such as protection against illegal searches. On the one hand, according to the strict constructionists, there is no general right to privacy. Loose constructionists, on the other hand, assert that a general right to privacy can be inferred from the rights that were explicitly listed by the framers. Privacy rights have taken center stage in many court cases, including *Roe v. Wade* (1973).

CHECKS ON THE COURTS

The legislative and executive branches check the power of the judiciary branch in several ways. The main way of limiting the courts' power lies with **judicial implementation,** the process by which a court's decision is enforced. The executive branch must enforce court decisions, but if the president or governor disagrees with a ruling, he or she sometimes ignores it or only partially enforces it. Legislatures can also limit the courts through the power of the purse. If Congress refuses to appropriate funds for implementing a Supreme Court decision, that decision will not be enforced. Congress and state legislatures also have the power to amend the Constitution, which they can do to counter a court ruling.

Sample Test Questions

1. Describe the common law tradition and precedent.

2. What is judicial review? How did the Supreme Court get this power?

3. What is an amicus curiae brief?

4. True or false: Judicial activists favor an expansive role for the courts.

5. True or false: Presidents spend a great deal of time deciding whom to nominate to the Supreme Court.

6. A court of appellate jurisdiction can hear which kinds of cases?

A. Cases that have been appealed from a lower court
B. Cases involving foreign governments
C. Civil cases
D. Criminal cases

7. According to the tradition of senatorial courtesy, a senator of the president's party has the power to do what?

A. Accept the president's nominee for a federal judgeship in his or her state
B. Approve the president's nominee for a federal judgeship in his or her state
C. Reject the president's nominee for a federal judgeship in his or her state
D. Interview any nominee to the federal bench

8. What happens when the Supreme Court issues a writ of certiorari?

A. The government must produce a person in court and press charges or release the person.
B. State courts must rule in a case.
C. The Court agrees to hear an appeal from a lower court.
D. The Court declines to hear a case.

9. Where are the majority of cases heard?

A. U.S. District Courts
B. U.S. Courts of Appeal
C. State courts
D. The Supreme Court

10. What was Franklin Roosevelt attempting to do with court packing?

A. Expand the size of the Supreme Court so he could appoint friendly justices
B. Shrink the size of the federal court system
C. Increase the role of state courts
D. Take judicial power for the executive branch

ANSWERS

1. In a common law system, judges rely on past decisions for guidance on handling cases. A past ruling that informs court decisions is called a precedent.

2. Judicial review is the power of a court to determine whether a law or government action is constitutional. The Supreme Court gave itself this power in the 1803 case *Marbury v. Madison.*

3. An amicus curiae ("friend of the court") brief is one filed by a group or person not a party to the case.

4. True

5. True

6. A

7. B

8. C

9. C

10. A

Suggested Reading

• Baum, Lawrence. *The Supreme Court.* 8th ed. Washington, D.C.: Congressional Quarterly Press, 2003.

Baum offers an in-depth exploration of how the Court functions and the role it plays in society.

• Carp, Robert A. *The Federal Courts.* 3rd ed. Washington, D.C.: Congressional Quarterly Press, 1998.

Carp's book presents a comprehensive view of the federal court system as a whole.

• Davis, Richard. *Seeking Justice: The Press, Public Opinion, and Interest Groups in the Supreme Court Nominations.* New York: Oxford University Press, 2005.

Supreme Court nominations are among the most public and controversial decisions a president can make, and they have a great impact on the law. Davis examines the role that the press and the public have in the nomination and confirmation process.

• Davis, Sue. *Justice Rehnquist and the Constitution.* Princeton, NJ: Princeton University Press, 1989.

The chief justice does not control the Supreme Court, but he can strongly influence the direction of the Court. Davis studies the impact of William Rehnquist on the Court.

• McGuire, Kevin T. *Understanding the Supreme Court: Cases and Controversies.* New York: McGraw-Hill, 2002.

The author explores important cases and the judicial philosophies that shape American law.

• Mezey, Susan G. *No Longer Disabled: The Federal Courts and the Politics of Social Security.* New York: Greenwood, 1988.

What sort of role do the courts play in shaping policy? Mezey explores that question with regard to disability policy.

• O'Brien, David M. *Storm Center: The Supreme Court in American Politics.* 5th ed. New York: Norton, 2000.

Storm Center is a classic study of the way the court fits into the American political system.

• O'Connor, Sandra Day. *The Majesty of the Law: Reflections of a Supreme Court Justice.* New York: Random House, 2003.

O'Connor, the Supreme Court's first woman and a key swing vote on the court, recounts her experiences on the Court and her views of the law.

• Sandler, Ross, and David Schoenbrod. *Democracy by Decree: What Happens When Courts Run Government.* New Haven, Conn.: Yale University Press, 2003.

Sandler and Schoenbrod are among the critics who charge that the courts have too much power. Their book evaluates the role of the courts in making policy.

Useful Websites

- www.findlaw.com

A database of Supreme Court cases since the 1970s.

- www.fjc.gov

The website of the Federal Judicial Center, a federal agency that researches, monitors, and educates the public about U.S. courts.

- www.law.umkc.edu/faculty/projects/FTrials/ftrials.htm

This website provides encyclopedia-style tidbits about some of history's most famous trials, including the LAPD–Rodney King trial and the Clinton impeachment trial.

- www.rominger.com/supreme.htm

This website has many links about the Supreme Court, including information on pending cases, as well as links to state courts systems and pending cases.

- www.supremecourtus.gov

The website of the Supreme Court of the United States. The site includes the Court's calendar of oral arguments, information for visitors, and links to information about the cases.

- www.uscourts.gov

The homepage of the federal court system.

POLITICAL PARTIES

8

Overview

The U.S. Constitution does not discuss or describe political parties. Indeed, many of the founding fathers feared the rise of parties: They felt that partisanship could tear apart the young nation. But political parties emerged almost as soon as the new government was established. Within a few years, John Adams ran for the presidency as a Federalist in 1796 and Thomas Jefferson ran as a Democratic Republican in 1800.

Today political parties continue to greatly influence American politics: They shape elections, define political disputes, and organize Congress. Our political leaders generally come from either the Republican or Democratic Party. Nevertheless, the American political system supports more than just these two parties, and third-party candidates often have lasting impacts on the politics, even if they rarely win major races.

How Political Parties Work

A **political party** is an alliance of like-minded people who work together to win elections and control of the government. Political parties compete against one another for political power and for the ability to put their philosophies and policies into effect.

Many voters demonstrate **party identification,** even though they do not formally belong to a party. So a voter might claim to be a Democrat, even though she does not pay dues, hold a membership card, or technically belong to that party. Other voters see themselves as **independents:** These voters do not belonging to any party, and they willingly vote for the best candidate regardless of that person's party affiliation.

The Rise of Independents

The number of people in the United States who identify themselves as independents has increased significantly in the past thirty years. Some scholars argue that this fact suggests that political parties are weakening. It is not clear, however, just how independent these people really are. Some scholars have argued that many people who call themselves independents always vote for the same party, just like partisans do.

Political socialization influences party identification. Family beliefs, education, socioeconomic conditions, and recent political events all help determine whether a person chooses to identify with a political party.

American Voter Identification

In the United States, the electorate breaks down roughly into thirds: One-third of voters identify themselves as Democrats, one-third as Republicans, and one-third as independents. These numbers, however, fluctuate to some degree, especially around elections.

PARTY ORGANIZATION

Party organization is the formal structure and leadership of a particular party. The major parties in the United States do not have a single party organization; rather, they have a series of organizations that cooperate to win elections. These organizations include the following:

- National party committees
- State party committees
- County party committees
- Party committees in Congress

Although the national party committee nominally functions as the head of the party, the national committee cannot force other party organizations to do what it wants. Sometimes different party organizations argue with one another about how to achieve their goals.

EXAMPLE: Following the 2004 presidential election, former Vermont governor Howard Dean became the chair of the Democratic National Committee. Working toward the 2008 elections, Dean clashed with Rahm Emmanuel, a representative from Illinois and the chair of the Democratic Congressional Campaign Committee, over how to spend party money. Dean wanted to spend the money building grassroots party organizations in every state (particularly in states that favor Republicans), whereas Emmanuel wanted to spend the money supporting candidates in specific races that are more likely to be won.

PARTY FUNCTIONS

In the United States, parties perform many functions:

- **Recruit candidates:** Parties want to win elections, so they must recruit people who are likely to win.
- **Organize elections:** Parties work hard to mobilize voters, encourage people to volunteer at the polls, and organize campaigns.
- **Hold conventions:** Every four years, the parties hold **national conventions** to formally declare the party's platform and to choose the party's presidential and vice-presidential nominees.
- **Unite factions:** Parties are not centered on a person but on a set of policy positions known as the **party platform.** The platform brings together a wide range of people with similar interests.

- **Ensure plurality:** The out-of-power party articulates its views in opposition to the ruling party. By doing this, the opposition party gives the public an alternative.

> **A Platform Made from Planks**
>
> The term *party platform* once had a more literal meaning: Candidates literally stood on a platform to explain their positions on issues. Political scientists use the word *plank* to refer to a position on a particular issue.

National Conventions

Convention delegates are the party members or officials who vote on nominations and ratify their party's platform. Delegates are **party activists,** people who believe so strongly in the ideology of their parties that they devote time and energy to working on the platform. Nowadays, conventions primarily serve as large-scale advertisements for the parties. In recent years, party leaders carefully choreographed conventions to present a united front and to put a positive face on their party. Controversial issues are sometimes avoided, whereas speeches aim for broad appeal.

> **Convention Disasters**
>
> A chaotic or ugly convention can harm a party's chance in the presidential election. The 1968 Democratic convention is perhaps the best example: While protesters fought with police outside, the convention turned chaotic when opponents of Democratic nominee Hubert Humphrey tried to speak out. The convention floor itself then turned violent. Humphrey secured the nomination but lost the election to Republican Richard M. Nixon.

The American Two-Party System

The United States has only two major political parties: the Democrats and the Republicans. These parties have a **duopoly**, meaning that they share almost all the political power in the country.

> **Parties in Other Democracies**
>
> Most democratic countries have more than two parties. In Israel, for example, twelve parties or party alliances held seats in the seventeenth Knesset. Japan has several major parties, including the Liberal Democratic Party, the Democratic Party of Japan, the New Komeito, and the Japanese Communist Party.

THE ELECTORAL SYSTEM

In the United States, a candidate wins the election by gaining a **plurality**, or more votes than any other candidate. This is a **winner-take-all system** because there is no reward for the party or candidate that finishes second. Parties aim to be as large as possible, smoothing over differences among candidates and voters. There is no incentive to form a party that consistently gets votes but cannot win an election. As a result, two political parties usually dominate plurality electoral systems to the disadvantage of smaller third parties, just as the Democrats and the Republicans dominate the American political system. No one person or organization prevents third parties from forming, but the plurality system itself usually hinders their efforts to win votes.

The United States also has mostly **single-member districts**, meaning that each legislative district sends only one member to the legislature. There is no benefit to finishing second. Some countries use **multiple-member districts**, which makes it easier for minor parties to succeed because there are more members winning seats in the legislature.

The Electoral College

The Electoral College exacerbates the winner-take-all system because in all but two states, whoever wins the most popular votes wins all of the state's electoral votes in the presidential election. The electoral rules favor a two-party system, and minor parties have a very difficult time competing in such a system. Even successful third-party candidates often fail to get a single electoral vote.

EXAMPLE: In the 1992 presidential election, independent candidate H. Ross Perot received nearly 19 percent of the popular vote, but he did not get a single electoral vote. Other recent third-party candidates—including John Anderson in 1980, Perot again in 1996, and Ralph Nader in 2000—also failed to win electoral votes. The last third-party candidate to win any electoral votes was George Wallace in 1968's tumultuous election.

Proportional Representation

Many other democratic legislatures use **proportional representation** instead of plurality to determine how seats are allocated to political parties. Parties win seats in the legislature in rough proportion to the percentage of the popular votes the party wins. A party that receives 30 percent of the votes, for example, will get roughly 30 percent of the seats in the legislature. In multiparty systems, parties can achieve electoral success without winning a majority, so there is less reason to form giant parties that strive for the majority.

ADVANTAGES AND DISADVANTAGES

There are a few advantages of the American two-party system:

- **Stability:** Two-party systems are more stable than multi-party systems
- **Moderation:** The two parties must appeal to the middle to win elections, so the parties tend to be moderate.
- **Ease:** Voters have only to decide between two parties.

But there are also a few disadvantages to our system, including the following:

- **Lack of choice:** Both parties tend to be very similar, limiting voters' options.
- **Less democratic:** A percentage of people will always feel marginalized by the system.

REALIGNMENT

Scholars use the term **realignment** to describe a major shift in the political divisions within a country. Realignment marks a new change in direction for the party that redefines what it means to be a member of that party. It usually occurs when a new issue challenges the old party lines and splits its members. The issue is often **crosscutting:** Both major parties are split on a matter, and some Democrats find they agree with Republicans more than other Democrats. When the issue becomes critically important, the parties shift around the axis of the new issue, and a new party system emerges.

Critical Elections

A **critical election** often indicates that a realignment has occurred. Critical elections do not cause realignments. A critical election is a sign, not a cause, of a realignment.

SOFT MONEY

Until recently, political parties were able to indirectly provide large amounts of money to candidates. The campaign finance laws passed in the mid-1970s limited donations to campaigns: Each person could only donate $1,000 to a campaign for the general election. Individual donors, however, could give unlimited amounts of money to parties and some political groups. Political scientists call this type of unregulated donation **soft money.** Although the parties could not use soft money to help candidates directly (by donating it to a campaign, for example), the parties could spend it in ways that helped their candidates. Parties use soft money to sponsor the following:

- **Voter registration and GOTV drives:** The party can selectively register voters who are likely to support the party. During get-out-the-vote (GOTV) efforts, parties wage campaigns to encourage voting and target people likely to vote for the party.
- **Issue ads:** The Supreme Court ruled that as long as an ad does not explicitly say "vote for candidate X" or "vote against candidate Y," the ad is not considered a campaign ad. Therefore, parties can run ads attacking the opponent and saying good things about their nominee.

In 2002, Congress passed the **Bipartisan Campaign Reform Act,** popularly known as the **McCain-Feingold bill,** which banned soft money. Parties could no longer raise unlimited amounts of unregulated money. However, parties have responded by delegating some of their duties to **527 groups** (named after section 527 of the Internal Revenue Code). These private organizations are not officially affiliated with the parties and can therefore raise and spend money in much the same way that parties could before the reform law. For this reason, some critics allege that campaign finance reform did nothing but weaken the parties.

527s in 2004

In the 2004 campaigns, 527 groups on both sides played a big part. On the Democratic side, groups such as America Coming Together and Emily's List spent large amounts of money, whereas the Swift Boat Veterans for Truth and the Club for Growth did the same on the Republican side. Other noteworthy 527 groups during the 2004 election cycle include Progress for America (conservative) and Moveon.org (liberal).

HISTORY

Most Americans look favorably on the two-party system because it has dominated much of American politics from the very beginning. The Republican and Democratic parties have existed for more than 150 years, and that history gives them a legitimacy that third parties do not have. The two-party system is also self-perpetuating. Children grow up identifying with one of the two major parties instead of a **third party** because children tend to share their parents' political views.

Polarizing Issues

Throughout much of American history, central issues have divided the electorate. In the early decades of the republic, for example, the extent of federal power dominated politics. Some political scientists might argue that today's polarizing issues include abortion and gay marriage. Such polarizing issues have helped maintain the two-party system in the United States: Each party rallies around one side of the issue at hand.

The Early Republic: Federalists Versus Antifederalists (1792–1800)

The first political issue that divided American statesmen was the ratification of the Constitution. On one side were the Federalists, who wanted to ratify the Constitution in order to create a stronger national government; the Antifederalists, on the other side, feared that the Constitution would strip people of the liberties they had just won in the Revolutionary War. Although the Constitution was ratified, this early political division extended into the first decades of the republic. The Federalists allied themselves to Alexander Hamilton and President John Adams, while Thomas Jefferson rallied the Antifederalists, who had begun calling themselves the Democratic Republicans. Neither faction was a true party in the modern sense, though, because both lacked strong cohesion.

The "Era of Good Feeling" (1800–1824)

Following Jefferson's victory in the presidential election of 1800, the Federalists faded away as a serious political threat, so that by the time of James Monroe's presidency (1817 to 1825), almost all Americans identified with the Democratic Republicans. Because of the absence of party competition, this period has been dubbed the "Era of Good Feeling." The public still debated and fought over issues but not within the context of distinct political factions.

The Jacksonian Era: Democrats Versus Whigs (1824–1850)

The first modern political party was the Democratic Party, which formed in the wake of the highly contested presidential election of 1824, when Andrew Jackson won the popular vote but did not win a majority of electoral votes. The House of Representatives chose John Quincy Adams to be the next president. In response, Jackson's supporters organized the Democratic Party to oppose the Adams Administration. The

Democrats rebounded in four years and elected Jackson to replace Adams in 1828. The Democrats were also the first major **grassroots** party, building support from the ground up. Those disparate politicians who opposed Jackson's policies formed a temporary coalition known as the Whig Party.

The Antebellum Period: Democrats Versus Republicans (1850–1860)

Over the next few decades, slavery emerged as a hugely divisive issue, as pro-slavery forces fought abolitionists with increasing intensity. Neither the Whigs nor the Democrats could respond adequately to the new issue. As a result, both parties split in two along sectional lines.

The Republican Party formed in the late 1840s and early 1850s out of abolitionist Democrats and northern Whigs. The Democrats, on the other hand, now consisted primarily of Southerners and rural Westerners. In 1860, the Republicans nominated Abraham Lincoln. Northern Democrats nominated Stephen Douglas, whereas Southern Democrats nominated John C. Breckenridge. Lincoln narrowly won the race with promises of maintaining the Union, but his election nevertheless prompted South Carolina and several other Southern states to secede.

The Reconstruction Era (1868–1896)

The northern Republicans and southern Democrats continued to vie for power in the decades after the Civil War. Blacks were able to vote for a brief period after the war, and they mostly voted Republican, in part because they associated the Democrats with slavery and the Republicans with emancipation. Democratic efforts to dissuade blacks from voting also encouraged many blacks to vote Republican.

Strong Parties and Patronage

During the nineteenth century, political parties were strong, powerful organizations. At times, the head of a party organization wielded even more power than elected officials from that party. One important source of power was the party's ability to choose nominees. Until fairly recently, party leaders chose people to run for office, with little or no input from the public. Leaders met in **caucus,** or informal closed meetings, to set the party platform and choose nominees. The party could punish a recalcitrant member by refusing to nominate that person for the next election, which meant that the member would lose his or her job. At times, party organizations doled out government jobs and contracts were given out to allies in return for political **patronage.** These party organizations are called **machines** because they transform favors and patronage into votes.

The Gilded Age (1880–1896)

The next great issue to divide America was industrialization, as massive corporations began hording capital and dominating the unregulated marketplace. To challenge the big-business trusts, poor western farmers united to form a powerful third party, the People's Party, or **Populists.** The Democratic Party incorporated much of the Populist platform into its own platform in the election of 1896, which inadvertently killed the Populists as a potent third party. Republican William McKinley defeated the Democratic Populist challenger William Jennings Bryan and established a new era of Republican dominance. Except for the election of 1912, the Republicans won every presidential election between 1896 and 1932.

Progressivism (1896–1932)

Another social movement, called Progressivism, swept through the nation in the first two decades of the 1900s. Like the Populists, Progressives fought for government regulation of big business and more political power for the average American. Progressivism was bipartisan, which meant that Progressive politicians could be found in both the Republican and Democratic political parties. For example, both Republican Theodore Roosevelt and Democrat Woodrow Wilson were Progressives. A feud between President William Howard Taft—a traditional conservative Republican—and the Progressive Roosevelt split the party and prompted Roosevelt to found the Progressive Party. Roosevelt won a surprising number of popular and electoral votes in the three-way election of 1912 but divided Republican voters so deeply that the more organized Democrats managed to elect Woodrow Wilson. Wilson's battle to convince the Senate to ratify the Treaty of Versailles to end World War I all but killed the Progressive movement, and voters elected conservative Republican presidents until the election of 1932.

The Depression and the New Deal (1929–1941)

Republican dominance ended with the Great Depression, which began with the stock market crash of 1929. Frustrated with Republican president Herbert Hoover, many voters turned to the Democrats. The Democratic nominee in 1932, Franklin Delano Roosevelt, proposed to revive the economy with a legislative package of relief and reform known as the New Deal. Roosevelt won and successfully put America on the road to recovery.

The New Deal Coalition (1936–1968)

The **New Deal coalition** formed the backbone of Democratic success in the mid-twentieth century. This coalition consisted of groups who supported the New Deal, including workers, labor unions, Catholics, Jews, and racial minorities. The South continued to be overwhelmingly Democratic, and after 1932, African American voters moved in large numbers to the Democratic Party. For the next three decades, the Democratic Party dominated American politics.

In the 1950s, a committee of respected political scientists called for **responsible parties,** parties that were strong enough not only to propose specific and substantive policies but also to carry them out if elected. In general, American parties are not very responsible because they cannot force members to follow the platform, unlike their counterparts in other countries. Because parties no longer have much control over their candidates, the vision of responsible party government is unlikely to be fulfilled anytime soon.

The Civil Rights Movement and Vietnam (1960s)

The New Deal coalition splintered in the 1960s because of the civil rights movement and American involvement in Vietnam. The Democratic Party included nearly all white southerners, who still saw the Republicans as the party that invaded their homeland during the Civil War. At the same time, most African Americans were now Democrats. The tension between these groups caused the New Deal coalition to split in the late 1960s, and large numbers of southern whites switched to the Republican Party. By the 1980s, much of the South was solidly Republican.

The critical election came in 1968. The Vietnam War, along with civil rights, caused stark divisions. George Wallace, the Democratic governor of Alabama, broke away from the Democrats and ran as a third-party candidate, which greatly hurt the Democrats. Republican Richard Nixon consequently eked out a narrow and bitterly fought victory. The chaotic election of 1968 also marked a decline in American political parties.

Following the election, the Democrats worked to change the way their party operated, focusing heavily on the process of choosing nominees. Political scientists call the process of opening party leadership to new people **party reform.** The Democrats aimed at making convention delegates look more like party voters by including more women and minorities. The easiest way to achieve this goal was to hold primary elections, which allow voters to directly participate in the party nomination process. Beginning in 1972, the Democrats made increasing use of the primary election, taking great power away from party leaders. Republicans followed suit, in part because Democratic-controlled state governments forced them to do so.

The Contemporary Party System (1968–Present)

Republicans have fared very successfully since the election of 1968, particularly in presidential races; since 1968, only two Democrats have been elected president, Jimmy Carter in 1976 and Bill Clinton in 1992 and 1996. Some scholars believe that the breakdown of the New Deal coalition produced a realignment that allowed the Republicans to dominate. Others, however, argue that instead of realignment, the United States is experiencing **dealignment,** the loosening of party ties. Since the 1970s, more voters have identified themselves as independents, not belonging to either party. More people seem willing to cross party lines and vote for the other party. More voters are also engaging in **split-ticket voting,** voting for both Republicans and Democrats for different offices in the same election. Split-ticket voting has produced a number of **divided governments** in which one party controls the presidency while the other controls at least one house of Congress.

The Reagan Democrats

The so-called Reagan Democrats were notorious for crossing party lines in the 1980s. These mostly blue-collar workers traditionally voted Democrat but were drawn to Reagan's toughness and social conservatism. The Reagan Democrats helped Reagan win two terms in office.

Political parties today no longer have the ability to dictate nominees or control massive patronage. Candidates function independently from the party leaders, charting their own strategies and ignoring or dismissing the party platform.

EXAMPLE: In 1996, Republican presidential nominee Bob Dole told reporters that he had not even read his party's platform.

As the importance of parties has decreased, there has been a rise in **candidate-centered politics,** in which people tend to focus on the candidates instead of party labels when voting, particularly when electing presidents. Today, parties primarily provide services such as money, expertise, lists of donors, and name recognition to candidates and campaigns. Although candidates do not have to do everything party leaders say, they often work closely with their party leadership in order to win favors and party support. Some races are still **party-centered,** especially when voters know little about the candidates.

What's in a Name?

Political parties sometimes change their names. In 1977, the Prohibition Party renamed itself the National Statesmen Party. However, the party's vote total went down dramatically in the 1980 election, so it changed the name back—and regained some votes during the 1984 election.

Third Parties

Third parties face many obstacles in the United States. In all states, the Democratic and Republican candidates automatically get on the ballot, whereas third-party candidates usually have to get thousands of signatures on petitions just to be listed on the ballot. The state and federal governments, which make rules governing elections, are composed of elected Democratic and Republican officials, who have a strong incentive to protect the existing duopoly. Also, third-party candidates often face financial difficulties because a party must have received at least 5 percent of the vote in the previous election in order to qualify for federal funds.

Coke and Pepsi

The two political parties are a lot like the two giants of the cola world, Coke and Pepsi. Although each wants to win, they both recognize that it is in their mutual interest to keep a third cola from gaining significant market share. Coke and Pepsi, many people have argued, conspire to keep any competitor from gaining ground. For example, in supermarkets, cola displays at the end of the aisles are often given over to Coke for six months of the year and Pepsi for the other six. Competitors such as Royal Crown face an extremely difficult challenge. The Democrats and the Republicans function in much the same way.

SOME IMPORTANT THIRD PARTIES

Party	Dates	Success(es)
Anti-Masonic Party	1828–1832	First party to hold a convention to nominate candidates
Prohibition Party	1867–present	Has nominated a candidate for president in every election since 1872
Progressive Party	1912	Elected a number of candidates to state legislatures, Congress, and even the U.S. Senate. Deflected enough votes from Republican William Howard Taft to hand the presidency to Democrat Woodrow Wilson in 1912.
American	1968–present	Won electoral votes (for George Wallace)
Libertarian Party	1971–present	Some members have won local elections.
Green Party	1984–present	Some members have won local elections.

THE APPEAL OF THIRD PARTIES

Third parties appeal to people for a number of reasons:

- **Ideology:** People who feel strongly about a particular issue might be drawn to a third party that focuses exclusively on that issue.

  EXAMPLE: The Greenback Party focused on the monetary system, and the Prohibition Party sought to ban the consumption of alcohol. The Populist Party, meanwhile, grew out of the Populist movement, and the Republican Party developed primarily out of the abolitionist movement.

- **Dissatisfaction with the status quo:** Some third parties form when part of a major party breaks off in protest and forms a **splinter party.**

  EXAMPLE: In 1912, Theodore Roosevelt led a group of dissidents out of the Republican Party to form the splinter Progressive Party.

- **Geographical location:** Third parties can be closely tied to a specific region, which can increase their appeal. Chicago's Harold Washington Party, for example, seeks to carry on the legacy of Harold Washington, the city's first African American mayor.

The Problem with Charismatic Leaders

Some people join third parties because of the charismatic personality of the party's candidate. If the leader leaves the party, however, the party often collapses, which is what happened to the Reform Party in the mid-1990s. Founded by Ross Perot after his first presidential bid in 1992, the Reform Party served as Perot's base for his 1996 campaign. After Perot decided not to run again, however, the Reform Party's political clout declined dramatically. In 2000, the party split in two over the candidacy of former Republican Pat Buchanan. Neither Buchanan nor his Reform Party rival gained many votes, and the party has largely disappeared from the national stage.

THE ROLE OF THIRD PARTIES

Despite their lack of success in the polls, third parties can affect American politics in a number of ways:

- **Introduce new ideas:** Third parties propose many government policies and practices.

  EXAMPLE: The Populist Party introduced ideas that influenced some economic policies of the New Deal, whereas the Anti-Masonic Party was the first party to use a convention to nominate its candidates, in the mid-nineteenth century.

- **Put issues on the agenda:** Third parties can force the major parties to address potentially divisive problems.

  EXAMPLE: In 1992, neither Bill Clinton nor George H. W. Bush talked much about the budget deficit until independent candidate Ross Perot emphasized it in his campaign.

- **Spoil the election:** Third parties can cost one party an election by playing the **spoiler.** If a third party draws enough votes away from a major party, it can prevent that party from winning. It is impossible to know for sure what would have happened had the third-party candidate not run, but in some cases, it seems that the third party probably cost one candidate the election.

> *EXAMPLE:* Some pundits argued that Ralph Nader's bid in the 2000 presidential election may have cost Al Gore the presidency by siphoning away votes in key states such as Florida.

- **Keep the major parties honest:** A leftist party can challenge the Democratic Party, for example, on social justice issues, whereas a conservative party can pose problems for the Republican Party. Because third-party candidates usually have little chance of winning, they can speak more frankly than their major party rivals, addressing facts and issues that the major parties would often prefer to ignore.

Sample Test Questions

1. What is a political party?

2. Why does the United States have a two-party system?

3. Why do some object to the two-party system?

4. True or false: Fusion occurs when two parties nominate the same candidate for an office.

5. True or false: Many of the ideas proposed by the Progressives aimed at reducing the power of party machines.

6. What is realignment?

A. When one party takes the presidency away from the other
B. The emergence of a new political alignment and a new balance between the parties
C. The loosening of party ties as more people see themselves as independent
D. The shifting of power from a national party organization to a state party organization

7. What is a party machine?

A. Any unpopular party
B. A term for *party in the electorate*
C. Party efforts to get out votes during an election
D. A powerful party organization that transforms patronage and favors into votes

8. Party in the electorate focuses on which of the following?

A. Party identification among voters
B. The way parties run their organizations
C. The process of nominating candidates for office
D. The party structure in Congress

9. Which of the following is true of responsible parties?

A. They do not lie to the public.
B. They are able to enact their party platform if elected.
C. They offer responsible policies in their platform.
D. They seek to improve government, not win elections.

10. Which third party is the only one to win a presidential election and displace another major party?

A. Libertarian Party
B. Progressive Party
C. Democratic Party
D. Republican Party

ANSWERS

1. A political party is an organization that seeks to influence government by electing officials to office.

2. A number of factors contribute to the two-party system, including the electoral system, legal barriers to third parties, history and tradition, and political socialization.

3. Some feel that the two-party system is undemocratic because it does not represent significant parts of the population and that it greatly limits the electoral choices Americans have.

4. True

5. True

6. B

7. D

8. A

9. B

10. D

Suggested Readings

• Black, Earl, and Merle Black. *The Rise of Southern Republicans.* Cambridge, Mass.: Harvard University Press, 2002.

A study of the major shift in party alignment over the last few decades: the move of white southerners from the Democratic Party to the Republican Party.

• Green, John C., and Daniel Shea, eds. *The State of the Parties: The Changing Role of Contemporary Parties.* 2nd ed. Lanham, Md.: Rowman and Littlefield, 1996.

A number of top-notch scholars analyze the changing roles of the parties as the parties adapt to open-nomination systems and campaign finance laws.

• Greenberg, Stanley B. *The Two Americas: Our Current Political Deadlock and How to Break It.* New York: Thomas Dunne Books, 2004.

Greenberg studies the division of America into red states and blue states.

• Keith, Bruce E., et al. *The Myth of the Independent Voter.* Berkeley: University of California Press, 1992.

The authors argue that the rise in independent voters is an illusion because most so-called independents behave exactly like party loyalists.

• Nader, Ralph. *Crashing the Party: How to Tell the Truth and Still Run for President.* New York: St. Martin's Press, 2002.

Nader recounts his iconoclastic run as the Green Party nominee in 2000, including his role as a spoiler.

• Rosenstone, Steven J., Roy L. Behr, and Edward H. Lazarus. *Third Parties in America.* 2nd ed. Princeton, NJ: Princeton University Press 1996.

An excellent account of the history and impact of third parties.

- Sundquist, James L. *Dynamics of the Party System: Alignment and Realignment of Political Parties in the United States*. Revised ed. Washington, D.C.: Brookings, 1983.

One of the classic works on realignment. Sundquist provides ample detail in describing the history of party shifts.

Useful Websites

- www.democrats.org

The Democratic National Committee's site offers information and links to candidates and local organizations. The site also contains the Democratic Party platform.

- www.gp.org

The web site of the Green Party, a fairly new but prominent third party.

- www.lp.org

The Libertarian Party is the most successful third party in the United States.

- www.politicalindex.com/sect8.htm

The National Political Index has extensive links to political parties, both major and minor.

- www.politics1.com/parties.htm

A great site with information about the major parties and about 50 third parties active in the United States.

- www.rnc.org

The Republican National Committee's site offers information and links to candidates and local organizations. The site also contains the Republican Party platform.

INTEREST GROUPS

9

Overview

The famous French writer on American government and society Alexis de Tocqueville once wrote that America was a nation of joiners. This facet of American political life has not changed since de Tocqueville made his observation in the nineteenth century. Americans are much more likely to join political and social organizations than people in other countries. Although most political scientists agree that this unique trend has a positive impact on democracy, the political power wielded by these groups sometimes dominates the political process at the expense of individuals and society as a whole. For example, many Americans these days feel that politicians listen more to special interests than to average voters, and John McCain centered his 2000 presidential bid around attacks on the power of interest groups.

Interest groups come in all shapes and sizes. They range from very liberal to very conservative and everything in between. Lobbyists pursue nearly every imaginable goal, from tax credits to fundamental revisions of American political culture. The National Rifle Association, the American Association of Retired Persons, the National Organization for Women, and the World Wildlife Fund are all examples of interest groups.

Types of Interest Groups

An **interest group** is an organization of people who share a common interest and work together to protect and promote that interest by influencing the government. Interest groups vary greatly in size, aims, and tactics. Political scientists generally divide interest groups into two categories: economic and noneconomic.

ECONOMIC GROUPS

Economic groups, which seek some sort of economic advantage for their members, are the most common type of interest group. Money has significant influence in capitalist societies, so economic interest groups are numerous and powerful. These groups are usually well funded because members willingly contribute money in the hopes of reaping greater political influence and profit.

Economic groups work to win **private goods,** which are benefits that only the members of the group will enjoy. When a labor union agrees to a contract, for example, its members benefit from the contract, whereas nonunion members do not. If there is no private good incentive, people might choose not to join (especially if there is a membership fee or dues). There are four main types of economic groups: business groups, labor groups, agricultural groups, and professional associations.

Business Groups

Business groups are the most common type of interest group; more than half of all registered lobbyists work for business organizations. Some business lobbyists work for a single corporation, lobbying solely for that company. Businesses also form associations with companies from the same industry to promote all of their interests. For example, the American Petroleum Institute works on behalf of oil companies. Some groups act on behalf of business in general. The U.S. Chamber of Commerce, for example, seeks pro-business policies in general, not just policies that help one part of the economy.

Because they are usually well funded, business groups tend to be very influential. They work to promote the interests of private companies and corporations by seeking tax cuts, regulatory changes, and other pro-business benefits. Business groups do not always agree with one another, however. What benefits one industry may harm another, so advocates for those industries quite often work against one another.

Labor Groups

Labor groups represent unions, which work to increase wages and improve working conditions for both skilled and unskilled workers. Individual workers have very little power, but banded together, they can wield significant influence. Labor unions have been a significant part of American economic and political life since the late nineteenth century. At the peak of the unions' influence, roughly one-third of American workers belonged to labor unions.

In recent decades, however, union membership has declined so that fewer than one-fourth of the nation's workers belong to any union. The American Federation of State, County, and Municipal Employees; the United Food and Commercial Workers International; and Service Employees International are among the largest and most influential labor unions. The AFL-CIO (American Federation of Labor–Congress of Industrial Organizations) is an umbrella organization of labor unions that cooperate in order to expand their influence. Labor unions spend much of their time and energy dealing with employers, but they also play a political role. Unions mobilize voters and donate money to help candidates who they feel will benefit workers.

Splits in the Labor Movement

The decline of labor unions has caused some people to question union leadership. In 2005, for example, a number of very prominent unions pulled out of the AFL-CIO because they could not agree on a political strategy. Leadership elections have also turned nasty. Although organized labor's political influence remains, some pundits argue that these disputes further diminish the power of unions.

Agricultural Groups

Agricultural groups represent the interests of farmers. Farmers have been organized for centuries to protect themselves against price fluctuations and other issues. In the United States, farmers' groups, such as the Grange movement, have played an important role in politics, which continues today: The federal government spends large amounts of money supporting farmers and influencing what crops are grown. Not all agricultural groups agree on the same policies. Some groups, such as the Farm Bureau, tend to work most closely with large agribusinesses, whereas others, such as the Farmers Union and the Grange, do more to protect family farms.

Professional Associations

Many professionals have formal organizations that set ground rules for the profession, regulate practices, and promote standards of conduct. Professional associations also lobby the government on issues related to their profession. The American Medical Association, for example, fights against laws it feels undercut physicians' autonomy. Similarly, the National Education Association, a professional association for teachers, lobbies for policies it feels will benefit teachers and students.

> **Interest Groups and Prescription Drugs**
>
> Prescription drugs are more important to health care than ever before. Interest groups have played a strong role in the rules governing prescription drugs, from influencing the process of drug approval by the Food and Drug Administration to regulating the price and distribution of pharmaceuticals. When Congress added prescription drug coverage to Medicare in 2004, many felt that pharmaceutical companies had influenced Congress to forbid negotiations over drug prices.

NONECONOMIC GROUPS

Noneconomic groups (sometimes called **citizens' groups**) are interest groups that fight for causes instead of working for material gain. Unlike economic groups, which work for private goods, noneconomic groups seek **public goods** (also called **collective goods**), which benefit everyone in society, not just members of the group. Instead of **material incentives,** these groups offer their members a variety of **selective incentives,** including the following benefits:

- **Purposive benefits:** The emotional and psychological benefits members receive knowing they have contributed to a cause they feel is worthwhile
- **Solidarity benefits:** The social benefits members receive after meeting new people and friends they worked with to promote the cause
- **Informational benefits:** The educational benefits members receive after having learned more about the issues that matter to them

There are four main types of noneconomic groups: public interest groups, single-issue groups, ideological groups, and government groups.

Public Interest Groups

Public interest groups claim to work for the good of the whole society, not just one part of it. Not surprisingly, public interest groups often have very different ideas as to how to improve society. Many public interest groups tackle a number of related issues. Greenpeace, for example, works to protect ecosystems around the world and to educate the public about dangers to the environment. The nonpartisan public interest group Democracy 21 seeks to strengthen democracy by lobbying for election and campaign finance reforms.

Single-Issue Groups

Single-issue groups work solely on one specific issue. These groups tend to be very strongly driven, composed of members who are passionately committed to the particular cause. Over the last few decades, the number of single-issue groups has grown greatly; there are now groups covering a broad range of issues. Well-known single-issue groups include the National Rifle Association, which lobbies against gun control legislation, and Operation Rescue, which works to ban abortion.

Ideological Groups

Whereas single-issue groups have a very narrow focus, ideological groups have much broader aims rooted in a strongly held philosophy. Ideological groups often work to change cultural norms, values, and prevailing stereotypes. Conservative ideological groups include the Christian Coalition and the Traditional Values Coalition, whereas liberal ideological groups include the NOW and the National Organization for the Advancement of Colored People.

Government Groups

Government groups represent the interests of other governments. Many cities and state governments, for example, have lobbyists in Washington to act in their interest. Most foreign governments also hire lobbyists to promote their interests in Congress and the White House.

> **Catchin' a Ride**
>
> People who reap the benefits from public goods without actually contributing to the group that won those goods are known as **free riders.** The free rider phenomenon is particularly troublesome for noneconomic interest groups, especially ideological interests groups, which have trouble recruiting active members who are willing to contribute time, money, and energy to winning a public good that will benefit everyone.

SOME MAJOR INTEREST GROUPS		
	Type of Group	Example
Economic	Business	National Association of Manufacturers
	Labor	International Brotherhood of Teamsters
	Agricultural	American Farm Bureau Federation
	Professional Association	American Bar Association
Noneconomic	Public Interest	League of Women Voters
	Single Issue	The Environmental Defense Fund
	Ideological	Christian Coalition
	Government	National League of Cities

Strategies Used by Interest Groups

Organized groups are more effective than unorganized ones. A well-organized group can wage a coordinated campaign that incorporates many different tactics. Organization can also make up for size: A well-organized small group often has a bigger impact than a large poorly organized one.

Lobbyists employ a number of tactics and offer lawmakers a number of benefits to achieve their goals, including persuasion, information, material incentives, economic leverage, disruption, and litigation.

ACCESS

The key to lobbying is access: To influence an official, one must be able to speak to that official. Given how busy members of Congress and other government officials often are, getting access poses a major challenge. Sometimes a lobbyist can only get two or three minutes of the official's time, so the lobbyist must be prepared to make the pitch very quickly.

Some types of people have an easier time getting access than others. Some lobbying organizations use these types of people to help gain access. Actor Michael J. Fox, for example, has lobbied for increased funding for Parkinson's disease research. Both Angelina Jolie and Bono have also successfully lobbied Congress for their causes.

A Profitable Profession

Former government officials, especially high-ranking ones, can often earn large salaries by working as lobbyists, which makes lobbying an attractive profession for retiring members. These officials are often in great demand as lobbyists because they know many people in government and can therefore get access easily. Bob Dole, for example—who used to be a senator from Kansas and was the Republican Party's presidential nominee in 1996—is one of the most famous former officials now working as a lobbyist in Washington, but there are many others.

PERSUASION AND INFORMATION

Lobbyists work to persuade governmental officials. Lobbyists offer arguments, evidence, and research to support their groups' positions. Many government officials do not have the time to research issues themselves, so they rely on information from trusted interest groups and lobbyists to keep them informed and up to date. Publishing their findings also allows interest groups to influence public opinion, which, in turn, often influences the policy decisions of lawmakers.

MATERIAL INCENTIVES

Although persuasion is a key part of lobbying, interest groups also provide some material incentives to government officials. Laws limit government officials from taking gifts, but they can still be wined and dined. Also, lobbyists can hold informational seminars for officials, flying them to places such as the Florida Keys or a golf resort to educate them about issues.

ECONOMIC LEVERAGE

Interest groups can use economic power as a weapon to get what they want. In most cases, economic power means money: Rich interest groups can contribute to campaigns, run advertisements, pay for research, and build a strong presence in Washington. Interest groups can leverage their economic power in other ways too, though. Labor unions, for example, often seek change by striking or by threatening to strike. Boycotting, or refusing to buy a particular company's goods, is another effective method groups use to accomplish their goals.

DISRUPTION

Interest groups sometimes stage protests in order to disrupt activities, generate publicity, and apply pressure on those they oppose. Disruptions can include strikes, pickets, riots, and sit-ins. In the 1960s, student civil rights groups used sit-ins to peacefully protest the Jim Crow laws and institutions in the South.

LITIGATION

In the United States, interest groups often achieve their goals through litigation, by suing groups they oppose. In the 1940s and 1950s, for example, the NAACP brought numerous lawsuits against segregated school systems, culminating in the landmark *Brown v. Board of Education* decision of 1954. Many other groups have used the courts to achieve their goals.

The Inside Game: Lobbying

Interest groups influence government using variants on one of two strategies, the inside game and the outside game. The **inside game** refers to attempts to persuade government officials through direct inside contact. Another term for the inside game is **lobbying.** Washington is filled with thousands of lobbyists, covering every imaginable issue and viewpoint. Lobbyists usually work for interest groups, corporations, or law firms that specialize in professional lobbying.

The Origin of Lobbying

The term *lobbying* comes from the way interest groups played the inside game in the nineteenth century. Many members of Congress and other government officials would gather and eat together at the Willard Hotel in Washington, D.C. People seeking to influence the government waited for the members in the lobby of the hotel, talking to them as they came in and out.

SUCCESSFUL LOBBYING

To lobby successfully, interest groups need a great deal of money. Washington, D.C., is one of the most expensive cities in America, so simply maintaining an office there can be very costly. Interest groups also pay for meals, trips, and other operational expenses, which can be significant. Money alone does not make an interest group influential, but a lack of money is usually crippling. Lobbyists also need to be reputable because a lobbyist who lies to a member of Congress, for instance, could be shunned or lose clients. Therefore, being honest is in the best interest of lobbyists.

TARGETS OF LOBBYING

Lobbyists try to influence officials working in all three branches and in the federal bureaucracy.

Lobbying the Legislative Branch

Interest groups spend hundreds of millions of dollars a year to lobby members of Congress on a range of issues. These groups try to affect the legislation being generated in Congress. Sometimes lobbyist speak with congresspeople directly, but lobbyists also testify at congressional hearings. The Senate publishes ethics guidelines to explain the complex federal laws that govern the interaction among congresspeople and lobbyists. Many corporations and foreign countries donate money to interest groups and thus help sponsor lobbyists in Washington.

Lobbying the Executive Branch

Although some lobbyists have direct access to the president, most have access only to the lower levels of the executive branch. Interest groups particularly target regulatory agencies, which have the ability to set policy affecting commerce and trade throughout the country. Some scholars have claimed that lobbying of regulatory agencies has resulted in agency capture, effectively handing control of the agency over to the industries it was intended to regulate.

Lobbying the Judicial Branch

Interest groups work to influence the courts in a number of ways. Interest groups often file **amicus curiae** (friend of the court) **briefs,** presenting an argument in favor of a particular issue. Sometimes interest groups file lawsuits against the government or other parties. For example, the NAACP worked for years to bring civil rights cases to the Supreme Court. The American Civil Liberties Union also makes extensive use of the courts.

The Outside Game: Public Pressure and Electoral Influence

Besides lobbying, interest groups also play the **outside game** by trying to convince ordinary citizens to apply pressure on their government representatives. Interest groups playing the outside game often rely on grassroots activism and electoral strategies to achieve their goals.

GRASSROOTS ACTIVISM

Grassroots activism consists of mobilizing large numbers of people to achieve the interest group's goal. By mobilizing thousands (or millions) of voters, an interest group can demonstrate to government officials that the public strongly supports its particular cause. Some grassroots efforts are general, trying to motivate as many people as possible, whereas others are more targeted. An interest group, for example, might target a member of Congress by holding rallies in his or her district and encouraging his or her constituents to write letters. A member of Congress who receives tens of thousands of letters endorsing health care reform, for example, is likely to pay attention to the group that sponsored the letter-writing campaign. In fact, most grassroots activists rely on a number of tactics to achieve their goals, such as the following:

- **Rallies and marches:** Bringing together thousands of people generates excitement and determination among supporters.

  EXAMPLE: In late spring 2006, a number of groups staged a rally for Darfur (a war-torn region of the Sudan) on the national mall in Washington, D.C. The groups demanded that the American government take a more active role in stopping the violence in Darfur.

- **Letter-writing campaigns:** Interest groups often encourage members to write to their senator or member of Congress, seeking to demonstrate their influence through the number of letters sent. Interest groups make it easy for their members by providing them with form letters that require only a signature.

- **Petitions:** A group can also write a petition advocating a certain position on an issue and collect signatures. The effect is similar to that of letter-writing campaigns.

- **Hill visits:** Sometimes an interest group will arrange for its members to visit Capitol Hill to meet with members of Congress. Although this is a form of lobbying, it is also a grassroots effort because it puts members of Congress in contact with their constituents.

- **Institutional advertising:** Although not strictly a form of grassroots activity, institutional advertising, which aims at advancing the image of an organization, can influence public opinion, thereby affecting policy and lawmakers.

The Importance of Rallies

Staging a mass rally in Washington is often taken as a sign that a group wields important influence. Such rallies act as bonding experiences for those attending and can be landmark events in the nation's history. The March on Washington in 1963, for example, was a watershed in the civil rights movement. Nearly every American has heard Martin Luther King, Jr.'s, "I Have a Dream" speech, delivered during the march.

ELECTORAL STRATEGIES

Most elected officials want to be reelected, so they listen to people who can help or hinder that reelection. Interest groups take advantage of this situation by rallying voters to their cause and contributing money to reelection campaigns.

Rallying Voters

Most interest groups cannot legally encourage their members to vote for or against a particular candidate, but they can achieve the same effect by informing their members of candidates' stances on issues. For example, for years the Christian Coalition has issued "voter guides," which describe the candidates' positions on issues that are particularly important to group members, such as abortion. Other groups (including the American Conservative Union and the Americans for Democratic Action) play the **ratings game** by publishing the positions of all members of Congress on key issues with the hope of swaying voters.

PACs and Campaign Contributions

Politicians also listen to people and groups who can donate lots of money. Interest groups are not allowed to donate money to campaigns directly, but they can contribute money through their **political action committee (PAC).** Theoretically independent of interest groups, PACs can solicit donations from group members and then give that money to candidates they support. A PAC can only give $10,000 ($5,000 in the primary campaign, $5,000 in the general election campaign) to each candidate during an election, but they can give money to as many candidates as they wish.

Most money that PACs donate goes to support particular candidates, but PACs sometimes fund opposing candidates to punish the politicians they normally support who have not been paying attention to the PAC's interest group. The vast majority of incumbents win reelection, but in a close race, a PAC's money can be very important.

Soft Money

From the 1970s until 2002, interest groups could both give and use **soft money,** which is unregulated money. The Bipartisan Campaign Reform Act of 2002, however, banned the use of soft money. Interest groups are still looking for loopholes in the new regulations, and it is not clear yet what the long-term impact of the law will be.

The Pros and Cons of Interest Groups

Interest groups generate a great deal of controversy. Some critics even blame interest groups for many of the problems in America. Other people, however, see interest groups as a vital component of the American democratic system.

PLURALISM

Pluralism is the idea that democratic politics consists of various interest groups working against each other, balancing one another out so that the common good is achieved. President James Madison first put forth this idea in an essay called *Federalist Paper No. 10* (1787), which urged New Yorkers to ratify the Constitution. According to Madison, competing interest groups are necessary to good government because they not only give people a means of contributing to the democratic process but also prevent any one minority from imposing its will on the majority. Interest groups therefore are a vital party of a healthy democracy.

Flaws in Pluralism

Critics of pluralism contend that there is no such thing as the common good because there are so many conflicting interests in society: What is good for one person is often bad for others. They argue that the interest groups interfere with democracy because they seek benefits for a minority of people rather than the greater good of the majority. The National Rifle Association, for example, has repeatedly blocked new gun control legislation despite the fact that a majority of Americans actually want stricter gun laws. Other critics argue that the interest group system is really effective only to economic interest groups, which have greater financial resources at their disposal. Nearly two-thirds of lobbyists in Washington represent economic groups. Critics also argue that interest groups tend to ignore the interests of the poor in favor of middle- and upper-class Americans, who have more time and money to contribute.

Hyperpluralism

Other scholars have argued that interest groups have been too successful and use the term **hyperpluralism** to describe political systems that cater to interest groups and not the people. These critics argue that too many interest groups lead to **demosclerosis,** the inability of government to accomplish anything substantial. These critics contend that the U.S. government cannot make serious changes, even if those changes are needed, because competing interest groups stymie the government from governing the country effectively.

Sample Test Questions

1. What are the basic types of interest groups?

2. What is lobbying?

3. What is a free rider? Why do free riders create problems?

4. True or false: Interest groups can give unlimited amounts of money to political campaigns.

5. True or false: Grassroots activism refers to attempts to persuade government officials by direct, personal contact.

6. What does an interest group demonstrate by staging large rallies?

A. It has a great deal of money.
B. It has strong organizational skills.
C. Many people passionately care about the interest group's issue.
D. The group is very professional.

7. What is a PAC?

A. A partisan action committee
B. A political action committee
C. A policy action commission
D. A political activism club

8. What is soft money?

A. Unregulated campaign contribution money
B. All money donated by PACs
C. All money donated by interest groups
D. Paper money

9. What is a massive letter-writing campaign an example of?

A. Grassroots activism
B. The inside game
C. Lobbying
D. A worthless tactic

10. Which of the following best defines demosclerosis?

A. The shutting down of the government because no budget was passed
B. The inability of the government to make any significant changes due to the power of interest groups
C. Paralysis of interest groups
D. An excess of rallies shutting down traffic in Washington

ANSWERS

1. The basic types of interest groups are economic groups (including business groups, labor groups, agricultural groups, and professional associations) and noneconomic groups (including public interest groups, single-issue groups, and ideological groups).

2. *Lobbying* refers to an interest group's effort to persuade government officials through personal contact.

3. Free riders are people who benefit from the work of an interest group without actually contributing to the group's efforts. Many people do not feel the need to help interest groups—particularly noneconomic interest groups—when they know that they will benefit from the group's activities regardless of their input.

4. False

5. False

6. C

7. B

8. A

9. A

10. B

Suggested Reading

• Birnbaum, Jeffrey H., and Alan S. Murray. *Showdown at Gucci Gulch*. Reprint, New York: Vintage, 1988.

A readable and fascinating account of interest group activity during the debates over tax reform in the mid-1980s.

• Cigler, Allan J., and Burdett A. Loomis, ed. *Interest Groups Politics*. Washington, D.C.: Congressional Quarterly Press, 1983.

A well-respected study of the strategies, tactics, and impact of interest groups.

• Day, Christine. *What Older Americans Think: Interest Groups and Aging Policy.* Princeton, NJ: Princeton University Press, 1990.

Senior citizens have great influence on American politics because they vote in large numbers and are served by interest groups, such as AARP. Day examines how interest groups devoted to senior issues interact with their constituents, paying close attention to the impact the groups have on policy.

• Lowi, Theodore J. *The End of Liberalism.* 2nd ed. New York: Norton, 1979.

Lowi examines the impact of the rise of interest groups on American democracy.

• Olson, Mancur, Jr. *The Logic of Collective Action.* Rev. ed. Cambridge, Mass.: Harvard University Press, 1971.

Olson's account of why people join interest groups—and why noneconomic groups have trouble recruiting and keeping members—was groundbreaking, and the book remains very influential.

• Rozell, Mark J., and Clyde Wilcox. *Interest Groups in American Campaigns.* Washington, D.C.: Congressional Quarterly Press, 1999.

Two top political scientists explore the role that interest groups play in campaigns.

Useful Websites

- http://api-ec.api.org/frontpage.cfm

Homepage of the American Petroleum Institute.

- www.aarp.org

AARP is the nation's largest interest group, with millions of members. It wields significant influence over issues associated with aging.

- www.aflcio.org

The homepage of the AFL-CIO, a large umbrella organization for labor unions.

- www.nationalgrange.org

The website for the oldest general farm organization in America.

- www.nea.org/index.html

The homepage of the National Education Association.

- www.nih.gov/sigs/

A list of scientific special interest groups.

THE MEDIA

10

Overview

The United States probably has one of the most varied and expansive news media industries in the world. Americans have hundreds of cable channels to choose from, thousands of newspapers and magazines, many radio shows, and countless websites and news blogs. With the rise of twenty-four-hour television news stations, most Americans have access to the latest news almost immediately. Because the vast majority of people rely on the media to keep them up to date, the media wields significant power: It decides what is newsworthy and runs or publishes stories accordingly. For these and other reasons, the media is a significant facet of American government. Many people lament media bias, although these same people disagree about which way the bias runs. To understand American politics fully, we must therefore seek to understand the role of the media.

Types of Media

The term *news* **media** refers to the groups that communicate information and news to people. Most Americans get their information about government from the news media because it would be impossible to gather all the news themselves. Media outlets have responded to the increasing reliance of Americans on television and the Internet by making the news even more readily available to people. There are three main types of news media: print media, broadcast media, and the Internet.

PRINT MEDIA

The oldest media forms are newspapers, magazines, journals, newsletters, and other printed material. These publications are collectively known as the **print media.** Although print media readership has declined in the last few decades, many Americans still read a newspaper every day or a newsmagazine on a regular basis. The influence of print media is therefore significant. Regular readers of print media tend to be more likely to be politically active.

The print media is responsible for more reporting than other news sources. Many news reports on television, for example, are merely follow-up stories about news that first appeared in newspapers. The top American newspapers, such as the *New York Times,* the *Washington Post,* and the *Los Angeles Times,* often set the agenda for many other media sources.

The Newspaper of Record

Because of its history of excellence and influence, the *New York Times* is sometimes called the *newspaper of record*: If a story is not in the *Times,* it is not important. In 2003, however, the newspaper suffered a major blow to its credibility when *Times* journalist Jayson Blair admitted that he had fabricated some of his stories. The *Times* has since made extensive efforts to prevent any similar scandals, but some readers have lost trust in the paper.

BROADCAST MEDIA

Broadcast media are news reports broadcast via radio and television. Television news is hugely important in the United States because more Americans get their news from television broadcasts than from any other source.

Television News

The main broadcast networks—ABC, CBS, and NBC—each have a news division that broadcasts a nightly news show. For the past fifty years, most Americans watched one or more of these broadcasts. Since the 1980s, however, cable news channels have chipped away at the broadcast networks. CNN and MSNBC both broadcast news around the clock. Because the cable news channels are always broadcasting news programs, many people who want to follow a story closely tune in to these stations first. The relatively new Fox network news program has also drawn numerous viewers away from the big three networks.

Radio News

The other type of broadcast media is radio. Before the advent of television in the 1950s, most Americans relied on radio broadcasts for their news. Although fewer Americans rely on radio as their primary news source, many people still listen to radio news every day, especially during morning and evening commutes. Local news stations have a particularly large audience because they can report on local weather, traffic, and events.

> **Talk Radio**
>
> Since the 1980s, talk radio has emerged as a major force in broadcasting. Talk radio is a radio format in which the hosts mix interviews with political commentary. As a result, many talk radio shows are highly partisan. Conservatives have a strong hold on American talk radio through programs hosted by influential commentators, such as Rush Limbaugh and Sean Hannity.

THE INTERNET

The Internet is slowly transforming the news media because more Americans are relying on online sources of news instead of traditional print and broadcast media. Americans surf the sites of more traditional media outlets, such as NBC and CNN, but also turn to unique online news sources such as weblogs. Websites can provide text, audio, and video information, all of the ways traditional media are transmitted. The web also allows for a more interactive approach by allowing people to personally tailor the news they receive via personalized web portals, newsgroups, podcasts, and RSS feeds.

Weblogs—known colloquially as **blogs**—have become very influential since the start of the twenty-first century. Leading bloggers write their opinions on a variety of issues, and thousands of people respond on message boards. Although many blogs are highly partisan and inaccurate, a few have been instrumental in breaking big stories.

Transforming Traditional Media

Bloggers are not only transforming traditional media sources but holding them more accountable too. When CBS news anchor Dan Rather challenged President George W. Bush's National Guard service record on television in 2004, bloggers countered by questioning Rather's sources. It soon became clear that Rather's information was dubious at best, prompting CBS to issue a public apology. Many media insiders believe that this forced Rather into an early retirement.

THE MEDIUM IS THE MESSAGE

Media scholar Marshall McLuhan once said that "the medium is the message." He meant that the medium, or manner, through which the message is transmitted shapes the meaning of the message. Different types of media have different strengths and weaknesses, and how people perceive a story depends on how they receive it. For example, television is primarily a visual media. Strong pictures and video affect television viewers more than words, and pictures convey emotion better than arguments or discussion. Television viewers, therefore, are more likely to remember how a story made them feel than the actual details of the story. Print media, in contrast, are better than visual media at communicating details and information. An average newspaper story, for example, contains substantially more facts than a comparable television story. This is not to say that television news is inferior to print media; the two media simply communicate information differently.

EXAMPLE: A debate in 1960 between presidential candidates Richard Nixon and John F. Kennedy demonstrated that the medium truly is the message. Many people listened to the debate on the radio, whereas others watched it on television. Although a majority of radio listeners felt that Nixon had won the debate, a majority of television viewers thought that Kennedy had won.

Functions of the Media

The media has immense power within the American democracy because just about all Americans get their news from the media rather than from other people or other sources. Media coverage shapes how Americans perceive the world and what they consider to be important. Voters and politicians alike must pay attention to the media. In the American political system, the media perform a number of functions important to the democratic process. The media reports the news, serves as an intermediary between the government and the people, helps determine which issues should be discussed, and keeps people actively involved in society and politics.

REPORTING THE NEWS

Perhaps the most important role of the media in politics is to report the news. As noted above, the vast majority of people must trust the media to provide them with information. Democracy requires that citizens be informed because they must be able to make educated voting choices.

> **Media Bias**
>
> These days, politicians often complain of bias in the media, usually a liberal bias against the views of conservative politicians. They complain that the media's ability to decide which stories to report often reflects its partisanship. Although this is true to some extent, most major newspapers and television news stations report the same stories more or less objectively. Bias is often restricted to the media outlet's commentary and opinion pages.

Types of Reporting

For much of American history (until the early twentieth century), most news media were clearly and openly biased. Many newspapers, for example, were simply the voices of the political parties. This type of journalism is called **partisan journalism.** Other newspapers practiced **yellow journalism,** reporting shocking and sordid stories in order to attract readers and sell more papers. **Objective reporting** (also called *descriptive reporting*) did not appear until the early twentieth century. Newspaper publishers such as Adolph Ochs of the *New York Times* championed objective journalism and praised reporters for simply reporting the facts. Although most journalists today still practice objective journalism, more and more are beginning to analyze and interpret the material they present, a practice called **interpretive reporting.**

Yellow Journalism

The media has influenced politics throughout American history. The most prominent—and notorious—example is the role of William Randolph Hearst's newspapers in starting the Spanish-American War in 1898. According to the legend, Hearst's papers ran many stories chronicling the cruelty of Spanish colonial rule. When the American battleship *Maine* exploded under mysterious circumstances, Hearst seized the moment, alleging that the Spanish had destroyed the ship. War soon followed. Few media moguls have this much direct influence, but with media consolidation, some worry that the media has too much power.

BEING THE COMMON CARRIER

The media plays a **common-carrier role** by providing a line of communication between the government and the people. This communication goes both ways: The people learn about what the government is doing, and the government learns from the media what the public is thinking.

SETTING THE AGENDA

Journalists cannot report on an infinite number of stories, so they must choose which are the most newsworthy. By choosing which stories to present to the public, the news media helps determine the most important issues; in other words, the journalists set the agenda. **Agenda-setting** is crucial because it shapes which issues will be debated in public. Sometimes political scientists refer to agenda-setting as **signaling** because the media signals which stories are the most important when they decide what to report.

Pack Journalism

Critics allege that journalists often copy one another without doing their own investigating. When one newspaper runs a story, for example, many others will run similar stories soon afterward. Critics refer to this tendency as **pack journalism.**

ACTING AS THE PUBLIC REPRESENTATIVE

The media sometimes acts as a **public representative** by holding government officials accountable on behalf of the people. Many people argue that the media is ill equipped to play this role because the media does not face the same type of accountability that politicians face. Serving as the representative of the public, moreover, could undermine the media's objectivity because the act of representing the people might require reporters to take a position on an issue.

EXAMPLE: The classic example of **watchdog journalism,** or activist reporting that attempts to hold government officials and institutions accountable for their actions, is the Watergate investigations of Bob Woodward and Carl Bernstein. The *Washington Post* reporters doggedly pursued allegations of campaign misdeeds and presidential crimes despite the fact that many Americans did not care. Journalists have exposed many other government scandals and misdeeds, including the Iran-Contra affair and the Lewinsky scandal.

Attack Journalism

Since the Watergate scandal brought down a president, investigative journalism has become more prestigious, and many reporters try to make a career around uncovering scandals. Some people complain, though, that all reporters want to be the new Woodward or Bernstein, interested only in breaking the next big story. These critics say that investigative journalism has become **attack journalism:** Journalists only care about bringing down a prominent person, not about the truth or the common good. Critics of attack journalism believe that President Bill Clinton's impeachment in 1998 was the result of attack journalism and partisan politics. The rise of attack journalism has brought to light questions about the proper role of journalism.

SOCIALIZING PEOPLE

In the United States, the media plays a big role in socializing people to American society, culture, and politics. Much of what young people and immigrants learn about American culture and politics comes from magazines, radio shows, and television. Many people worry that young people are exposed to too much violence and sex in the media, knowing the effect it will have on children's views and development.

PROVIDING A POLITICAL FORUM

The media also provides a public forum for debates between political leaders. During campaigns, opposing candidates often broadcast advertisements and debate with each other on television. Many voters learn a great deal about the candidates and the issues by watching these ads and debates. Even during years without elections, though, the news media allows elected official to explain their actions via news stories and interviews.

Government Regulation of the Media

Even though the Constitution guarantees freedom of the press, the government does regulate some media. Print media are largely unregulated, and newspapers and magazines can print nearly anything as long as they don't slander anyone. The Internet has also gone largely unregulated, despite congressional efforts to restrict some controversial content. Broadcast media, however, are subject to the most government regulation. Radio and television broadcasters must obtain a license from the government because, according to American law, the public owns the airwaves. The **Federal Communications Commission (FCC)** issues these licenses and is in charge of regulating the airwaves.

> **FCC Police**
>
> The FCC also acts as a police agency of the airwaves, and it can fine broadcasters for violating public decency standards on the air. In extreme cases, the FCC can even revoke a broadcaster's license, keeping him off the air permanently. The FCC has fined radio host Howard Stern numerous times for his use of profanity, for example, and fined CBS heavily for Janet Jackson's "wardrobe malfunction" during the halftime performance at the Super Bowl in 2004.

MEDIA DOCTRINES

The FCC has also established rules for broadcasts concerning political campaigns:

- The **equal time rule,** which states that broadcasters must provide equal broadcast time to all candidates for a particular office.
- The **right of rebuttal,** which requires broadcasters to provide an opportunity for candidates to respond to criticisms made against them. A station cannot air an attack on a candidate and fail to give the target of the attack a chance to respond.
- The **fairness doctrine,** which states that a broadcaster who airs a controversial program must provide time to air opposing views.

The FCC has not enforced the fairness doctrine since 1985, and some allege that the FCC has taken a lax approach to enforcing the other rules as well.

MEDIA CONSOLIDATION

The government has also regulated ownership of media outlets to ensure that no one broadcaster monopolizes the market. Since the 1980s, however, the government has loosened restrictions on media ownership, and Congress passed the Telecommunications Act in 1996 to allow companies to own even more media outlets.

Due to the loosening of ownership restrictions, more and more media outlets are falling under the control of a few giant corporations, a tendency called **media consolidation.** The Hearst, Knight Ridder, and Gannett corporations own most of the nation's newspapers, whereas Clear Channel Communications owns many radio stations. Large companies also own the major networks and other television stations. The Walt Disney corporation, for example, owns ABC and ESPN, along with the Disney Channel, and Viacom owns CBS and MTV. Rupert Murdoch's Media Corporation, meanwhile, owns all of the Fox channels, several radio networks, satellite television providers, and newspapers in many countries. And Time-Warner owns dozens of magazines, including *Time, Life,* and *Sports Illustrated,* as well as the CNN and Turner television networks.

Critics of Media Consolidation

Critics contend that media consolidation limits consumers' choices because a small number of companies own all the media outlets. They argue that consolidation is not competitive and that corporate owners might restrict or manipulate news coverage. Some critics also lament the homogenization of American culture due to media consolidation. Because radio and television formats have become increasingly uniform, people throughout the country receive the same broadcasts.

Cable Exceptionalism

It is not clear if the FCC has the authority to regulate cable television. The FCC is entitled to regulate those who broadcast over the airwaves because the people (not the broadcasters) own the airwaves. Cable television, however, is not sent over the airwaves: Cables transmit the programs directly into people's houses. Presumably this means that cable television cannot be regulated, but some members of Congress have still sought to do so.

Sample Test Questions

1. Why is the media so important in a democracy?

2. What did Marshall McLuhan mean when he said that "the medium is the message"?

3. What is media consolidation, and why do some people worry about it?

4. True or false: Conservatives have dominated political talk radio for most of the last few decades.

5. True or false: Most articles in newspapers can be classified as interpretive news reports.

6. Why can the FCC regulate broadcast media, but not print media?

A. The First Amendment does not cover broadcast media.
B. More people watch TV than read newspapers.

C. The public owns the airwaves, and broadcasters only rent them from the government.
D. Print media companies have more money to fight government regulation.

7. What did the 1996 Telecommunications Act allow?

A. Companies to own more media outlets
B. The government to regulate cable television
C. The government to strongly enforce the fairness doctrine
D. The government to seize stations from defiant companies

8. What do media critics sometimes use the term *pack journalism* to describe?

A. The fact that journalists are all liberal
B. The fact that journalists all dress alike
C. The prominent role of broadcast media
D. The tendency of journalists to follow and imitate each other

9. Which of the following is *not* a function of the media?

A. Socialization
B. Encouraging people to rally 'round the flag
C. Reporting the news
D. Providing a forum for political debate

10. What do newspapers that are affiliated with particular political parties practice?

A. Yellow journalism
B. Objective journalism
C. Partisan journalism
D. Interpretive journalism

ANSWERS

1. The media is the primary source of political information for most people, so it plays a crucial role in democracy.

2. McLuhan's comment refers to the fact that the way a message is transmitted affects how the message is received. Television, for example, is a visual medium, so viewers are most likely to be affected by images. Print media tends to provide more facts and details than television.

3. Media consolidation is the trend toward fewer corporations owning most media outlets. Some people worry that media consolidation will limit choices, bias news coverage, and make the country more homogeneous.

4. True

5. False

6. C

7. A

8. D

9. B

10. C

Suggested Reading

• Bagdikian, Ben H. *The Media Monopoly.* 6th ed. Boston: Beacon Press, 2000.

Bagdikian raises concerns about consolidation and the growing power of the media.

• Hess, Stephen. *Live From Capitol Hill: Studies of Congress and the Media.* Washington, D.C.: Brookings, 1991.

Although the president gets most of the media coverage, Congress is not ignored. Hess examines how the media and members of Congress use and help one another.

- Jamieson, Kathleen Hall, and Paul Waldman. *The Press Effect.* New York: Oxford University Press, 2002.

An in-depth, critical examination of the role of the media in American politics.

- Kurtz, Howard. *Spin Cycle: Inside the Clinton Propaganda Machine.* New York: Free Press, 1998.

Kurtz explores the strategies the Clinton Administration used to handle the media.

- McLuhan, Marshall. *Understanding Media: The Extensions of Man.* Reprint, Cambridge, Mass.: MIT Press, 1994.

McLuhan's best-known work is the source of his statement that the "medium is the message."

- Patterson, Thomas E. *Out of Order.* New York: Vintage, 1994.

Patterson sharply criticizes the role of the media in elections by arguing that its fascination with the horse race element of campaigns undercuts its abilities to cover the issues.

Useful Web Sites

- www.cmpa.com

The Center for Media and Public Affairs is a nonpartisan organization that investigates news coverage for bias.

- www.fark.com

A site that consolidates stories from many sources, providing links to the original stories for more detail.

- www.fcc.gov

The homepage for the Federal Communications Commission includes information on broadcasting regulations.

- www.mediachannel.org

Media Channel's website has links to many media sources from around the world.

THE POLITICAL PROCESS

11

Overview

Although many world governments claim to act in the best interests of the people they govern, only democracies actually represent the will of the people. Elections give voice and agency to every person in the political community and allow all interested citizens to directly engage in politics and participate in the discussion of how the society will be ruled. Elections are therefore the most fundamental component of democracies.

Not all elections are the same. In fact, national, regional, and local governments employ a variety of voting systems to meet their constituents' needs. Also important is the question of which people in the community are allowed to vote. Elections can serve different purposes too, for that matter. Some elections determine who will lead the community, whereas other elections ask voters to express their opinions on specific laws, taxes, and other issues. For these reasons, understanding elections and voting systems is essential to understanding democratic systems of government.

Elections

Although American citizens age eighteen and older in all states have the right to vote, the manner in which they vote varies considerably from state to state and even from county to county. The U.S. Constitution gives states the right to determine how elections are run (with some limits), but states often delegate some of this power to local governments.

TYPES OF BALLOTS

The ballots used in elections have changed significantly in American history. Originally, political parties printed their own ballots, listing only their candidates. Voters took ballots from the party of their choice and deposited them in the ballot box within full view of other voters. As a result, vote choices were public. Since 1888, however, state governments have printed ballots that list all candidates for all offices. Votes are cast in secret. Because Australia was the first country to adopt the secret ballot, this ballot is called the **Australian ballot.**

Elections in the United States use one of two kinds of Australian ballots:

1. The **office-block ballot** (also called the **Massachusetts Ballot**): Candidates are grouped by office.

2. The **party-column ballot** (also called the **Indiana Ballot**): Candidates are grouped by party.

Political parties do not like office block ballots because these ballots encourage people to vote for candidates from different parties (a practice known as **split-ticket voting**). Instead, political parties prefer party-column ballots because these ballots make it easy to choose candidates only from a particular party. Some of these ballots even allow voters to choose all of a party's candidates by checking a single box, or pulling a single lever, a practice called **straight-ticket voting.**

Partisan Battles over Ballots

Political parties tend to support whatever ballot helps them get the most votes. In the 1998 election, the Democratic Party in Illinois won big, in part because of a very effective campaign to get voters to vote straight-ticket Democrat. After the election, Republicans in the Illinois state legislature sought to forbid those ballots with a single box, which allowed a straight-ticket vote.

VOTING MACHINES

Americans vote using a wide variety of machines:

- **Mechanical voting machines:** Voters flip switches to choose candidates and then pull a lever to finalize their vote.

- **Punch-card machines:** Voters mark their choices on a card using a pencil and then deposit their cards into a machine, which then tallies the vote based on the card's holes.

- **Touch-screen machines:** Similar to ATMs, these increasingly popular machines "read" the voters' choices.

But these methods have serious problems. Mechanical voting machines frequently break down, but many of the companies that made the machines have gone out of business. Punch-card machines are fallible because punching does not always create a complete hole (leading to debates about hanging and pregnant chads, as in the 2000 presidential elections). Many computer security experts see touch-screen voting as dangerously insecure. Others point out that most touch-screen machines leave no paper documents, a huge problem in cases of recounts.

Florida 2000

The 2000 election in Florida and other states was shocking because of the inconsistency and imprecision of voting in many jurisdictions. Even within a single state, precincts use a wide variety of voting machines. And jurisdictions often have very different rules for counting votes and holding recounts. After the 2000 election, many wanted to standardize voting, but so far little has been done for one major reason: cost. Purchasing the same voting machines for all precincts would be prohibitively expensive.

ABSENTEE BALLOTS

Traditionally, people vote by filling out a ballot at their local polling precinct or voting center. But some voters, such as college students or people serving in the military, cannot get to their polling place to vote. The states allow these voters to use **absentee ballots.** Absentee voters usually receive their ballots in the mail several weeks before the election, fill them out, and mail them back to state election officials.

VOTING BY MAIL

Usually states have provided absentee ballots to those who had good reasons for not being able to go their polling place. In recent years, though, some states have made it easy for anyone to vote by mail, in an effort to encourage voting. In 2000, for example, Oregon allowed all voters in the presidential election to mail in their ballots. Voter participation surpassed 80 percent, a remarkable number. Due to this success, Oregon has completely abandoned precinct voting.

But voting by mail has its critics. These people argue that voting by mail allows people to make their final choice early in the campaign, before debates or other events that could substantially change the race. Still others feel that voting in person at precincts builds a sense of civic-mindedness, which is not possible through voting by mail. Supporters of voting by mail argue that the increased turnout outweighs these criticisms.

Online Voting

Many people think the future of voting is on the Internet, which would allow people to vote as easily and quickly as they send email. Some states have experimented with online voting. Critics fear that online voting has the potential to compromise the secret ballot or to encourage voter fraud, and so online voting remains in its experimental stages.

Running for Office

Americans elect thousands of officials at all levels of government. The people who run for office vary greatly in terms of ideology, goals, campaign strategies, and outlooks, but all must campaign to win.

ELIGIBILITY

All federal offices have eligibility requirements, some more stringent than others. The eligibility requirements for elected federal offices are summarized in the following table.

ELIGIBILITY REQUIREMENTS FOR FEDERAL OFFICES	
Office	Requirements
Representative	At least 25 years old, a citizen for at least 7 years, and a resident of the state he or she represents
Senator	At least 30 years old, a citizen for at least 9 years, and a resident of the state he or she represents
President and Vice President	At least 35 years old, a natural-born citizen, a U.S. resident for at least 14 years

TRAITS OF OFFICE SEEKERS

Most elected officials are older, white males and usually wealthier than the average citizen. In the last few decades, more women and minorities have taken office at the state and federal levels, but they hold office in disproportionately low numbers. Following the 2002 elections, for example, just sixty-two women served as members of the House. After the 2004 elections, only one African American served in the Senate. The homogeneity of officeholders does not reflect the diversity of the population of the United States.

Professional, Ambitious, and Driven

Most people who run for office are professionals, such as businesspeople, doctors, and, above all, lawyers. Blue-collar workers and manual laborers occasionally run for office, but not in proportion to their numbers. Because they are predominantly professionals, candidates are, on the whole, more educated than the average citizen.

> **Political Scientist as Politician**
>
> Thus far, only one president has had an academic background. Woodrow Wilson held a PhD in political science and both taught at and served as the president of Princeton University before entering politics.

All office seekers, however, are ambitious. Running for office—even a low-level one—is extremely demanding. Only people with a strong commitment to winning will put up with the intense schedule of campaigning. At higher levels, candidates face even more challenges.

> *EXAMPLE:* Presidential candidates often campaign for eighteen hours a day. But the last few days of a presidential campaign are particularly grueling. Candidates give up sleep to campaign nonstop for the last few days. At the end of the 2000 campaign, Democrat Al Gore campaigned for forty-eight hours straight, attending rallies at all hours of the day. His opponent, Republican George W. Bush, followed a similarly grueling schedule.

PRESIDENTIAL CANDIDATES

The longest, most difficult, most expensive, and most visible campaigns are those for president. The process begins when a candidate chooses to run. Then he or she must win the party nomination, endure the primaries, attend the national convention, and, ultimately, campaign in the general election.

Choosing to Run

Candidates usually spend the two years before the first primary raising money, cultivating support from important party activists, and getting their name known by the public. Many people spend a number of months preparing to run for office only to eventually decide not to run because they cannot generate enough support or they find the process too demanding.

Winning the Nomination

After candidates enter the race, they must fight for the party's nomination with the other candidates. Before 1972, party leaders chose nominees through negotiation and compromise. Since the early 1970s, the parties have opened up the nomination process to voters through **primary elections:** The winner of a primary becomes the party's nominee. In a **closed primary,** only party members may vote; most states hold this type of primary. In an **open primary,** all voters, regardless of party, may vote as long as they participate in only one primary.

In the presidential campaign, a candidate must win a majority of **convention delegates** in order to win the nomination. Each state holds either a primary or **caucuses** (meetings of party members to select a candidate). Candidates win a number of delegates based on how many popular votes they receive in these primaries; these delegates go to their party's national convention to vote for the party's nominee. The candidate with the most delegates wins the nomination. **Superdelegates** are prominent party members (including elected officials and party organization leaders) who automatically get to vote in the national convention. Winning delegates also helps candidates raise money: The more delegates they win, the more legitimate they appear as contenders. The candidate who appears to have the lead is called the **front-runner.**

The Big Mo

Momentum—dubbed "the big mo" by President George H. W. Bush—is crucial in the primary campaign. Supporters will often abandon a candidate who appears to be faltering. Momentum seems to have a life of its own: A candidate who has momentum surges forward, even if other candidates have more money or endorsements. Often, a candidate who gets momentum early can run away with the race. In most presidential campaigns, the eventual winner is apparent long before the final primaries.

Front-Loading Primaries

Over the past few election cycles, many states have moved their primaries up to an earlier date, a process called **front-loading.** Due to front-loading, the nominations are decided early, usually by the end of March, even though the national conventions do not meet until late summer. States do this in order to maximize the impact they have on the nomination. States with primaries toward the end of the campaign have little impact because one candidate has emerged as the clear winner. Front-loading also limits the time in which party members disagree about candidates and potential nominees, allowing the party to unite in preparation for the general election.

EXAMPLE: In 1988, a group of southern states agreed to hold their primaries on the same day, early in the campaign, in order to increase the chance of nominating a moderate southerner. Since then, many states have held primaries on the same date in March, now known as **Super Tuesday,** during the election year.

The National Convention

Every four years, the major parties hold massive conventions, whose major purpose is to choose the party's nominees for president and vice president. Delegates from across the country arrive, meet with party leaders, and vote on a number of matters. The **credentials committee** established by each party decides which delegates are legitimate and therefore allowed to participate.

> **Delegate Controversy**
>
> Most of the time, certification by the credentials committee is a formality. Every now and then, however, a dispute arises that forces the credentials committee to make unpleasant choices. At the 1964 Democratic convention, for example, two different slates of delegates claimed to represent Mississippi: an all-white group opposed to civil rights and a mixed-race group supporting civil rights. In this case, the credentials committee accepted the pro–civil rights group, but in doing so, they alienated many southern whites.

Parties officially nominate their candidates at national conventions. Delegates chosen in primaries gather together and vote for the party's nominees; they also approve their party's platform. In theory, conventions could be bitterly fought affairs, but in practice, the voting is a formality: By that point, the party's nominee has become clear. Conventions have become highly staged and scripted and serve primarily to rally the party behind the nominees.

The General Election Campaign

The general election commences after the conventions. Candidates from Republican, Democratic, and independent parties vie for votes by giving speeches, shaking hands, holding rallies, proposing policies, courting the media, and debating one another. In modern campaigns, the media relentlessly follows candidates and polls likely voters, so coverage often seems akin to sports reporting on pennant races. Many voters rely heavily on the debates to make their choice.

Debates in the Television Age

Although presidential candidates have debated for a long time, the television age changed the character of debates. In 1960, the debates were broadcast for the first time on television. Many people were drawn to the visual appeal of John F. Kennedy: He appeared attractive, athletic, and confident, while Nixon (who was suffering from the flu) appeared uncertain and unattractive. Many famous moments in recent political history occurred during the debates. In 1980, for example, Republican Ronald Reagan began his attack on Democrat Jimmy Carter by saying, "There you go again," to thunderous applause. George H. W. Bush, meanwhile, hurt himself in the televised presidential debates when he repeatedly looked at his watch while Bill Clinton was speaking. Even though Bush was merely timing Clinton's speech, many viewers misinterpreted the action as a reflection of boredom and disinterest, which led to drop in the polls for Bush.

The Electoral College

The **Electoral College** officially decides the presidential election. Each state has the same number of electoral votes as it has total seats in Congress. In most states, all of the state's electoral votes are awarded to the presidential candidate who receives the most popular votes in that state, whereas the losing candidates receive none. Presidential candidates, therefore, usually focus their energies on winning the popular vote in the large states that have many electoral votes or in states in which the voters are deeply divided. Republicans stand little chance of winning liberal California and New York, for example, and Democrats are no longer popular in conservative Texas, but both parties have spent millions of dollars on campaigns in recent presidential elections in the populous swing states of Florida and Ohio.

Campaign Finance Reform

Political campaigns, especially presidential ones, cost a lot of money to run. During the 2004 presidential race, for example, both major party candidates spent more than $100 million. Generally, the candidate with the bigger war chest tends to win the race. Campaign finance laws limit the amount of money people and corporations may donate to a campaign, as well as dictate how candidates may spend that money.

EARLY ATTEMPTS AT REGULATING CAMPAIGN FINANCE

For much of American history, there were no regulations at all on campaign finance: Anyone could give as much as he or she wished, and candidates could spend all they had in any way they saw fit. Two landmark laws in the early twentieth century regulated campaign finance for the first time:

- The **corrupt practices acts:** This series of laws, starting in 1925, limited expenditures by congressional candidates and controlled corporate contributions to candidates.
- The **Hatch Act:** Passed in 1939, this act limited the political actions of federal civil servants and restricted contributions by political groups.

THE REFORMS OF THE 1970s

The 1970s saw the first significant campaign finance reforms. In 1971, Congress passed the **Federal Elections Campaign Act (FECA),** which began to substantially regulate campaign contributions. It limited spending on media advertisements, required disclosure of all donations over $100, and restricted the amount of money candidates could donate to their own campaigns.

Watergate and the 1974 Reforms

The Watergate scandal exposed a wide range of illegal activities being performed by the Nixon Administration, among them campaign finance law violations. For example, the Nixon reelection campaign had a large "slush fund" of cash to be used for covert purposes. In response to these revelations, Congress toughened campaign finance regulations by amending FECA and by doing the following:

- Creating the **Federal Election Commission,** an independent regulatory agency that monitors campaign finance
- Introducing public financing for presidential campaigns (both primary and general election campaigns); candidates who qualify can receive assistance in paying for their campaigns
- Imposing limits on campaign spending by presidential candidates who accept federal funding
- Limiting contributions to campaigns (no person can donate more than $2,000 to a candidate in an election and no more than $25,000 total to all campaigns; political groups were limited to $5,000 per candidate)
- Requiring that campaigns disclose all contributions

In 1976, Congress allowed businesses, unions, and political groups to form **political action committees (PACs)** in order to give money to candidates. PACs are significant because they allow a variety of organizations to donate money to campaigns. Also, although each person can only donate $5,000 to a PAC, he or she may donate $5,000 to as many PACs as he or she wishes. The PACs can then, in turn, donate the money to the campaigns.

LOOPHOLES IN THE REFORMS

Since the 1970s, campaigners have found a number of ways around the reforms of the 1970s:

- **Soft money:** The new laws placed few limits on political parties and PACs. Although these groups could not give unlimited contributions to campaigns, they could spend an unlimited amount of money (known as **soft money**) on such activities as voter education, registration drives, and getting out the vote.

> *EXAMPLE:* In 2002, several wealthy donors, including Haim Saban, whose $7 million donation was the largest in history, gave money to the Democratic National Committee to build a new headquarters.

- **Independent expenditures:** In *Buckley v. Valeo* (1976), the Supreme Court ruled that, based on the First Amendment, a candidate may spend his or her own money in whatever way he or she wishes. This means that wealthy candidates may legally donate millions of dollars to their own campaigns. Individuals and groups, for example, can spend as much as they wish on **issue advertising.** Such ads cannot directly say "vote for X" or "vote against X," but they can say virtually anything else.

> *EXAMPLE:* Most issue ads are clearly designed to sway voters. An ad supporting a candidate may say flattering things about the candidate and conclude by saying, "Call X and tell her you appreciate her work." An attack ad can portray a candidate very negatively and finish by saying, "Call Y and tell him he's wrong."

- **Bundling:** This is the practice of collecting donations from a number of people, then sending them together as a large payment to the candidate. The large donations might make a candidate feel indebted to the people giving the money.

MCCAIN-FEINGOLD BILL

For much of the 1990s, Senators Republican John McCain and Democrat Russ Feingold fought to reform campaign finance laws, aiming at restricting or banning soft money. In 2002, however, the two men finally generated enough support to pass the **McCain-Feingold bill,** now called the **Bipartisan**

Campaign Finance Reform Act. The House passed the bill as the Shays-Meehan Act, and President George W. Bush signed it into law. This act placed more stringent restrictions on campaign finance by doing the following:

- Banning all soft money donations to the national party organizations
- Limiting the time period during which independent groups can run issue ads

The new law did not ban soft money donations to local and state parties, although it did limit the amount of such donations. It also increased the amount of money an individual could donate to $4,000 and upped the limit on donations to all campaigns to $95,000 in each two-year election cycle. Many political scientists think that the bill might ultimately weaken political parties and strengthen independent groups, which can still raise and spend large amounts of money.

Voting

Voter turnout is the number of citizens who vote in a given election. Americans tend to vote in low numbers. For much of the last few decades, about half of eligible people voted in presidential elections; the numbers are even smaller for off-year congressional elections (usually about 35 to 40 percent) and lower in local elections (less than 25 percent).

> **Voting Elsewhere**
>
> Most democracies have much higher voter turnouts than does the United States. In Belgium, for example, turnout is usually about 90 percent. Some countries even forbid nonvoting: Those who do not vote must pay a fine.

EXPLANATIONS FOR LOW TURNOUT

Why do Americans vote in small numbers? Political scientists have suggested a number of reasons:

- **Inconvenience:** For many, getting to the polling place on election day is very difficult: Many people have to work, and some have trouble getting to their precinct.
- **Registration:** All voters must register ahead of the election (sometimes a month or more in advance); the registration process can be confusing and at times difficult to follow.
- **Similarity of the parties:** Some citizens believe the parties are very similar, so voting will not make a difference
- **Alienation:** People do not vote because they feel that the government does not care about them or listen to their concerns.
- **Frequency of elections:** Americans hold elections more frequently than most other democracies; voters find it difficult to vote on so many different days.
- **Lack of competitiveness:** Many races in the United States are very lopsided, so voters are likely to stay home, thinking the outcome is a foregone conclusion.

The Effects of Low Turnout

Some people argue that low turnout rewards Republicans because minorities, who tend to vote Democrat, are the least likely to vote. Others argue that election outcomes would be roughly the same even if everyone voted because the preferences of nonvoters are similar to those of voters.

THE MULTIPLE MEANINGS OF LOW TURNOUT

Some scholars and pundits fret over low turnout, convinced that low turnout undermines democracy. Democracy is government by the people, they argue, and when people do not vote, they give up their part of popular sovereignty. Low turnout also reflects a strong sense of alienation among the public, a bad sign for America's legitimacy.

Other scholars argue the opposite. Low turnout is a sign of a healthy democracy because it reflects satisfaction with the government. According to this view, people only vote when they feel threatened or angered about an issue. People who do not vote, then, are content with the status quo.

VOTING BEHAVIOR

Political scientists use the term **voting behavior** to describe what voters do and what motivates them to do it. Put differently, students of voting behavior seek to answer the question: Why do voters make the choices they do? A variety of factors affect whether and how a person votes, including a person's age, wealth, education, race or ethnicity, gender, religion, geographical location, partisanship, and issues at stake. Political scientists sometimes make generalizations about people's voting behavior based on these factors: Historically, women and African Americans have tended to vote Democrat, people from the South tend to vote Republican, and wealthier people tend to vote Republican, except for the extremely wealthy, who usually vote Democrat. The following table summarizes how some factors affect whether eligible voters vote.

WHO VOTES?

Factor	Effect
Age	Senior citizens vote in very large numbers, whereas young people (18–30) vote in small numbers
Education	Increased education leads to increased voting
Wealth	Wealthier people tend to vote more than poorer people, but the wealthiest people usually vote Democrat
Race	White people vote more than minorities
Competitiveness of Candidates	Overall, people are more likely to vote in hotly contested elections

Retrospective and Prospective Voting

Some political scientists contend that people engage in retrospective voting: Voters use the past few years to decide how to vote. In general, if a voter thinks that the country has done well over the last few years, he or she votes for the party in power. If the voter believes that the country has done poorly, he or she votes for the opposition party. Other scholars argue that Americans engage in prospective voting, which is voting with an eye to the future. People vote for the candidates that they believe will do the most to help the country in the next few years.

Sample Test Questions

1. What is the Australian ballot? Why does it matter?

2. Describe the difference between an open primary and a closed primary.

3. What are some reasons why voter turnout is low in the United States?

4. True or false: Young people are the most likely to vote.

5. True or false: The party-column ballot makes it easier to vote straight ticket.

6. What is one reason why some people *do not* criticize voting by mail?

A. It could undermine the secret ballot.
B. Voters might make their choices too early.

C. It might increase voting.
D. It could erode civic-mindedness.

7. What is front-loading?

A. Scheduling many primaries early in the campaign season
B. The momentum of a front-runner
C. Raising all of one's campaign money early
D. A process of creating ballots

8. The first real regulation of campaign finance came with which law?

A. Bipartisan Campaign Finance Reform Act
B. McCain-Feingold bill
C. The Pendleton Act
D. The corrupt practices acts

9. What is Super Tuesday?

A. Inauguration Day
B. The day on which many primaries are held
C. The day of the general election
D. The last day for contributing money to a presidential campaign

10. What are political scientists who study voting behavior seeking to understand?

A. Why members of the House vote the way they do
B. Why people make the vote choices they do
C. The benefits and drawbacks of different voting machines
D. Rules deciding what counts as a vote and what does not

ANSWERS

1. The Australian ballot is a secret ballot: No one can see for whom one votes. It allows voters to avoid pressure to vote for a specific candidate and undercuts selling votes.
2. In an open primary, someone does not need to belong to a party to participate, but that person can only vote for one party's candidates. In a closed primary, only party members may vote; most states hold this type of primary.
3. Some explanations for low turnout include inconvenience, registration, similarity of the parties, alienation, frequency of elections, and lack of competitiveness.
4. False
5. True
6. C
7. A
8. D
9. B
10. B

Suggested Reading

• Bimber, Bruce, and Richard Davis. *Campaigning Online: The Internet in U.S. Elections.* New York: Oxford University Press, 2003.

A thoughtful study of how the Internet affects campaigns.

• Faucheux, Ronald A. *Running for Office: The Strategies, Techniques, and Messages Modern Political Candidates Need to Win Elections.* New York: M. Evans, 2002.

Faucheux's book aims to provide advice on campaigning to first-time candidates; it's also useful to students of elections.

• Patterson, Thomas E. *The Vanishing Voter.* New York: Knopf, 2002.

Patterson studies why turnout has dropped in the United States and theorizes about the consequences of low voter turnout on American democracy.

• Sabato, Larry J., ed. *Overtime! The Election 2000 Thriller.* Reading, Mass.: Addison Wesley Longman, 2001.

A number of political scientists comment on the unusual presidential election of 2000.

• Skocpol, Theda. *Diminished Democracy: From Membership to Management in American Civic Life.* Norman: University of Oklahoma Press, 2003.

Skocpol examines the trend of citizens drifting away from civic participation.

Useful Websites

• http://vote-smart.org

Project Vote Smart offers a great deal of information on voting and elections, from campaign finance to voting records.

• www.fairvote.org

The Center for Voting and Democracy provides information on how different election rules affect campaign strategies on this website.

• www.fec.gov

The website for the Federal Election Commission, which regulates campaign finance in federal elections.

- www.opensecrets.org

The Center for Responsive Politics maintains this site, which contains a wealth of information on campaign finance. It also contains a list of major donors and interest groups.

- www.rockthevote.org

MTV's Rock the Vote is an attempt to get young people to learn about—and participate in—American politics.

- www.vanishingvoter.org

The John F. Kennedy School of Government at Harvard University runs this site, which provides information on voter participation and tries to encourage people to register and vote.

CIVIL LIBERTIES AND CIVIL RIGHTS

12

Overview

"We hold these truths to be self-evident, that all men are created equal." So wrote Thomas Jefferson in the Declaration of Independence in 1776, but his conception of equality was vastly different from our own. Still, the Founding Fathers fought to create a free and equal society, in which Americans were free from religious persecution and other restrictions on their individual liberties. The civil rights movement, which began in earnest in the 1950s, was born when African Americans demanded that they be given equal protection under the law. Their demonstrations set the stage for other groups to begin agitating for new laws as well.

Today, we take such freedoms as the right to privacy and freedom of speech for granted. But our civil liberties and rights are the result of many years of agitation and activism. Plus, our conceptions of civil rights and liberties have evolved since Jefferson's day. Recent events such as the debate over gay marriage and the war on terror ensure that our conceptions of liberty and equal rights will continue to evolve in the years to come.

THE BILL OF RIGHTS

Civil liberties protect us from government power. They are rooted in the **Bill of Rights,** which limits the powers of the federal government. The government cannot take away the freedoms outlined in the Bill of Rights, and any action that encroaches on these liberties is illegal.

LIMITS AND THE BILL OF RIGHTS

Amendment	Right(s) Granted
1st	Freedoms of speech, press, assembly, petition, and religion
2nd, 3rd, 4th	Right to bear arms, protection from having troops inside one's home, protection from unreasonable search and seizure
5th, 6th, 7th, 8th	Due process, right to trial by jury, protection from cruel and unusual punishment
9th, 10th	Those rights not enumerated by the Bill of Rights

THE STATES

The Bill of Rights applies mostly to the federal government, so citizens were not protected from the states' encroaching on their civil liberties. The Fourteenth Amendment, ratified in 1868, protects citizens against state infringements of the rights and liberties guaranteed in the Constitution. In the early part of the twentieth century, courts began the practice of **incorporation,** enforcing the Fourteenth Amendment by forcing state governments to abide by the Bill of Rights. To do so, courts urged **selective incorporation** by asking the states to incorporate select parts of the Bill of Rights rather than all ten amendments. By 1969, however, the entire Bill of Rights had been incorporated by the Supreme Court.

Types of Civil Liberties

The Constitution guarantees many types of civil liberties, including freedom of speech and the press, freedom of religion, and the rights of the accused. Over time, Americans have expanded their civil liberties to include the right to privacy.

FREEDOM OF SPEECH AND THE PRESS

The First Amendment grants citizens freedom of speech, press, petition, and assembly, all essential for citizens to communicate freely in a democracy. Citizens must have the right to criticize the government for democracy to function properly. The courts have granted Americans wide-ranging freedoms of speech and expression.

Unprotected Speech

Not all speech is protected, however. In some cases, the government has the legal right to regulate what Americans say and print. Free speech must first pass a number of tests:

- **Clear-and-present-danger test:** Speech that has the potential to cause harm or that constitutes a clear-and-present danger to the government is not protected.

- **Bad-tendency rule:** Speech that might lead to some sort of "evil," such as the violent overthrow of the government, is not protected.

- **Obscenity test:** Speech that is considered obscene is not protected, even though Americans have different opinions on what material might be considered obscene.

- **Slander test:** Speech that states something about a person or group that is known to be false is not protected because such speech (known as **slander**) can damage people's otherwise good reputations.

- **Libel test: Libel,** or printed material that slanders others, is also not protected; one important exception relates to public figures: People are free to print anything they want about public figures so long as they do not demonstrate **actual malice** (a reckless disregard for the truth with the aim of hurting the person).

Symbolic Speech

Any action that demonstrates a particular political viewpoint is known as **symbolic speech.** Generally, the courts have protected symbolic speech, such as the burning of draft cards or of the American flag, under the First Amendment.

Restrictions

In some trials, judges issue **gag orders,** which restrict what journalists can report about the trial. **Prior restraint** is a governmental act that stops the publication of materials thought to be damaging or slanderous; in recent years, the government has had a difficult time exercising prior restraint.

EXAMPLE: In 1971, the Nixon Administration tried to prevent the *New York Times* from publishing classified documents called the *Pentagon Papers* that detailed how the government waged the Vietnam War. The Supreme Court argued that the government could not block the publication of the *Pentagon Papers* because otherwise the government would be determining what newspapers can and cannot publish.

FREEDOM OF RELIGION

The First Amendment includes two clauses that ensure freedom of religion:

1. The **free exercise clause:** Congress cannot forbid the practice of any religions.
2. The **establishment clause:** Congress cannot make laws that establish specific religions as state religions.

Separation of Church and State

Thomas Jefferson interpreted the establishment clause to mean that there needs to be a "wall of separation between Church and State." The courts have interpreted the clause to mean the following:

- The government cannot set up a church.
- The government cannot aid one religion or prefer one religion over another.

Government Aid to Religious Schools

Many of the recent conflicts over the establishment clause have concerned the role of religion in government-funded schools. In *Lemon v. Kurtzman* (1971), the Supreme Court held that the government cannot give money directly to religious schools. The Court developed the three-part ***Lemon* test** to determine the situations in which the government may give money to religious institutions. The government can only fund religious schools if the aid money follows these three conditions:

1. It will be used for secular purposes.

2. It will not be used to advance or inhibit religion.

3. It will not be used to encourage the government to become involved with the religion.

School Vouchers

A recent controversy over the establishment clause concerns **school vouchers,** government money given to parents to help pay for tuition at private schools. Some states and municipalities have created voucher programs to help parents get their children out of poorly performing public schools. Opponents of the program argue that voucher programs violate the *Lemon* test by inadvertently funding religious schools, because many parents choose to send their children to private religious schools. In a 2002 case, the Supreme Court ruled that voucher programs do not violate the establishment clause because parents could use them to send their children to secular private schools.

School Prayer

In the landmark *Engel v. Vitale* case in 1962, the Supreme Court ruled that school-sponsored prayer in public schools violates the establishment clause and is therefore illegal. The Court rejected all school prayer, even general prayers that do not name a specific deity or propose a particular belief. Nevertheless, the Court has also ruled that religious clubs and organizations can meet on school property, as long as no student is required to attend. The Court has also held that schools cannot begin graduation ceremonies or school events with a prayer.

School Prayer Today

Despite the Supreme Court's decisions, school prayer continues in some public schools, largely due to lack of complaint or protest. If no one objects to a school's prayer, then the courts will not order the school to stop. Moments of silence also fall under the category of "school prayer."

Free Exercise of Religion

The Bill of Rights does not protect all forms of religious expression. For example, murder in the name of religion is still murder and is therefore illegal. Similarly, the government sometimes overrules parents whose religious beliefs conflict with certain medical practices by requiring the parents to have their children vaccinated. The government has gone back and forth over the extent to which it can restrain religious activities.

EXAMPLE: The Religious Freedom Restoration Act in 1993 required the government to accommodate religious behavior unless there is a compelling reason not to. The Supreme Court struck down parts of the act in 1997, claiming that Congress overstepped its authority. In fact, the Court has upheld the rights of some religious groups to use illegal substances, such as peyote, during religious ceremonies.

The Right to Gather

The Bill of Rights forbids the government from preventing the peaceful assembly of people, regardless of why those people have gathered. In a famous example, in 1978, the Supreme Court held that the neo-Nazi Nationalist Socialist Party of America (NSP) had the right to march through Skokie, Illinois, home to a sizable Jewish population. The American Civil Liberties Union argued on behalf of the NSP.

THE RIGHTS OF THE ACCUSED

The Constitution gives many rights to people accused of crimes. The Founding Fathers sought to protect citizens of the United States from a government that would arrest and detain them without cause or trial, which is what Great Britain often did to American colonists before the Revolutionary War. According to the Constitution, a person accused of a crime has these rights:

- **Writ of habeas corpus,** or the right to be presented to a judge and hear charges as to why he or she is being held; the government cannot hold people for no reason (Article I, Section 9)
- Protection against searches and seizures without probable cause (Fourth Amendment)
- Protection from self-incrimination (Fifth Amendment)
- Quick arraignment and a speedy trial (Sixth Amendment)
- Legal counsel (Sixth Amendment)
- Not be tried more than once for the same crime (Sixth Amendment)
- Trial by jury (Sixth Amendment)
- Protection from cruel or unusual punishment (Eighth Amendment)

The Warren Court and the Rights of the Accused

Chief Justice Earl Warren, appointed by President Dwight D. Eisenhower in 1953, led the Supreme Court through many landmark civil rights and civil liberties cases. Some of the rights that the Warren Court established have been scaled back, but most of the basic principles have remained:

- **The exclusionary rule:** In *Mapp v. Ohio* (1961), the Court ruled that all evidence must be submitted to the judge before the jury sees it in all state and federal criminal trials.

If the judge decides that the evidence has been obtained illegally, the prosecution will not be able to use the evidence during the trial.

- **The right to an attorney:** In ***Gideon v. Wainwright*** (1963), the Court ruled that the government must provide for an attorney to represent those defendants in all criminal cases who cannot afford an attorney on their own.

- **The right to a Miranda warning:** In ***Miranda v. Arizona*** (1966), the Court ruled that police must inform the accused of his or her rights, including the right to remain silent during interrogation.

Exceptions to the Exclusionary Rule

Since the 1980s, the Court has admitted some illegally obtained evidence under two exceptions to the exclusionary rule:

- **Inevitable discovery:** Evidence is admissible at trial if the police would have eventually discovered the illegally obtained evidence through the course of their investigation anyway.

- **Good faith:** Evidence is admissible from police officers who honestly believe that they acted in compliance with the law.

THE RIGHT TO PRIVACY

Privacy is never explicitly mentioned in the Constitution, yet many Americans believe that they have an inherent right to privacy. In practice, Americans today believe their right to privacy includes access to birth control, the freedom to have abortions, freedom from persecution for some sexual behaviors, and the right to die as one chooses.

Birth Control and Abortion

In *Griswold v. Connecticut* (1965), the Supreme Court ruled that states could not ban the use of contraception because such a ban violated the right to privacy. Justice William O. Douglass argued that several amendments implied a right to privacy, particularly the Ninth Amendment, which states explicitly that the list of rights in the Constitution is not exhaustive.

In 1973, the Supreme Court ruled in the case ***Roe v. Wade*** that the government cannot ban abortion within the first trimester. The Court's ruling is rooted in the woman's right to privacy, which gives her the right to decide what to do with her body. Since *Roe,* the courts have limited abortion in a number of cases. In *Webster v. Reproductive Health Services* (1989), the Supreme Court ruled that states could ban the use of public funds for abortion. Three years later, in *Planned Parenthood v. Casey,* the Court ruled that states could require pre-abortion counseling, a waiting period of twenty-four hours, and parental permission for girls under eighteen years old.

Rights of Abortion Protesters

In 1994, Congress passed the Freedom of Access to Clinic Entrances Act, which created a buffer zone around clinics in which no one could protest or harass the health care providers or patients on their way into and out of the clinics. Despite claims that the law violated free speech rights, the Supreme Court upheld the law in 1997.

Dying and Death

Many people now argue that the right to privacy extends to the right to choose one's death. According to this view, people can choose to end their lives as they see fit. A decision in 1976 by the New Jersey Supreme Court held that a person could choose to refuse treatment for a terminal illness. Most courts have held, though, that people do not have a constitutional right to suicide, on their own or with a doctor's assistance.

Dying with Dignity

In 1997, Oregon passed the Death with Dignity Act, which legalized physician-assisted suicide under certain conditions. Texas passed a similar law in 1999.

The Civil Rights Movement

Slavery was legal in roughly half of the states up until the Civil War. After the war ended, the Constitution was amended three times to end slavery and ban discrimination against blacks. But discrimination and segregation did not end until the significant Supreme Court cases of the 1950s.

RECONSTRUCTION AMENDMENTS (1865–1870)

Adopted between 1865 and 1870, the Reconstruction Amendments to the Constitution form the legal basis for the protection of civil rights:

- **The Thirteenth Amendment** (1865) makes slavery and involuntary service illegal.
- **The Fourteenth Amendment** (1868) declares that anyone born in the United States is a citizen of both the United States and of the state in which the person resides; it also contains three key clauses:

    1. The **privileges and immunities clause** states that no state can be deprive a citizen of the privileges and immunities of citizenship.
    2. The **due process clause** states that no person can be deprived of life, liberty, or property without due process of law.
    3. The **equal protection clause** declares that all citizens have the equal protection of the law.

- The **Fifteenth Amendment** (1870) declares that no person, including former slaves, can be denied the right to vote on the basis of race

EARLY CIVIL RIGHTS LAWS (1860s–1870s)

To supplement the Reconstruction Amendments, Congress passed several civil rights laws in the 1860s and 1870s. These laws gave the president the authority to use the military to enforce civil rights for blacks and made it illegal for states to restrict voting along racial lines.

THE JIM CROW LAWS AND SUPREME COURT DECISIONS (1880s–1900s)

After the federal troops withdrew from the South at the end of Reconstruction in 1877, white southerners quickly took over state governments and openly flouted the recent laws designed to protect the rights of former slaves. Several state governments in the South went so far as to legalize discrimination of blacks; these laws are known as the **Jim Crow laws.**

Even though the Fifteenth Amendment gave all men the right to vote, the southern states employed a variety of tactics to prevent blacks from voting, including the following:

- **Whites-only primaries:** Nonwhites were barred from primaries because Democrats argued that political parties were private organizations and thus not subject to antidiscrimination laws.

- **Literacy tests:** Blacks were required to pass complex tests that were graded by white election officials in order to vote.

- **Poll taxes:** Some states required people to pay a fee in order to vote.

- **Grandfather clause:** If a person could prove that his grandfather was eligible to vote prior to 1867, he could bypass the literacy tests and other barriers; because no blacks could vote at that time, they had to pass the difficult literacy tests.

Several Supreme Court decisions also weakened the civil rights amendments. In ***Plessy v. Ferguson*** (1896), the Court held that the state government could segregate public transportation and thus established the **separate but equal** doctrine: Blacks could be forced into separate accommodations, including theater seats and hotels, as long as the accommodations were equal to those given to whites.

THE NAACP (1909–1940s)

The National Association for the Advancement of Colored People (NAACP) was founded in 1909. Energetic and talented lawyers such as Thurgood Marshall (later the first African American Supreme Court justice) began fighting racial segregation and discrimination via the courts.

BROWN V. BOARD OF EDUCATION *AND DESEGREGATION (1950s)*

Encouraged by the NAACP, several black families around the country challenged school segregation laws by demanding that their children be allowed to attend white schools. These cases eventually reached the Supreme Court, where they were then consolidated into a few cases. In 1954, the Court issued a landmark ruling in ***Brown v. Board of Education of Topeka, Kansas,*** that overturned *Plessy v. Ferguson* by stating that the separate but equal doctrine was unconstitutional and that segregation in public schools was illegal.

In 1955, the Court issued another ruling (sometimes called *Brown 2*) that ordered lower courts to enforce integration "with all deliberate speed." The phrase was intentionally vague, however. *Brown 2* was an attempt to force an end to segregation without creating mass unrest. Many white southerners angrily protested the *Brown* decision, and many schools remained segregated. Although the courts ended **de jure segregation** (segregation imposed by law), **de facto segregation** (segregation due to residential patterns and economic factors) persisted.

THE BUS BOYCOTT (1955–1956)

In 1955, an African American woman named Rosa Parks refused to move to the colored section of a bus in Montgomery, Alabama. Her act of civil disobedience set off a yearlong boycott of the Montgomery bus system led by Dr. Martin Luther King, Jr. In 1956, a federal court ordered the end of segregation of the Montgomery bus system.

KING AND NONVIOLENCE (1957–1960s)

In 1957, King formed the Southern Christian Leadership Conference to organize campaigns to end segregation and discrimination. King advocated nonviolent tactics and encouraged peaceful marches, protests, and other acts of civil disobedience to achieve his goals. King's peaceful approach had a tremendous impact on the nation because it contrasted so strongly with white southerners' violent responses to his campaigns. In 1963, for example, the police commissioner of Birmingham, Alabama, ordered that his officers attack black protesters with dogs, fire hoses, and cattle prods. Many Americans saw this on television and were horrified by southern police brutality. King's civil rights campaign culminated in the 1963 March on Washington. Speaking to several hundred thousand people on the national mall—and millions more watching on television—King delivered the "I Have a Dream" speech, calling for a color-blind society and an end to discrimination.

CIVIL RIGHTS LEGISLATION (1960s)

In the mid-1960s, Congress passed several laws in an attempt to end discrimination:

- **The Civil Rights Act of 1964,** which banned discrimination on the basis of race, religion, color, gender, and national origin. The act outlawed segregation in all public facilities, authorized the federal government to force desegregation in schools, and established equal rights in the workplace.
- **The Voting Rights Act of 1965,** which outlawed discriminatory exam requirements for voter registration and

allowed the federal government to take over the registration process in states with a history of discrimination. Both measures dramatically increased voter registration by African Americans in the South.

- **The Civil Rights Act of 1968,** which eliminated discrimination in housing and made it easier for minorities to secure loans and mortgages.

AFFIRMATIVE ACTION (1970s–PRESENT)

Affirmative action programs try to rectify past discrimination by giving minorities and women special consideration when employees are hired and students are admitted into universities. Proponents argue that affirmative action rights past wrongs and helps erase the effects of racism and other bias. Critics argue that affirmative action unfairly discriminates against whites, a phenomenon known as **reverse discrimination.**

The Bakke Case

In 1978, the Supreme Court ruled in its first affirmative action case, ***Regents of the University of California v. Bakke.*** The Court upheld affirmative action but argued that although race could be a factor in admissions decisions, it could not be the only factor.

Recent Crusades for Equal Rights

The late twentieth century and early twenty-first century witnessed many groups agitating for equal rights, including women, seniors, the disabled, and gays and lesbians.

WOMEN

Like African Americans, women have had to struggle to win equal protection under federal law. The Constitution explicitly gives men power and rights that were not given to women, including the right to vote.

The First Women's Movement (1840s–1920s)

In 1848, a group of women met in Seneca Falls, New York, to organize the **suffrage movement.** The Seneca Falls activists were disappointed when the Fifteenth Amendment extended the right to vote to black men, but not women. Women did not win the right to vote until the **Nineteenth Amendment** was ratified in 1920.

The Second Women's Movement (1960s)

The civil rights movement of the 1950s galvanized many women to create their own movement for civil rights. **Feminism,** the movement that seeks social, political, and legal equality for women, gained strength. In 1966, several feminists formed the National Organization for Women (NOW) to promote their goals, including the Equal Rights Amendment.

ERA

The **Equal Rights Amendment (ERA)** was proposed to amend the Constitution to ensure that everyone had equal rights regardless of gender. After Congress approved the ERA in 1972, it was sent to the states for ratification. Not enough states ratified it, however, which killed the amendment.

In the 1960s, several court cases argued that **gender discrimination** violated the Fourteenth Amendment's equal protection clause. In many cases, the courts have struck down discriminatory laws. The 1964 Civil Rights Act forbids gender discrimination in the workplace, and some women have used this law to fight **sexual harassment,** which is unwanted and inappropriate physical or verbal conduct of a sexual nature that creates an uncomfortable work environment or interferes with a person's ability to do his or her job.

SENIORS

In 1967, Congress passed the Age Discrimination in Employment Act (ADEA), which prohibits any age discrimination unless age is a clear and necessary qualification for the job. In 1978, Congress amended the ADEA to ban **mandatory retirement** rules for most employees.

THE DISABLED

The Civil Rights Act of 1964 did not protect people with disabilities. Congress has since passed several laws prohibiting discrimination against the disabled:

- **The Rehabilitation Act** (1973), which banned discrimination against the disabled in any program receiving government funding. A 1978 amendment to the act required buildings constructed with federal money to accommodate the disabled with ramps, elevators, and other special equipment.
- **The Education for All Handicapped Children Act** (1975), which required public schools to make provisions for students with disabilities.
- **The Americans with Disabilities Act** (1990), which required all public buildings to be handicapped accessible and forced employers to make all reasonable accommodations for disabled workers. Employers also cannot discriminate against the disabled when hiring.

GAYS AND LESBIANS

Throughout much of the twentieth century, many states had laws that criminalized homosexual acts. In 2003, the Supreme Court declared such laws against sodomy illegal in *Lawrence v. Texas,* because they violate the due process clause of the Fourteenth Amendment. The Court decided that state governments cannot criminalize consensual adult sexual behavior.

Sample Test Questions

1. What are civil liberties and rights?

2. Why is the Fourteenth Amendment so important in civil rights?

3. What does *incorporation* mean?

4. True or false: The Constitution explicitly grants Americans a right to privacy.

5. True or false: The Supreme Court has upheld all elements of the Americans with Disabilities Act.

6. Which Supreme Court case overturned the "separate but equal" doctrine?

A. *Plessy v. Ferguson*
B. *Brown v. Board of Education of Topeka, Kansas*
C. *Griswold v. Connecticut*
D. *Miranda v. Arizona*

7. What is prior restraint?

A. A form of civil rights protest
B. Arresting someone before they commit a crime
C. Preventing something from being printed
D. Stopping a person from voting

8. In 2003, the Supreme Court upheld affirmative action as long as it does what?

A. Applies to gender, not race

B. Aims at diversity and includes race as one factor among many
C. Favors children of University of Michigan graduates
D. Is limited to law school admissions

9. Which clause is *not* part of the Fourteenth Amendment?

A. The privileges and immunities clause
B. The due process clause
C. The equal protection clause
D. The establishment clause

10. What did the Supreme Court order in *Gideon v. Wainwright?*

A. The police must inform suspects of their rights when they are arrested.
B. The government must pay for an attorney for defendants who cannot afford one.
C. Searches should require a warrant based on probable cause.
D. The government cannot ban contraception.

ANSWERS

1. Civil liberties are individual freedoms that the government cannot take away. Civil rights are the rights of equality before the law.

2. The Fourteenth Amendment is important to civil rights because it includes three clauses that established much of the constitutional framework for civil rights: the privileges and immunities clause, the due process clause, and the equal protection clause, all of which apply to state governments.

3. *Incorporation* is a legal term; it means that states are bound by the Bill of Rights.

4. False

5. False

6. B

7. C

8. B

9. D

10. B

Suggested Reading

• Abraham, Henry J. *Freedom and the Court.* New York: Oxford University Press, 2003.

Abraham analyzes the effects of the Supreme Court on civil rights and civil liberties.

• Anderson, Terry H. *The Pursuit of Fairness: The History of Affirmative Action.* New York: Oxford University Press, 2004.

Anderson presents an objective study of a very controversial policy.

• Heymann, Philip B., and Juliette N. Kayyem. *Protecting Liberty in an Age of Terror.* Cambridge, Mass.: MIT Press, 2005.

Heymann and Kayyem offer specific recommendations about how to balance national security and civil liberties.

• Howard, John R. *The Shifting Wind.* Albany: State University of New York Press, 1999.

Howard explores civil rights decisions by the Supreme Court from the Civil War until the 1950s.

- Hull, N. E. H., and Peter Charles Hoffer. *Roe v. Wade: The Abortion Rights Controversy in American History.* Lawrence: University of Kansas Press, 2001.

The authors present a comprehensive account of the battles over abortion rights.

- Leone, Richard C., and Anrig Greg, Jr., eds. *The War on Our Freedoms: Civil Liberties in an Age of Terrorism.* New York: Public Affairs, 2003.

This collection of essays by experts in a variety of fields discusses the effects of the War on Terror on American civil liberties.

Useful Websites

- www.aclu.org

The American Civil Liberties Union is the most prominent—and the most controversial—civil liberties group in the United States.

- www.cdt.org

The Center for Democracy and Technology provides information on how the spread of technology affects privacy.

- www.findlaw.com/casecode/supreme.html

This site is an excellent source for information on Supreme Court decisions, including ones concerning civil rights and civil liberties.

- www.naacp.org

Homepage for the National Organization for the Advancement of Colored People, a crucial organization in the end of segregation.

- www.nclr.org

The National Council of La Raza is an organization that works to improve the lives of Hispanics, including fighting for civil rights.

13

PUBLIC POLICY

Overview

The term *public policy* covers the whole range of government actions designed to improve life in the United States. How much we pay in sales tax or into social security, whether the Clean Air Act is enforced, how many food stamps a family can receive, how best to patrol the borders, and even whether children need to pass a test before graduating from high school are all matters of domestic policy. Because domestic policy covers so much, people have widely divergent opinions about what constitutes the "right" policy. People also disagree about how best to create and implement such policies.

How Policy Gets Made

Public policy is any rule, plan, or action pertaining to issues of domestic national importance. Public policy solves internal problems, such as how to protect citizens from toxic waste or how to ensure that all children get equal access to education. In order to be made official, public policy legislation goes through five steps:

1. The national agenda
2. Formulation
3. Adoption
4. Implementation
5. Evaluation

Incrementalism

Changes in American domestic policy occur slowly. Many interest groups will fight against making radical changes, and many lawmakers are reluctant to change things too quickly. Political scientists call this phenomenon **incrementalism** because policy gets tweaked slightly over time rather than dramatically altered all at once.

THE NATIONAL AGENDA

When something becomes a concern for a significant number of people, that concern becomes part of the **national agenda,** the list of things that the public wants the government to address. An issue becomes part of the national agenda for any of the following reasons:

- **As part of a larger trend:** Some trends, like the rise in violent crime in the 1980s and early 1990s, lead people to demand government action, especially for stronger federal law enforcement.
- **After a major event:** Sometimes, a single event forces an issue onto the agenda. The September 11th attacks, for example, led many Americans to demand an increase in national security. Likewise, the Exxon Valdez oil spill in 1989 prompted many to call for environmental protection.
- **Through an interest group:** An interest group or members of a social movement work to raise public awareness of an issue. If enough people get involved, the issue can get put on the national agenda.
- **Speeches:** Prominent politicians attempt to put an issue on the agenda through speeches. The president is particularly able to do this due to the amount of media coverage of the White House.

After an issue gets put on the national agenda, people will begin petitioning the government to take action.

FORMULATION

Policy formulation determines how the government will respond to problems on the national agenda. Although people may agree that a particular problem exists, they might strongly disagree about how to remedy it. Members of Congress, executive branch officials, and interest groups may all propose solutions, which then prompt intense debate in the media and in Congress.

EXAMPLE: The budget surplus was one of the key issues in the election of 2000. In the last few years of the Clinton Administration, the federal government ran a surplus for the first time in years, and many people had ideas about what to do with the extra money. Republican candidate George W. Bush pledged to return money to the public in the form of tax cuts, whereas Democrat Al Gore advocated using the money for some social programs, demonstrating how different people can offer radically different solutions to issues on the national agenda.

ADOPTION

After debating the issue and proposals, the federal government chooses one policy solution and then passes new laws to adopt the new policy.

EXAMPLE: After winning the 2000 presidential election, George W. Bush worked with the Republican-controlled Congress to enact the tax cuts he had promised.

IMPLEMENTATION

After a policy gets adopted, it must be implemented. The federal agencies charged with implementing the policy must determine exactly how they will carry it out. The federal bureaucracy promulgates the laws passed by Congress into specific policy, drawing up the rules and guidelines for putting the law into practice.

> *EXAMPLE:* The Federal Election Commission (FEC) was charged with enforcing the Bipartisan Campaign Finance Reform Act after it was passed in 2002. To do so, the FEC had to determine the nuts and bolts of how the law worked and had to create rules governing the enforcement of the new law.

EVALUATION

People begin judging and evaluating a policy once it has been put into effect. Feedback might come from the people whom the policy serves, bureaucrats who monitor the implementation, and pundits and reporters who care about the issue.

> *EXAMPLE:* Many different public interest groups and think tanks, including the powerful Cato Institute and the Heritage Foundation, evaluate government policies.

Welfare

Welfare policies help those in economic need. These programs are also known as **public assistance.** The basic method of distributing public assistance funds is via **income transfer:** The government takes money from wealthier citizens through taxes, then gives some of that money to citizens with low or no income. Because funds are redistributed from the rich to the poor, we call such policies **redistributive policies.**

POVERTY IN AMERICA

The U.S. government established a standard for dealing with income inequality during President Lyndon Johnson's War on

Poverty in the 1960s. This standard, known as the **poverty line,** determined that those families that earn less than three times their annual budget for food would be considered poor and in need of public assistance.

EXAMPLE: In January 2006, the U.S. Department of Health and Human Services determined the national poverty line to be approximately $20,000 for a family of four.

Debating the Standard

Many people argue that the federal poverty standard is inaccurate because it focuses so much on the cost of food and not enough on housing costs. These critics claim that because housing prices have risen faster than food prices, the poverty standard does not accurately measure how much money a family needs to survive. According to these critics, there are substantially more poor people in the United States than the current standard suggests.

BASIC WELFARE PROGRAMS

Welfare consists of a variety of policies with different goals:

- **Supplemental Security Income (SSI):** Offers aid to elderly and disabled people who do not qualify for social security benefits
- **Food stamps:** Gives low-income people coupons with which to purchase food
- **Earned Income Tax Credit (EITC):** Refunds some or all of a family's social security taxes
- **Public housing:** Creates and subsidizes apartments and other dwellings for low-income families

- **Rent vouchers:** Provides grants to low-income individuals to help defray housing costs

- **Medicaid:** Provides low-cost medical care to those on welfare

> **Corporate Welfare**
>
> The federal government has many policies designed to stimulate the economy by assisting businesses. For instance, the government subsidizes some agricultural products and offers tax credits for various types of research. Critics of such programs accuse the government of promulgating "corporate welfare."

Crime and Law Enforcement

The local, state, and federal governments in the United States all play an important role in fighting crime. Generally, the federal government sets the basic parameters of law enforcement and provides money and other aid to state and local agencies that then enforce the law.

THE POLITICS OF CRIME

Some politicians campaign on a "law and order" platform, promising to crack down on crime and impose harsh sentences on those found guilty of committing crimes. Scholars debate the efficacy of government anticrime programs. During the 1990s, for example, violent crime fell dramatically. President Clinton and the Democrats claimed credit, citing the strong economy and the new crime bill passed in the early 1990s. Some critics, in contrast, point to other causes for the dip in crime, including demographics (the age groups most likely to commit violent crimes shrank) and the vast increase in the number of prisons. It is never easy to explain why the crime rate rises or falls.

Abortion and Crime

Perhaps the most controversial argument advanced to explain the drop in crime came from economist Steven Levitt (co-author of the best-selling *Freakonomics* [2005]). Levitt argued that the Supreme Court ruling in *Roe v. Wade* in 1973 led to the drop in crime. He contended that unwanted children born into poverty are more likely to become criminals. But after *Roe v. Wade,* more women chose to have abortions rather than have unwanted babies, which had the additional effect of lowering the crime rate in the late 1980s and early 1990s, around the time these children would have been teenagers. Needless to say, this theory has generated intense controversy.

GUN CONTROL

Gun control refers to policies aimed at regulating the ownership and use of firearms. Proponents of gun control argue that tighter restrictions will reduce the number of guns on the streets and consequently decrease the amount of violent crime in the United States. Critics of gun control argue that the Constitution prohibits the federal government from regulating firearms because the Second Amendment states that citizens have the right "to bear arms." Many critics also believe that gun control disproportionately affects law-abiding citizens because gun control laws will not deter the people who are most likely to commit crimes.

THE WAR ON DRUGS

The federal government has made its War on Drugs a national priority since the 1980s because high drug use presents a public health concern and increases the violent crime rate. As part of this war, the government has passed laws imposing harsh sentences on drug dealers, and it has also acted to stop the flow of illegal drugs into the country.

Despite all the money spent and all the federal government's efforts, drug use has not declined, as illegal drugs continue to flow into the United States, prompting some people to argue that the U.S. anti-drug policy has failed. Some critics even argue that the War on Drugs has created more problems than it has solved.

EXAMPLE: Critics contend that the mandatory minimums and harsh sentences imposed on people for possessing even small amounts of illegal substances have contributed to overcrowding in prisons. In turn, prison overcrowding increases relapse rates; inmates are now more likely to commit crimes again because prisons are unable to provide adequate job training and counseling to all the inmates.

Although the federal government has not substantively changed its drug policies in decades, some state and local governments are experimenting with other methods of punishing those caught breaking the law. Some states do not imprison first-time offenders, for example, or those caught with a small amount of drugs. Instead, the state sends them to rehabilitation programs. It is still too soon to know what effect these policies have had on drug use and crime.

Medical Marijuana

Some scientists believe that marijuana can alleviate symptoms of some diseases, such as improving eyesight in glaucoma patients and reducing the side effects of chemotherapy. As a result, some states—including Washington, California, Oregon, Arizona, Colorado, and Hawaii, among others—have legalized medical marijuana, allowing patients to legally obtain the drug with a doctor's prescription. The federal government, however, has disagreed with these states, arguing that marijuana should always remain illegal.

The Environment

Modern environmental policy in the United States began in the 1960s. Around this time, the environmental movement started to put pressure on the federal government to actively protect the country's resources and preserve the world's ecosystems.

THE NATIONAL ENVIRONMENTAL POLICY ACT

After an oil well exploded off the California coast in 1969, Congress passed the National Environmental Policy Act, a very important law in the history of environmental policy. The law required all federal agencies to conduct an **environmental impact statement** before taking any action that could affect the environment. The act also created the Council on Environmental Quality and the Environmental Protection Agency (EPA).

OTHER KEY ENVIRONMENTAL LAWS

Since the National Environmental Policy Act, Congress has passed other laws regulating pollution and cleaning up the environment, as explained in the table on the next page.

Environmentalism Versus Growth

Environmental policy must balance the needs of the environment with the need for a strong economy. Critics of environmental policies claim that EPA regulations hurt the economy by limiting growth. Businesses spend time and money complying with these laws, which hurts their efficiency and decreases their profit margins. Smaller profits, in turn, mean fewer jobs. Environmentalists reject these claims, arguing that a healthy environment trumps all other economic considerations.

IMPORTANT ENVIRONMENTAL LAWS SINCE 1970		
Law	**Date**	**Purpose/Impact**
Clean Air Act Amendments	1970	Restricted air pollution and authorized the EPA to enforce air quality standards
Clean Water Act	1972	Set goal of cleaning up waters by 1983
Federal Environmental Pesticide Act	1972	Banned the use of pesticides that are harmful to humans, animals, and crops
Clean Water Act	1974	Set federal standards for drinking water
Resource Conservation and Recovery Act	1976	Encouraged resource conservation and authorized federal control of hazardous waste
Comprehensive Environmental Response, Compensation, and Liability Act	1980	Established a "superfund" for cleaning up toxic waste
Clean Air Act Amendments	1990	Required reformulated gasoline to be used in large cities and reduced some gases
Food Quality and Protection Act	1996	Authorized the federal government to regulate the use of pesticides in food production
Chemical Safety Information, Site Security, and Fuels Regulatory Relief Act	1999	Regulated security and risk management plans at chemical and fuel plants
The Small Business Liability Relief and Brownfields Revitalization Act	2002	Provided funds to clean up brownfields (environmentally damaged urban areas)

Social Security

Launched in 1935 as part of Franklin Roosevelt's New Deal, the term **social security** refers to a federal social insurance program that seeks to keep retired people and the elderly out of poverty. All employers and workers are automatically taxed a certain portion of their wages—7.5 percent for workers as of 2007. This money is then paid out to people who have retired from the work force or who are unable to work.

Many people erroneously believe that social security functions as a pension system and that retired people withdraw money from an account filled with funds saved from a lifetime of working. In reality, social security money exists in one enormous account, funded by today's working people. Workers' taxes pay to support today's retirees. As a result, the money a person gets from social security is not always the same as the amount he or she has put in: Some people will receive more, and some people will receive less. Social security is an **entitlement program,** which means that certain people are entitled to benefits from the federal government.

THE WORKER-TO-RETIREE RATIO

Because social security relies on current workers to pay for benefits to current retirees, the ratio between workers and retirees is important. Ideally, each retiree is supported by a large number of workers so that each worker only has to pay a small part of the retiree's benefits. As baby boomers grow older, however, more retirees will be eligible for benefits, which reduces the ratio and increases the amount each worker must contribute to social security. In 1946, the ratio was roughly forty workers per one retiree. Researchers project that by the time the baby boomers have all retired in 2030, the ratio will have shrunk to two workers per one retiree.

THE SOCIAL SECURITY CRISIS

Many people worry about an impending social security crisis of having to fund too many retirees from the salaries of too few workers. Although the program has been running a surplus for many years, eventually people will be drawing social security benefits at a rate faster than workers can contribute. This deficit will force the government to either find money elsewhere to maintain benefits or drastically cut those benefits. Analysts also worry that a social security deficit will hurt the federal budget because many agencies have been borrowing from the current social security surplus. These agencies will eventually have to repay their debts to the social security program, causing massive upheaval in federal finances.

Solutions

Politicians and political scientists have proposed a number of ways to save social security before the crisis hits:

- **Raising taxes:** Raising payroll taxes—either by increasing the payroll tax rate or by raising or eliminating the ceiling on income subject to the social security tax—would generate more social security funds.
- **Reducing benefits:** Cutting benefits would save money.
- **Means-testing:** Reducing benefits given to the rich would increase the amount of social security money available to the poor.
- **Privatizing:** Allowing workers to decide how much to invest in Social Security is an extremely controversial program because it forces workers to take responsibility for their contributions.

Education

Democratic societies extol education as a means of providing people with equal opportunities, a goal that American political culture values. Americans have always left education to state governments and have shied away from too much federal control. As a result, American students do not always receive equal educational opportunities.

THE FEDERAL ROLE IN EDUCATION

For most of American history, the federal government played little or no role in education. Education was thought to be a local issue, best regulated by local and state governments. In 1965, with the passage of the Higher Education Act and the Elementary and Secondary Education Act, the federal government provided funding for education for the first time. In 1979, Congress created the Department of Education, which heralded a new level of federal involvement in education. Recently, many education advocates have pushed for stronger accountability from teachers and schools. This accountability comes in the form of standardized tests, which evaluate students' basic skills and knowledge. A school with low-scoring students would be punished for failing to help or adequately educate students.

THE NO CHILD LEFT BEHIND ACT

In the 2000 presidential race, Republican candidate George W. Bush pledged to regulate accountability on the federal level. After becoming president, Bush worked with Democrats and Republicans in Congress to pass the **No Child Left Behind Act (NCLB)** in 2001. The act provided more money to schools but required all schools in the country to meet certain educational standards in return.

NCLB has provoked controversy. The powerful teachers' lobby, the National Education Association, has argued that the act forces teachers to change their curricula and essentially teach only to the tests. Other critics contend that the federal government has not provided nearly enough funds to help schools adhere to the NCLB parameters. Finally, some critics claim that NCLB functions like an unfunded mandate, forcing state and local governments to spend money to meet the law's standards.

School Vouchers

Government-funded **school voucher programs** give low-income parents vouchers that can be used to pay for tuition at a private school of the parents' choice. Voucher programs have sparked much controversy. Some critics argue that the vouchers violate the separation of church and state because parents might use the government money to send their kids to religious schools. Others argue that the money used as vouchers could be used to improve the public school system, thereby eradicating the need for parents to send their kids to private schools.

Sample Test Questions

1. Briefly describe the stages of the policy process.

2. What is a redistributive policy?

3. What is incrementalism?

4. True or false: The federal government allows doctors to prescribe marijuana for medicinal purposes.

5. True or false: The No Child Left Behind Act dropped standardized testing requirements for schools receiving federal money.

6. Which of the following policies provides a tax refund on all or part of a poor family's social security tax?

A. Temporary Assistance to Needy Families

B. Earned Income Tax Credit
C. Food stamps
D. Supplemental Security Income

7. The National Environmental Policy Act required all federal agencies to conduct a(n) ________ prior to taking any major action.

A. Means-testing
B. Cost-benefit analysis
C. Environmental impact statement
D. Tax assessment

8. Which of the following is *not* a solution to the social security crisis?

A. Increasing federal contributions
B. Raising taxes
C. Reducing benefits
D. Privatizing

9. Under the No Child Left Behind Act, what will happen to a school that continues to fail to meet federal standards?

A. It will be taken over by the federal government.
B. It will be forced to allow students to transfer elsewhere.
C. It will be turned into a private school.
D. It will be given tax credits.

10. How does means-testing reduce benefits?

A. By privatizing the distribution of benefits
B. By tapering off benefits over time
C. By giving everyone an average benefit
D. By giving smaller benefits to wealthy people

ANSWERS

1. The policy process contains the following steps: (1) getting the issue on the national agenda; (2) formulation of policy options; (3) adoption of a policy; (4) implementation of the policy; (5) feedback leading to evaluation of the policy.

2. A redistributive policy (also called an income transfer policy) transfers money from one group to another.

3. Incrementalism is the tendency of American policy changes to happen gradually with no revolutionary change.

4. False

5. False

6. B

7. C

8. A

9. B

10. D

Suggested Reading

• Diamond, Peter. *Social Security Reform.* New York: Oxford University Press, 2002.

An in-depth look at the problems facing social security, with some thoughts on possible remedies.

• Melnick, R. Shep. *Between the Lines: Interpreting Welfare Rights.* Washington, D.C.: Brookings, 1994.

Melnick explores the role of the courts in welfare policy.

• Rosenbaum, Walter A. *Environmental Politics and Policy.* 5th ed. Washington, D.C.: Congressional Quarterly Press, 2001.

A thorough study of the making of environmental policy.

• Van Dunk, Emily, and Anneliese M. Dickman. *School Choice and the Question of Accountability.* New Haven, Conn.: Yale University Press, 2003.

Van Dunk and Dickman examine school voucher programs and other methods of school choice to assess their effectiveness.

Useful Websites

• www.cdc.gov

At the home site for the Centers for Disease Control and Prevention, visitors can get information on diseases, vaccinations, and other health-related issues.

• www.census.gov

The United States Census Bureau compiles a great deal of statistical data about the United States.

• www.epa.gov

The website of the Environmental Protection Agency, the chief federal agency charged with enforcing environmental laws.

• www.fbi.gov

The best-known federal law enforcement agency is the Federal Bureau of Investigation. Its website offers extensive data on crime in the United States.

• www.ssa.gov

The Social Security Administration runs the social security program. Its website contains statistics and information about the program.

FOREIGN POLICY

14

Overview

For most of the twentieth century, the United States defined its foreign policy in relation to the Soviet Union, as the two countries battled each other for dominance during the Cold War. Although the two countries themselves never came to blows, they engaged in social, political, and economic competition around the globe. Following the collapses of the Soviet Union in 1989, many Americans began turning their attention toward domestic policy.

This trend changed with the terrorist attacks of September 11, 2001. Since then, foreign policy has returned to center stage, and politicians and candidates hotly debate foreign policy issues. An old adage states that politics stops at the water's edge, meaning that the United States should not let political disputes influence foreign policy. In reality, though, partisan politics have a great impact on foreign policy.

Tools of Foreign Policy

The term **foreign policy** refers to a state's international goals and its strategies to achieve those goals. Foreign policymakers follow the same five steps with which public policy gets made:

1. **Agenda setting:** A problem or issue rises to prominence on the agenda.
2. **Formulation:** Possible policies are created and debated.
3. **Adoption:** The government adopts one policy.
4. **Implementation:** The appropriate government agency enacts the policy.
5. **Evaluation:** Officials and agencies judge whether the policy has been successful.

Unlike domestic policy, however, foreign policymaking usually involves fewer people and less publicity. In the United States, the president serves as the chief diplomat and is charged with running American foreign policy. The president employs three tools to conduct foreign policy:

1. Diplomacy
2. Foreign aid
3. Military force

DIPLOMACY

Diplomacy is the act of dealing with other nations, usually through negotiation and discussion. Diplomacy involves meetings between political leaders, sending diplomatic messages, and making public statements about the relationship between countries. The American president, for example, often hosts leaders and chief diplomats of other nations at the White House in order to discuss a variety of issues. Most diplomacy occurs behind the scenes as officials hold secret negotiations or meet privately to discuss key issues.

Approaches to Diplomacy

States generally pursue diplomacy in one of three ways:

- **Unilaterally:** The states acts alone, without the assistance or consent of any other state.
- **Bilaterally:** The state works in conjunction with another state.
- **Multilaterally:** The state works in conjunction with several other states.

There are pros and cons to each of these three approaches. Acting unilaterally, for example, allows a state to do what it wants without compromise, but it must also bear all the costs itself. Acting with allies, on the other hand, allows a state to maintain good relations and to share the diplomatic burden, but this often requires compromise.

American Isolationist Versus Internationalist Attitudes

Americans have always debated what role the United States should play on the global stage. Those people who advocate a strategy of largely ignoring the rest of the world are called **isolationists.** In contrast, those people who advocate taking an active role in world affairs are called **internationalists.** Since World War II, U.S. foreign policy has taken an active leadership role in international politics.

FOREIGN AID

States often help each other to improve relations and achieve their own foreign policy objectives. There are two types of foreign aid:

1. **Military aid:** States donate, sell, or trade military equipment and technology to affect the military balance of power in certain key regions of the world

2. **Economic aid:** States donate or loan money to other counties to boost economic development.

MILITARY FORCE

In some cases, states use military force or the threat of military force to achieve their foreign policy objectives. The use of military forces often involves stronger states pressuring weaker states to get what they want.

EXAMPLE: The practice of forcing a weak state to comply with a stronger state via the threat of force is sometimes called Finlandization. In the final days of World War II, Finland reached a peace agreement with the Soviet Union. Even though both countries knew that the Soviets could have easily overwhelmed the Finns, neither wanted war, and the Soviets preferred to use their military elsewhere. The terms of the peace treaty basically gave the Soviets everything they wanted, so much so that Finland almost became a puppet of the Soviet Union.

Deterrence

Deterrence refers to the build up of military force as a threat to warn another state not to pursue a particular course of action.

EXAMPLE: Throughout the Cold War, the United States relied on the strength of its nuclear and conventional weapons to deter the Soviet Union from invading western Europe.

American Foreign Policy Concerns

As the greatest military and economic power in the world, the United States has taken an active role in international politics. The United States values security and stability, both at home and abroad, above all else, and focuses on a number of areas to achieve those ends:

- Terrorism
- Nuclear proliferation
- Free trade

- Humanitarianism
- Environmental issues

TERRORISM

Terrorism has been used by groups of all ideological and political views, from the leftist Red Brigades in Europe to the right-wing terrorist Timothy McVeigh, who bombed a federal building in Oklahoma City in 1994. A number of foreign and domestic terrorists have launched attacks against American interests since the early 1980s. In 1982, a suicide bomber killed 241 American military personnel in Lebanon. A group of Islamic fundamentalists attempted to destroy the World Trade Center in 1993, and al Qaeda attacked American embassies in Africa in 1998. Al Qaeda's devastating, coordinated attacks on September 11, 2001, prompted officials in Washington to make combating terrorism the central focus of American foreign policy.

September 11th

Using passenger planes as weapons, nineteen terrorists damaged the Pentagon in Washington, D.C., and destroyed the twin towers of the World Trade Center complex in New York City, killing nearly 3,000 people in the process. The terrorist network al Qaeda carefully planned the attack to protest American foreign policy in the Middle East.

The War on Terror

Following the attack, President George W. Bush rallied the nation to fight back against the terrorists responsible. The United States successfully led a coalition force in an invasion of Afghanistan, where the governing Taliban regime had sheltered and aided the core leadership of al Qaeda, including Saudi exile Osama bin Ladin. Bush also created the Department of Homeland Security to coordinate efforts at home to prevent future terrorist attacks.

Bush's War on Terror broadened the scope of the American response from fighting al Qaeda and other groups intent on attacking the United States to fighting all terrorists around the world. Since 2002, the United States has funded many wars on terror being fought by other governments in Asia, Africa, Europe, and Latin America. The United States has even sent military consultants to other countries. As a result of these wars, a few terrorists groups, including the Irish Republican Army, have voluntarily renounced violence.

Terrorism and Other States

Many states around the world have lived with the threat of terrorism for far longer than the United States. Irish Republican Army terrorists frequently attacked English civilians in London in the 1980s, for example, to protest British control of Northern Ireland. Israel suffers from frequent terrorist attacks too: at one time from the Palestinian Liberation Organization and currently from Hamas, an Islamist terrorist organization based in Lebanon.

The Bush Doctrine

In 2002, President Bush argued that the United States has the right to eliminate its enemies before they attack American interests, a policy now known as the Bush Doctrine. Although previous presidents had always believed that the United States could defend itself by striking its enemies first, Bush was the first president to put that policy into effect when he authorized the invasion of Iraq in 2003 to prevent dictator Saddam Hussein from using weapons of mass destruction against the United States and its allies. Numerous critics, however, have challenged the Bush Doctrine, claiming that this largely unilateral policy has damaged American integrity abroad. Other critics have contended that the Bush Doctrine has undermined America's ability to criticize other aggressive states.

NUCLEAR PROLIFERATION

The United States has worked hard to prevent other countries from acquiring and developing nuclear weapons. The United States worries that rogue states might use nuclear technology irresponsibly to attack their enemies without thinking of the global repercussions. In 1968, the **Nuclear Non-Proliferation Treaty** tried to stop the spread of nuclear weapons. At the time, only five states had nuclear weapons: the United States, the Soviet Union, Great Britain, France, and China, all of which had a permanent seat on the United Nations Security Council. Nearly every country in the world signed the treaty, thereby agreeing not to seek or spread nuclear weapons.

Despite the agreement, however, a few states have still acquired or developed nuclear weapons, including India, Pakistan, and, most recently, North Korea. Most foreign policy analysts believe that Israel also has nuclear weapons, even though Israel refuses to reveal whether this is true. Iran is currently seeking to acquire nuclear technology, ostensibly to be used only for electrical power, even though few world leaders believe this claim.

Nuclear Arsenals Around the World

Although only a few states currently have nuclear weapons, many have sought to acquire them over the past few decades. Canada, Brazil, Argentina, Australia, South Korea, Japan, Egypt, Libya, Iraq, Germany, Poland, Serbia, Romania, Sweden, and perhaps Saudi Arabia have all launched nuclear weapon research programs at some point in the last forty years. South Africa also once had nuclear weapons but dismantled them in the early 1990s.

FREE TRADE

Since the end of World War II, the United States has led the way in creating a number of international institutions that govern international trade. The World Trade Organization (WTO) is the largest and most powerful of these institutions. It seeks to promote free trade among member nations by reducing or eliminating domestic subsidies and protective tariffs. WTO members must agree to abide by the organization's trade regulations, and almost all the world's countries are represented in the membership.

The governing body of the WTO has the authority to punish any member state that violates these rules. Many American laborers believe that such organizations hurt American industry and lead to outsourcing, transferring jobs formerly available to American workers to workers in other countries. Proponents of free trade—including the American government—however, argue that the benefits of free trade far outweigh the costs because free trade lowers the price of consumer goods and allows Americans to purchase more with their money.

HUMANITARIANISM

The United States has always been one of the major proponents of international human rights and has criticized many developing countries around the world for abusing those rights. President Jimmy Carter even made humanitarianism a major tenant of his foreign policy in the late 1970s. Since the end of World War II, the United States has also been the largest donor of international aid.

At the same time, the United States still lacks a codified humanitarianism foreign policy, responding to some global humanitarian crises (Somalia in 1992) but not others (Rwanda in 1996, Darfur in 2004). In fact, both conservative and liberal presidents and senators have refused to sign most international human rights treaties out of fear that Americans may be stripped of their rights as U.S. citizens when tried in international courts for crimes against humanity. This refusal has prompted much international criticism, especially in the wake of gross human rights violations, most notably at the American-controlled Abu Ghraib prison in Iraq in 2003 and at the American military detention center at Guantánamo Bay, Cuba.

Americans and foreign policymakers alike are divided on whether the United States should make humanitarianism a more formal component of its foreign policy. Proponents argue that the United States should promote human rights as the so-called leader of the free world and as the country with the most resources to help others. Others, however, argue that promoting human rights and sending troops on humanitarian missions achieves nothing tangible for the United States and could lead to wasteful uses of resources and the needless loss of American lives.

ENVIRONMENTAL ISSUES

Environmentalism has taken center stage in foreign policy as well. Many people around the world have realized that some environmental issues require transnational solutions, so they urge their political leaders to reach agreements over a variety of environmental matters. The most ambitious such agreement is the **Kyoto Protocol,** a 1997 treaty signed to curb global warming by reducing greenhouse gas emissions. A number of states, however, including China and the United States, have refused to sign the Kyoto Protocol, claiming that it had been formulated on faulty science. It remains to be seen whether the treaty can be effective without American participation.

Kyoto in America

Despite the fact that the president and the Senate have refused to sign the Kyoto Protocol, a number of state and local jurisdictions have adopted many of the treaty's requirements. Similarly, a number of corporations have voluntarily complied with some of the protocol's standards.

Regional Issues

The United States uses a variety of tactics to achieve the security and stability it seeks at home and abroad. Sometimes Washington acts as mediator to resolve disputes, such as when Presidents Jimmy Carter and Bill Clinton worked to restore peace between Israel and its Arab neighbors. Other times, the United States relies on trade because many policymakers believe that high levels of trade reduce the likelihood of militarized conflict. Finally, the United States has assumed the role of world policeman a number of times, sending troops on humanitarian missions or to punish rogue states that do not adhere to international codes of conduct.

THE MIDDLE EAST

Much of American foreign policy in the last three decades has centered around the Middle East, the swath of territory on the eastern Mediterranean where Europe, Asia, and Africa intersect. The region is also the birthplace of Judaism, Christianity, and Islam. What happens in the Middle East is vital to American interests. The Middle East is rich in oil, which drives the American economy; without oil, none of America's cars, planes, trains, ships, or industrial machinery would work.

Many rulers of oil-rich countries rely on the wealth generated by oil to sustain their undemocratic regimes and conservative theocracies, which, in turn, fuels dissatisfaction among the people. Some people express their frustration through sectarian violence against neighboring peoples of other faiths, and a minority of people even turn to terrorism to express their anger. Some theocratic regimes have supported the people's use of violence in the name of religious fanaticism. Peace and stability in the Middle East, therefore, would not only reduce violence in the region but would also curb terrorism abroad and stabilize the global economy.

Israel/Palestine

The key to stabilizing the Middle East lies in the resolution of the conflict between Israel and the Palestinians, an ethnic group currently under Israeli rule that seeks to carve out territory to establish its own country. Many neighboring Arab countries have declared their support for the Palestinians, and several have used the Israeli-Palestinian conflict to declare wars and holy wars against Israel. Some presidents, such as Jimmy Carter and Bill Clinton, have used their influence to help resolve these disputes peacefully. Other presidents' peace plans have been less successful. Many believe that peace will be harder to achieve in the wake of Israel's failure to destroy the Islamist group Hamas in 2006.

Iraq

Iraq has been at the center of American foreign policy since the Gulf War of the early 1990s, when the United States and its Allies liberated the oil-rich nation of Kuwait from its Iraqi occupiers. Rather than oust Iraqi dictator Saddam Hussein from power, the United States merely removed Iraqi forces from Kuwait and forced Hussein to end all his nuclear, chemical, and biological weapons programs. In 2003, President George W. Bush believed he had proof that these programs were still operational and therefore ordered the military to invade Iraq, remove Hussein from power, and establish a pro-American democratic government.

Poor management of the war, a shortage of troops, accusations of corruption, human rights violations, rampant sectarian and anti-American violence, and the lack of any weapons of mass destruction have all turned Iraq into a quagmire. Some Americans and foreign policymakers argue that the United States should pull out of Iraq immediately, whereas others say that the United States must remain and stabilize the country in order to keep Iraq from becoming a safe haven for terrorists.

Iran

The United States has had a rocky relationship with Iran since the late twentieth century. The United States and Britain, for example, orchestrated a coup against a democratically elected government to reinstall the pro-Western Muhammad Reza Pahlavi as the shah, or ruler, of Iran after he'd been deposed. The coup outraged Iranians and fueled suspicion of the West. In 1979, the Ayatollah Ruholla Khomeini overthrew the shah and then attacked the American embassy and held more than sixty Americans hostage for 444 days. The United States supplied Iraq with weapons and equipment in its war against Iran throughout the 1980s, driving the two countries even further apart.

In recent years, Iran has been trying to acquire nuclear technology, ostensibly to build nuclear power plants. The United States and the European Union, however, believe that Iran is trying to construct a nuclear weapon for protection against Western encroachment or for possible use against Israel. Iran is, therefore, at the center of American efforts to curb the spread of nuclear weapons, especially in light of the recent failure of the United States to prevent North Korea from developing nuclear weapons.

EUROPE

For all of the nineteenth and most of the twentieth century, Europe lay at the heart of American foreign policy. For the most part, the United States remained nominally neutral, hoping to trade with the great European powers and avoid becoming involved in their costly wars. World Wars I and II transformed the United States into a major military and economic superpower and prompted Washington to assume a leadership role in the postwar world.

The United States and its Western European allies waged much of the Cold War in Europe as well, carving the continent into spheres of influence. Since the fall of the Soviet Union in 1990 and the formation of the European Union in 1992, Europe has become one of the most politically and economically stable regions in the world. As such, it has become less of an American foreign policy concern. Nevertheless, the United States still has a number of vested interests in the region and has fostered democratization and humanitarianism.

Democratization

The collapse of the Soviet Union and the Iron Curtain surrounding the Eastern-Soviet bloc ushered in a new era for democracy and stability in Europe. Many Eastern European governments crumbled or voluntarily relinquished power in the wake of the fall of the Berlin Wall, including Poland, Hungary, Romania, and the former Yugoslavia and Czechoslovakia. Not all countries have made the full transition to democracy and the United States continues to support the peoples in Eastern Europe who are still struggling to end corruption and authoritarianism. The United States, for example, purportedly helped train many of the agitators who peacefully ousted the corrupt regimes in the Velvet Revolution in the Republic of Georgia in 2003 and the Orange Revolution in the Ukraine in 2004.

Peacekeeping

Although the United States welcomed the end of the Cold War, the demise of the Soviet Union and its satellite governments brought only chaos. Nowhere was this more evident than in Yugoslavia, where bitter ethnic rivalries and tensions between Serbs, Croats, Albanians, and Bosniaks led to the Bosnian War in the early 1990s and the Kosovo War in 1999, which the United States participated in through the North Atlantic Treaty Organization (NATO). The United Nations still maintains peacekeeping forces in Kosovo to prevent any further conflict.

Russia

A handful of foreign policy analysts argue that Russia remains a threat to American interests in Europe in spite of the collapse of the Soviet Union and the end of the Cold War. Even though Russia is no longer communist, Russian president Vladimir Putin has consolidated so much power in the early twenty-first century that many people have questioned whether the country is a democracy anymore. The NATO alliance remains in effect too, which has kept Moscow on its guard, and relations between the United States and Russia have chilled somewhat after several diplomatic spats. It remains to be seen what role Russia will play in Europe in the coming decades.

AFRICA

Africa has always been a relatively low priority for American foreign policymakers, simply because Africa has few tangible resources to offer the United States. American involvement in Africa has usually revolved around peacekeeping, either independently or as part of a larger United Nations force. Presidents Bill Clinton and George W. Bush have taken some steps to improve American foreign policy in Africa, particularly because Africa contains a significant Muslim population. Bush has also pledged millions of dollars to help fight the AIDS pandemic, which has ravaged much of the continent.

Peacekeeping

The last time the American troops served as peacekeepers in Africa was in 1992, to prevent warlords from stealing relief food intended for the starving civilians. Militia groups attacked and killed several U.S. marines, and many Americans at home wondered why the United States was in Somalia as they watched the body of a dead marine being dragged through the streets of Mogadishu on CNN. Politicians in Washington withdrew the troops immediately, and the United States has not sent a peacekeeping force to Africa since, not even to prevent genocide in Rwanda in the mid-1990s or in Darfur, Sudan, in the early 2000s. Clinton has since apologized for not sending troops to Rwanda. Some Americans have argued that the United States should use its vast resources to prevent genocide anywhere on the planet, regardless of whether doing so would directly benefit the United States.

ASIA

The United States trades heavily across the Pacific with a wide variety of partners and actively seeks to tap into the large markets of Asia, especially in China and India. The United States also takes an active interest in security matters in Asia.

Trade

Since the 1990s, China and India have developed rapidly, bringing more than a third of the world's population into the global market. American investors, business, and the federal government have vested financial interests in each of these emerging markets. Although India is quickly cornering the services and technology sectors, China has led the way in manufacturing. In fact, America's trade deficit with China has been one of the federal government's top concerns in recent years as the United States buys more goods from China than China buys from the United States. But many U.S. policymakers hope that increased trade with China will reduce the likelihood of any hostilities erupting between the two countries.

China

Despite high levels of trade in the past decade, the United States's relationship with China has soured considerably since the end of the Cold War. Beginning in the 1970s, China and the United States worked together to check the power of their mutual enemy, the Soviet Union. With the Moscow threat gone, however, neither country needs the other as it once did. China has sought more political authority in East Asia as it grows more powerful. The two countries butted heads on a number of occasions in recent years. Foreign policy analysts in both countries see the other country as their primary military threat, although tensions have died down considerably since China pledged its support for the American War on Terror in the aftermath of September 11th.

Taiwan

If China and the United States ever fought a war, it would be over Taiwan, a small but heavily populated island off the coast of China. The United States has always supported the government in exile in Taiwan, which for many years claimed to be the rightful government of mainland China. Over the years, Taiwan has moved toward democracy, and its capitalist economy has always been one of the strongest in Asia. Although the Taiwanese government no longer challenges the communist government in Beijing, many Taiwanese have pushed for independence, which Beijing would interpret as an act of war (because China still claims sovereignty over the island).

The United States has always supported the Taiwanese with economic aid and military equipment, and it is unclear how far Washington would go to protect a fellow democratic country. When the Chinese conducted missile tests off the coast of Taiwan in 1996, President Bill Clinton ordered two aircraft carrier groups to sail between Taiwan and the mainland as a warning to China. Both China and the United States have placed enormous pressure on Taiwan to refrain from declaring independence in order to prevent war.

Afghanistan

Shortly after the September 11th terrorist attacks, President George W. Bush issued an ultimatum to the ruling Islamist Taliban regime to hand over Osama bin Ladin and others in the al Qaeda leadership. When the Taliban refused, the United States and a coalition of allies invaded the country, ousting the Taliban, routing terrorists, and establishing a pro-Western government. Osama bin Ladin has eluded capture, but the American military continues to hunt al Qaeda cells.

North Korea

The United States is also concerned with communist North Korea, particularly ever since dictator Kim Jong Il declared that he had successfully developed and tested nuclear weapons in 2006. For many years after the end of the Korean War in 1953, North Korea threatened to destroy neighboring Japan and forcefully reunify North and South Korea. Almost all of the nation's scant resources go to feeding and maintaining the North Korean army, which is one of the largest in the world, with more than a million soldiers.

The North Korean people, meanwhile, have suffered numerous famines and survive only on food donations from China, Japan, South Korea, the United States, and the United Nations. The United States has called on other countries to impose harsh sanctions to punish North Korea for developing nuclear weapons. It remains to be seen how a nuclear-armed North Korea will change power relations in the region.

LATIN AMERICA

In 1823, President James Monroe issued the **Monroe Doctrine,** declaring that the European powers should not involve themselves in the Western Hemisphere. President Theodore Roosevelt amended this policy around the turn of the twentieth century with the Roosevelt Corollary to the Monroe Doctrine, which states that only the United States could interfere in Latin America. These two doctrines have dominated American foreign policy regarding Latin America ever since. In recent decades, the United States has been most concerned with immigration, trade, drugs, and the spread of socialism.

Immigration

Immigration issues dominate American relations with many Latin American countries, particularly those in Central America. In recent decades, the majority of American immigrants have come from Mexico, Cuba, El Salvador, the Dominican Republic, and Guatemala, among other countries. Each year, hundreds of thousands of people cross the border to work in the United States or permanently move to start new lives. The vast majority of these people come legally, but the increasing number of illegal immigrants has become a growing concern for ordinary Americans and U.S. politicians.

The issue of immigration has deeply divided Americans; some argue that illegal immigrants drain resources from the state governments, whereas others believe that all immigrants regardless of their legal status drive the economy. Bowing to political pressure, however, Congress passed the Sensenbrenner Bill in 2006 to erect a 700-mile-long fence along the Mexican border to help curb illegal immigration.

Trade

In recent years, the United States has sought to expand free trade in North America with the North American Free Trade Agreement (NAFTA) among the United States, Canada, and Mexico, which went into effect in 1994. Much like the larger World Trade Organization, NAFTA seeks to integrate these economies and reduce trade barriers and economic inefficiencies while simultaneously promoting regionalism. Critics have argued, however, that NAFTA is weak and has only succeeded in giving American jobs to Mexican workers, who work for lower wages. Proponents argue that free trade lowers the prices and raises the standard of living for the average American.

Drugs

Most of the illegal drugs that enter the United States come from Latin America, particularly Colombia. Washington has funneled millions of dollars into fighting drug cartels and cutting off cocaine production in Colombia since the Reagan Administration, with little visible success. Officials have also sought to increase border security, not only to prevent terrorists and illegal immigrants from entering the United States but also to curb the flow of drugs.

Socialism

American presidents since the Cold War have invoked the Monroe Doctrine to prevent the spread of communism and socialism in the Western Hemisphere. The most notorious example occurred in the early 1960s when the Central Intelligence Agency tried to depose and assassinate Cuban communist dictator Fidel Castro in the Bay of Pigs Invasion. Castro survived and retaliated by inviting the Soviet Union to install a number of nuclear missiles in Cuba to threaten the United States during the Cuban Missile Crisis. More recently, relations between the United States and Venezuela soured when Venezuela's socialist president Hugo Chavez denounced the United States as an imperialist world power.

Foreign Policymakers

Many people and groups shape American foreign policy, including the following:

- The president
- Cabinet departments
- Intelligence agencies
- Congress and the courts
- State and local governments
- The military-industrial complex

THE PRESIDENT

The president is the primary architect of American foreign policy. Article II of the U.S. Constitution names the president commander in chief of the armed forces and designates the president as the nation's chief diplomat. This role expanded and carried new weight as the United States became more of a global power during the twentieth century.

The National Security Council

The **National Security Council (NSC)** is a collection of security policy experts who are part of the White House Staff. The NSC, led by the national security adviser, advises the president on security issues.

> **Important National Security Advisers**
>
> Some of the nation's most powerful foreign policy experts were once national security advisers. President Richard Nixon appointed Henry Kissinger to the post, for example, and Kissinger helped formulate Nixon's foreign policy. President George H. W. Bush appointed Colin Powell to be his national security adviser, whereas President George W. Bush appointed Condoleezza Rice, one of his most trusted advisers, to the job. When she became secretary of state in 2005, Bush appointed Stephen Hadley to replace her.

The Joint Chiefs of Staff

Although the Constitution names the president as the commander in chief of the armed forces, each branch of the military also has its own head, known as the chief of staff. Together, these chiefs form the **Joint Chiefs of Staff (JCS),** a group that helps the president make strategy decisions and evaluates the needs and capabilities of the military.

CABINET DEPARTMENTS

Three cabinet departments usually take center stage in American foreign policy:

- **Department of State:** Engages diplomacy with other nations
- **Department of Defense:** Coordinates the American military around the world

- **Department of Homeland Security:** Protects America from terrorist attacks domestically and deals with natural disasters

> **Squabbling Secretaries**
>
> The secretaries of defense and state do not always agree with each other or with the president. In fact, sometimes the conflicts between the two lead to nasty infighting to get the president's favor. During the first term of George W. Bush, for example, Secretary of Defense Donald Rumsfeld frequently butted heads with Secretary of State Colin Powell, in particular over the prospect of invading Iraq.

Other Agencies

Although the State and Defense Departments are the primary foreign policy organizations in the cabinet, sometimes other departments play a role. When negotiating agricultural trade agreements, for example, the Department of Agriculture might play an important role. Specialized government organizations, such as the Office of the Trade Representative and the Export-Import Bank, also affect and influence foreign policy.

INTELLIGENCE AGENCIES

Many intelligence agencies work to provide the president with accurate, up-to-date information about the rest of the world. At the top of the intelligence services is the director of national intelligence, who coordinates the information that the various intelligence agencies gather. These agencies include the following:

- Central Intelligence Agency (CIA)
- National Security Agency (NSA)
- Defense Intelligence Agency (DIA)
- Army, Navy, and Air Force intelligence

The Importance of Intelligence

In order to conduct good foreign policy, officials must have accurate, reliable information. When the intelligence agencies fail to get quality information, policy often fails as well. In 1960, for example, the CIA dramatically underestimated popular support for Fidel Castro's regime in Cuba. Castro's military easily crushed the Bay of Pigs Invasion, embarrassing the United States and creating a foreign policy disaster for new president John F. Kennedy. But astute intelligence work in 1962 provided Kennedy with the information he needed a few years later during the Cuban Missile Crisis. Recently, much has been made about what President George W. Bush and his advisers knew and did not know before deciding to invade Iraq in 2003.

DOMESTIC INFLUENCES

Although the executive branch plays the primary role in conducting foreign policy, the legislative and judicial branches play roles as well.

Congress

Although the president determines foreign policy, Congress has the power of the purse and can therefore fund or refuse to fund the president's foreign policy programs. Congress can also force officials within the executive office to testify under oath about those policies and, in extreme cases, can pass laws to dictate policy to the president. The president sometimes also calls on Congress to endorse his choices, particularly with regard to the use of military force. Although the United States has not officially declared war on another country since 1941, the president has dispatched U.S. forces many times. In such cases, the president usually asks Congress to endorse the use of troops, and Congress usually complies.

EXAMPLE: On numerous occasions, Congress has granted the president authority to use military force without declaring war. The Gulf of Tonkin Resolution (1964), for example, authorized President Lyndon Johnson to use whatever force he deemed necessary to fight the Vietnam People's Army. Before the United States ousted Iraqi forces from Kuwait in 1990, President George H. W. Bush also sought approval from Congress.

Reagan and the Contras

In the 1980s, Republican president Ronald Reagan fought a major political battle with the Democratic-controlled Congress over giving aid to the Nicaraguan contras, a group attempting to overthrow the Marxist Sandinista government. President Reagan wanted to provide economic and military aid to the contras, whereas many Democrats argued against such aid. Eventually, Congress not only cut off funding but also made it illegal for the U.S. government to provide any money to the contras.

The Courts

The courts do not usually play a major role in foreign policy, but at times they have ruled about what the president and Congress can and cannot do. Recently, for example, federal courts have ruled that President George W. Bush overstepped his authority in detaining enemy combatants and wiretapping phone calls without a warning, but how this affects foreign or domestic policy remains to be seen.

State and Local Governments

State and local governments also play a role in foreign policy. These governments negotiate business deals with foreign governments and corporations, even hosting foreign dignitaries to promote trade deals. In some cases, local and state leaders work together with their foreign counterparts to reach informal policy agreements.

EXAMPLE: The American city of El Paso, Texas, is directly across the Rio Grande from the Mexican city of Juárez. The mayors of the two cities frequently reach informal agreements on matters that affect them both, such as pollution control and border crossings.

Public Opinion

Public opinion often shapes foreign policy, especially in recent decades. Mass demonstrations, rallies, and letter-writing campaigns can sway the opinions of lawmakers and other government officials. In the 1980s, for example, vocal opponents of President Ronald Reagan's policies in Central America contributed to Democratic electoral victories, which eventually changed American foreign policy in the region.

Public Opinion and the Vietnam War

During the late 1960s and early 1970s, many Americans regularly protested against American involvement in the Vietnam War. At times, even the president felt under siege by protesters. These protests influenced President Richard Nixon's decision to end the draft in 1970.

The Military-Industrial Complex

The defense budget of the United States is huge—about $400 billion a year. Many companies are eager to take advantage of that by getting defense contracts. Some people have argued that defense contractors play a major role in high defense budgets and foreign policy: Contractors actively work to increase the defense budget so that they can profit from it. Keeping the United States actively involved in conflicts around the world increases the defense budget and the demand for new weapons and technology. In his farewell address in 1961, outgoing president Dwight Eisenhower warned against the growing influence of the **military-industrial complex,** a coalition of defense contractors, the military, and members of Congress in districts that depend heavily on these contractors.

The Halliburton Controversy

Before he became vice president in 2001, Dick Cheney ran the Halliburton Corporation. Since the 2003 invasion of Iraq, Halliburton has received numerous contracts from the military. Critics allege that the military gave these contracts to Halliburton as a way of paying back Cheney's friends and associates. Others claim that only Halliburton can provide key services and that Cheney's relationship with the company is incidental.

Sample Test Questions

1. In what ways does the foreign policymaking process resemble the domestic policymaking process?

2. Describe the Bush Doctrine.

3. What is the military-industrial complex? Why do some people see it as a problem?

4. True or false: Foreign aid is a commonly used tool of foreign policy.

5. True or false: Congress usually defers to the president in matters of foreign policy.

6. Why was the Nuclear Non-Proliferation Treaty signed?

   A. To disarm countries with nuclear weapons
   B. To prevent the spread of nuclear weapons
   C. To regulate the use of nuclear power for energy
   D. To make nuclear technology accessible to all nations

7. The Department of Homeland Security was created following what event?

   A. The September 11th attacks
   B. The 1993 attack on the World Trade Center
   C. The 1998 attacks on American embassies in Africa
   D. The suicide bombing attack on U.S. marines in Lebanon

8. What does JCS stand for?

A. Judicial command staff
B. Joint Conference on Security
C. Joint command staff
D. Joint Chiefs of Staff

9. Which of the following options is *not* an American intelligence agency?

A. NEA
B. DIA
C. CIA
D. NSA

10. Which of the following is *not* an American foreign policy objective?

A. The proliferation of nuclear weapons
B. Environmentalism
C. War on Terror
D. Trade

ANSWERS

1. Foreign policy usually goes through the same basic steps—an issue gets on the agenda; policy alternatives are offered; the government adopts a policy; the policy is implemented; and the policy is evaluated. The difference is that the number of people involved is usually smaller.

2. The Bush Doctrine, put forward by President George W. Bush, argues that the United States should preemptively attack nations that could pose a threat to it.

3. The military-industrial complex is the alliance of the armed forces, defense contractors, and members of Congress whose districts rely heavily on the military. Some worry that it wields too much influence, increasing the size of the military in order to boost profits.

4. True

5. True

6. B

7. A

8. D

9. A

10. A

Suggested Reading

- Ambrose, Stephen E., and Douglas G. Brinkley. *Rise to Globalism: American Foreign Policy Since 1938*. 8th rev. ed. New York: Penguin, 1997.

This extremely readable book chronicles the emergence of the United States as a superpower after World War II.

- Hoge, James F., Jr., and Gideon Rose. *How Did This Happen? Terrorism and the New War.* New York: Public Affairs, 2001.

This collection of essays seeks to understand the rise of terrorism by Islamic fundamentalists from a multiplicity of perspectives.

- Nye, Joseph. *The Paradox of American Power: Why the World's Only Superpower Can't Go It Alone.* New York: Oxford University Press, 2002.

Nye argues that despite America's preeminent place in the world, it must adopt a multilateral approach to achieve its goals.

• Rashid, Ahmed. *Taliban: Militant Islam, Oil, and Fundamentalism in Central Asia.* New Haven, Conn.: Yale University Press, 2001.

Rashid, a reporter who spent a great deal of time in Afghanistan, explores the origins of Islamic fundamentalism and theorizes about its relationship to the United States.

Useful Websites

• www.brookings.edu

The Brookings Institution is one of the best-known think tanks. Its scholars conduct research on a variety of policy areas, including foreign policy.

• www.cfr.org

The Council on Foreign Relations has served as an unofficial think tank of the American foreign policy establishment for decades. Many top diplomats are also members of CFR.

• www.cia.gov

The website of the Central Intelligence Agency, the U.S. government's leading intelligence agency.

• www.csis.org

The homepage of the Center for Strategic and International Studies, which aims to promote global security and prosperity through in-depth research on international affairs.

• www.defense.gov

Another major player in the foreign policy process is the Defense Department.

- www.foreignpolicy-infocus.org

The website for the Global Affairs Agenda, an interest group that promotes a progressive foreign policy.

- www.intelligence.gov

The main website for the United States Intelligence Community (IC), the nonpartisan umbrella organization to which various departments and agencies, such as Navy Intelligence and the Defense Intelligence Agency, belong.

- www.state.gov

The U.S. State Department is the primary agency in conducting foreign policy. Its website provides a wealth of information about what it does.

- www.usip.org

The nonpartisan United States Institute of Peace promotes policies that encourage peace. Its website has links to briefings about violent hot spots worldwide.

APPENDIX

A+ Student Essays

American Political Culture

What role, if any, should religion play in politics and government? How might religion improve civil society?

Democratic societies have the unique problem of combating individualism in their citizens. Although democratic governments champion equality, they run the risk of allowing their citizens to become too concerned with themselves and their own lives. Such individualism erodes social bonds and, if left unchecked, would eventually ruin society. Religion, however, encourages people to become more involved in their communities and hence strengthens society as a whole. Coupled with the sense of mores, values, and such concepts as charity and goodwill, religious doctrines push people into social activism. For this reason, the United States should encourage its citizens to be active in whatever religion they choose.

French writer Alexis de Tocqueville argues in his book *Democracy in America* (1835) that democracies are inherently unstable because all the citizens are equal, less dependent on one another, and rely more heavily on themselves. As independence increases, fewer community ties are made. This democratic individualism allows people to become more like free-floating atoms than interdependent beings.

Religion, however, can curb independence and foster civic engagement. Broadly defined, religion is any belief in a god or a higher power that influences or controls one's destiny. This definition incorporates nearly all of the world's religions, from Christianity to Buddhism to Shintoism to Animism. The existence of gods or a god is crucial because such an existence establishes something higher and more significant than the human spirit. Equally important is the belief in the existence of an afterlife, a belief that the majority of people in the world also share. For Muslims, Jews, and Christians, there is a heaven or paradise. For Hindus, there is reincarnation into a better existence, and Buddhists believe in Nirvana. Likewise, many of these religions also have a counter-belief in a less desirable afterlife, such as hell or reincarnation into a lower class of being. The tension between both positive and negative forms of the afterlife helps resolve individualism.

In addition, religions provide mores for their followers, mores that benefit the state and civil society. Although each religion maintains its own sense of values, most faiths provide a common sense of morality and guidelines for dealing with other people. In nearly all religions, for example, it is wrong to kill or steal. Likewise, many religions promote peace, goodwill, and the Golden Rule: the notion that we should treat others as we would wish to be treated. These moral values strengthen the community.

These key features of religion curb individualism and prevent the collapse of society. The fear of a supreme being and the possible consequences of not performing well in this life encourage people to make investments now to attain heaven or paradise in the next life. This investment requires people to spend energy and time in this life. To do this, people cannot simply stay engrossed in their own affairs but must set their individualism aside to help others. Individuals with strong religious beliefs usually take an active role in the fate of society. Further, when people wholeheartedly believe in such mores, civic duties become voluntary. Individualism is curbed without hardship as people become willing to involve themselves in the community as part of their religious beliefs. As a result, the state benefits: Civic engagement becomes less of a chore and more of a personal joy. Citizens begin to care about one another, thereby ensuring the perpetuation of a civil society and the protection of civil liberties.

The Founding and the Constitution

Discuss the Constitution as a political document. In your view, is the Constitution liberal or conservative? Use specific examples to support your argument.

Even though political scientists hail the Constitution as the embodiment of the liberal enlightenment philosophy first outlined in the Declaration of Independence, the Constitution's framers actually designed the document to restrain democratic excess in the wake of the revolution and to unify Americans in a way that the Articles of Confederation had failed to do. Given the circumstances in which it was written, the Constitution, therefore, is a far more conservative document than most people realize.

The fifty-five men who gathered in Philadelphia in 1787 to draft the Constitution were all white, wealthy, property-owning individuals and not representative of the majority of Americans. Although these men certainly sought to expand political rights and privileges to a greater number of their fellow Americans, the framers' elite status and wealth made them wary of turbulence and political unrest. The loose confederation of states formed under the Articles of Confederation had proved ineffective in maintaining national order: States refused to cooperate, fund Congress, or honor the national debts. Worse, Congress had no ability to enforce its authority over the state legislatures. Shays' Rebellion, meanwhile, seemed to the framers to be a harbinger of perhaps even greater social upheaval in the near future. Delegates at the Constitutional Convention realized that they needed to create a stronger federal system of government in order to rein in the states, prevent another revolution, and resolve the young nation's financial woes.

But stronger government did not mean authoritarian government, and the delegates made certain that the new federal government would not have too much power over the people or over the individual state governments. The framers divided the government into three independent branches to further ensure that government would not and could not be monolithic. Their fear of centralized authority also led them to create an intricate system of checks and balances whereby each branch of government would have the authority to restrain the power of the other branches in some way so that no one branch would be able to dominate the others. They gave the president, for example, the ability to veto the laws that Congress creates. Congress, in turn, can override presidential vetoes with two-thirds approval in both houses. The Senate approves all presidential appointments to the judiciary branch, which itself eventually assumed the power of judicial review. In many ways, the framers safeguarded the liberty of the people by creating a government that would work slowly.

Yet while the framers wanted to protect the people from the government, they also wanted to protect the government from the people. Educated, semi-aristocratic patricians, the framers feared mob rule. They worried that commoners lacked the requisite knowledge and foresight to govern wisely and effectively and maintain stability. As a result, they wove many antidemocratic elements in the Constitution to ensure that only unbiased "best men" would serve in government. Senators, for example, served six-year terms and were originally appointed by the legislatures of the states they represented; not until the Seventeenth Amendment was ratified in 1913 could Americans elect their senators directly. Judges, moreover, were appointed by the president and served life terms, which the framers hoped would make them entirely independent from public opinion and the whims of the people. Even the president was to be elected through the Electoral College, a filtration system designed to prevent the people from electing someone the elites would deem unfit for the office.

Of course, the framers did have republican interests at heart when they drafted the Constitution, which created a government that allowed more people access to political power than ever before. At the same time, the framers feared disunity and democratic excess, and they sought to maintain stability by conservatively creating a stronger yet restrained federal government and by limiting the power of the people.

Federalism

Is federalism dead? Why or why not? Use specific examples to support your argument.

After deciding to forgo the Articles of Confederation, the framers of the Constitution decided to create a federal system of government in which the national government and the state governments would share political power. The framers hoped that federalism would not only allow state governments to meet the needs of a diverse body of people on the regional level but also that dispersed political power would prevent the national government from becoming too authoritative. Over the past two centuries, however, several events have fundamentally altered the balance of power among the federal government and the states, most notably the Civil War and the Great Depression. Although not dead, the federalist system is now radically different than the framers had originally intended.

The Civil War was the first major event in American history that redefined the relationship among the federal government and the states. Prior to the war, many southern politicians had been ardent proponents of states' rights, an antebellum euphemism for state supremacy. Southerners argued that states had the right to decide whether to obey the federal government's laws because the states had existed prior to the establishment of the national government and had, in fact, joined to draft the Constitution that had created that government. Most northerners, however, disagreed and believed the federal government and its laws were supreme over the states. The North's victory in the Civil War effectively ended this debate over states' rights and established the supremacy of the federal government over the states. From this point on, subordinate state governments had to obey all federal laws and statues, especially after the ratification of the

Fourteenth and Fifteenth amendments, which defined national citizenship and voting rights for all Americans regardless of which state they lived in.

Franklin Roosevelt's New Deal package, which attempted to combat the effects of the Great Depression, also gave the federal government more power vis-à-vis the states. The New Deal created a number of agencies that bypassed the states and directly provided relief to the people, such as the Works Progress Administration, the Civilian Conservation Corps, and the Agricultural Adjustment Administration. Roosevelt also gained more control over the economy with the Glass-Steagall Banking Reform Act and the creation of the Federal Deposit Insurance Corporation. Roosevelt ignored state politicians' objections when he created the Tennessee Valley Authority to provide power to one of the poorest regions in the country. The Federal Emergency Relief Act, meanwhile, earmarked $500 million to the states to be used for specific purposes, further strengthening Washington's power over individual state governments.

Many scholars have lamented the demise of federalism since the New Deal, believing that the states have no real political power left. Yet state governments still wield considerable power, especially in the years since the New Federalism of the 1970s. State governments, for example, still have the power to set education standards within their borders, which is why standardized test scores vary so drastically within the nation. The federal government has also been returning some powers to the states. Bill Clinton's 1996 welfare reforms allowed each state to spend federal dollars as it saw fit, with few stipulations. At the same time, however, this wave of New Federalism is nothing like the federalism envisioned by the framers, in which power was shared among states and the federal government more or less equally. It will be interesting to see whether this trend toward federalism continues or if the federal government will assume more power vis-à-vis the states in the coming years.

The Judiciary

Some people argue that the Supreme Court is undemocratic because it concentrates extraordinary political power into a body of nine appointed men and women. Others argue in favor of a judiciary independent of the caprice of public opinion. Which do you believe is the more valid viewpoint? Use specific examples to support your argument.

The Supreme Court has expanded its powers beyond mere arbitration as outlined in the Constitution. Today, the Court has become the *interpreter* of the Constitution. Consequently, the power of the judiciary branch now exceeds that of the other branches, resulting in a powerful, undemocratic branch of government that threatens the sovereignty of the American people.

The fact that only nine justices preside on the Supreme Court clearly indicates that the Court is undemocratic. So few individuals—particularly individuals who serve lifetime appointments and cannot be easily removed from power—should not have the ability to review laws for more than 300 million Americans. Once appointed to office by the president and approved by the Senate, the justices become entirely independent from politics and public opinion. Justices are left to interpret the Constitution as they see fit for as long as they live, and, more important, their opinions becomes law.

No other branch has such unrestricted power. The power of the U.S. Senate, for example, is divided among 100 men and women; that of the House of Representatives, among 435 members. Even though only one person heads the executive branch, both Congress and the people check the president's power; the legislature can overturn any presidential vetoes and must also approve all military actions. Further, individuals in the legislative and executive branches serve limited terms before the people must reelect them. The election process allows the public to determine the makeup of the legislature and the presidency. The Supreme Court, however, is not elected; therefore, it remains uncontrolled by the people and can rule as it pleases, regardless of whether the people agree with its decisions. Moreover, the opinions of these nine justices have the power to negate the legislation of the Congress, the orders of the president, and, consequently, the will of the people.

It would be far more democratic to grant the power of judicial review to the legislature. Granting Congress this authority would resolve two dilemmas. First, it would entrust the duty of constitutional interpretation to more than a small body of nine. Even if only one body of the legislature were given this power, judicial review would still be conducted by no fewer than the one hundred individuals in the Senate. Second, granting judicial review to Congress would also ensure the sovereignty of the people. If the elected representatives of the people are authorized to review the Constitution, the people ultimately control the core of the government.

Some might argue that if the legislature were to have the power of judicial review, chaos would ensue. Precedence could be undermined, and interpretations could be reversed with the election of each new batch of Congress members. The American legal system would lose its stability. But this fear is unfounded. Although Great Britain lacks a formal constitution, Parliament does have the authority of judicial review of its legal codes. Even though new governments are elected frequently, the judicial system in Great Britain does not fluctuate wildly but remains stable.

Others argue that the Supreme Court does not contradict the will of the people at all and actually preserves the republic and democracy by protecting the Constitution. Seen in this light, the

Court safeguards the Constitution from the masses, as well as from the whims of the legislature and its constituents, the American people. The American people, however, do not require protection from themselves. Such a statement implies that the people are incapable of governing themselves, which ironically goes against the very principle of democracy—that all people *do* have the capability to govern their own societies. Even if the justices on the Court truly have the best interests of the people in mind, the institution itself detracts from the fundamental principles of democracy. Only by granting judicial review to the legislature—and thus to the people—can democracy fully be realized.

Interest Groups

Are interest groups beneficial or detrimental to the American political system? Use specific examples to support your argument.

Even though political pundits deride interest groups as detrimental to American politics and government, interest groups actually have a significant positive effect that far outweighs any injury they may cause. Interest groups help promote good government and the maintenance of a pluralist society by giving ordinary Americans a means with which to participate in their government.

Critics have complained that American politics since the 1960s have been dominated by interest groups, which threaten democracy by taking government out of the hands of the people. These critics point out that two-thirds of all lobbyists in Washington represent self-serving interest groups that care only for themselves and that partisan political action committees donate hundreds of millions of dollars to political campaigns each election. They believe that too many interest groups lead to hyperpluralism and demosclerosis, the destruction of true democracy caused by government that favors special interests over the citizenry.

These arguments, however, give too much agency to institutions and not enough to individuals. However numerous or powerful, most interest groups are simply people, who have organized to better execute their constitutional right to petition the government. In fact, interest groups are the primary conduits through which the majority of Americans engage the government. Interest groups increase political participation within society, foster civic awareness and education, and, as some would argue, develop social capital among citizens who may not have come together otherwise. Interest groups have also secured some of the freedoms and liberties that Americans today often take for granted. The civil rights movement, for example, was rooted in the activism of the National Association for the Advancement of Colored People (NAACP) and the Southern Christian Leadership Coalition (SCLC). Without these organizations, the federal government might never have taken the initiative to secure the rights of black Americans. Interest groups, therefore, give voice to the people and help to promote and ensure democracy.

Even the founders recognized the vital importance of special-interest groups. James Madison, the proclaimed "Father of the Constitution" and author of the Bill of Rights, understood the benefits and necessity of interest groups to republican democracy. In his essay *Federalist Paper No. 10,* he argues that interest groups are both natural and unavoidable because large bodies of people invariably separate into a multitude of factions based on personal interest. Madison also believed that interest groups would lead to greater moderation in government. He argues that a multitude of competing interests will benefit American government: These interests will keep the government power in check by preventing any single majority of people from trampling the rights of the opposing minority. The more interest groups within the nation, the better the government and less likelihood of what he called a "tyranny of the majority."

Of course, American history is full of examples of majorities depriving minorities of their rights and civil liberties. It's also not difficult to single out some interest groups that seek only personal benefit, to the detriment of the common good. Nevertheless, interest groups foster good democracy by linking concerned and motivated individuals to the workings of government. A political system without interest groups would be sterile and would lack the pluralism republican government requires.

Foreign Policy

Some foreign policy analysts argue that promoting human rights serves no greater strategic or economic purpose and therefore has no serious place in American foreign policy. Should the United States work to promote human rights abroad, even in areas of the world where the United States has no specific military or economic interests?

Although promoting human rights may not achieve a specific strategic goal, doing so should be a key component of America's political strategy. As the most powerful and wealthiest democracy in the world, as well as the self-proclaimed leader of the free world, it would be immoral and even hypocritical for the United States not to make human rights an element of its foreign policy.

Almost every state shapes its foreign policy around specific strategic and economic concerns that affect or could potentially affect the welfare of the state and its people. The United States promotes free trade, international military security, and the expansion of democracy around the world—all in the interests of protecting the state and its people. In this sense, promoting human rights in developing countries seems to lie outside the scope of American national interests. Advocating on the behalf of Chinese dissidents, for example, or working to protect the lives of starving refugees in the Sudan would have no immediate impact on American security or trade. At the same time, however, promoting human rights sends a clear message to rogue nations and to the rest of the international community that the United States truly does intend to promote democracy and peace. The United States cannot claim to be the harbinger of peace and democracy while ignoring gross human rights violations. Moreover, making human rights a tenant of American foreign policy would put pressure on those countries seeking American business or financial and military support. Thus, promoting human rights abroad becomes a specific foreign policy goal, especially in an era when much of the world despises American hypocrisy after scandals in Iraq and Guantánamo Bay, Cuba.

It would be immoral for the United States to ignore human rights violations when it has both the capability and a high chance of success of righting those wrongs. Of course, there are cases in which the United States has no chance of succeeding. Some scholars have argued that the United States had little chance of success in protecting millions of starving people from warlords in Somalia in 1992. Americans at home watched their television sets in horror as Somali guerrillas ambushed and killed American soldiers, dragging their corpses through the streets of Mogadishu. An American pullout followed immediately, convincing many future foreign policymakers that the political cost of promoting human rights was too great. At the same time, avoiding human rights altogether is just as serious a mistake. The United States, along with the rest of the developed world, took no action in Rwanda in 1996 and watched as millions of people died unnecessarily. The United States has more recently taken a similar stance on the crisis in Darfur, choosing to allow slaughter rather than taking a strong international leadership role.

Promoting human rights should not be the core component of American policy, but it should be a key component. A human rights policy need not be zero sum, all or nothing, but our policy should be much firmer than it currently is. America could, for example, put more pressure on trading partners to obey international human rights laws and work with other developed and developing countries to resolve international human rights crises and to end genocide. And when the chance of success is high, the United States should once again shoulder more responsibility by taking an active role in providing humanitarian relief. Doing so would bring more credibility to the United States, increase its stature abroad, and allow it to resume its position as the leader of the free world.

Glossary

A

absentee ballot: A ballot, usually sent in the mail, that allows those who cannot go to their precinct on election day to vote.

absolutism: The belief that the government should have all the power and be able to do whatever it wants.

acquisitive model: A view of bureaucracies that argues agency heads seek to expand the size, budget, and power of their agency.

actual malice: Knowingly printing falsehoods in order to harm a person's reputation.

administrative adjudication: The bureaucratic function of settling disputes by relying on rules and precedents.

affirm: An action by the Supreme Court to uphold a ruling by a lower court; that ruling is now the legally binding one.

affirmative action: Measures to give minorities special consideration for hiring, school admission, and so on, designed to overcome past discrimination.

agency capture: The gaining of control (direct or indirect) over a government regulatory agency by the industry it regulates.

agency representation: A type of representation in which the representative is seen as an agent, acting on behalf of the district, who is held accountable if he or she does not do as the constituents wish.

agenda-setting: The power of the media to determine which issues will be discussed and debated.

amendment: A change to the Constitution.

American conservatism: The belief that freedom trumps all other political considerations; the government should play a small role in people's lives.

American exceptionalism: The view that the United States is different from other countries.

American liberalism: The belief that the government should promote equality in politics and economics.

Americans with Disabilities Act: The major law banning discrimination against the disabled, it requires employers to make all reasonable accommodations to disabled workers; it passed in 1990.

amicus curiae brief: Literally, a "friend of the court" brief. A brief submitted to the court by a group not involved in the case; it presents further arguments for one side in the case.

anarchism: The belief that all governments are repressive and should be destroyed.

appellate jurisdiction: The authority to review cases heard by lower courts.

appointment power: The president's power to appoint people to key federal offices.

appropriation: The act of Congress formally specifying the amount of authorized money that an agency can spend.

Articles of Confederation: America's first national constitution, which loosely bound the states under a weak national Congress.

attack journalism: Journalism that aims to undermine political leaders.

Australian ballot: A ballot printed by the government that allows voting to be secret.

authoritarian regime: A government that can do whatever it wants, without limits.

authority: The ability of the government to exercise power without resorting to violence.

authorization: A formal declaration by a congressional committee that a certain amount of money is available to an agency.

autocracy: A regime in which the government holds all the power.

B

bad-tendency rule: A rule to judge if speech can be limited: If the speech could lead to some sort of "evil," it can be prohibited.

***Bakke* case:** This Supreme Court Case decided in 1978 that affirmative action is legal as long as race is not the only factor considered.

balanced budget: When a government spends exactly as much as it takes in.

bicameral legislature: A legislature with two houses.

bilateral: A state acting in cooperation with another state.

bill: A proposed law or policy.

bill of attainder: A bill passed by the legislature that declares a person guilty of a crime.

Bill of Rights: The first ten amendments to the Constitution, which safeguard some specific rights of the American people and the states.

Bipartisan Campaign Finance Reform Act: A law passed in 2002 that banned soft money, put limits on issue advertising, and increased the amount people can donate to candidates; also called the *McCain-Feingold bill.*

bipolar system: An international system characterized by two superpowers that roughly balance each other.

blanket primary: A primary in which voters can choose candidates from more than one party; declared unconstitutional by the Supreme Court.

block grant: A grant-in-aid with few restrictions or rules about how it can be spent.

blog: A weblog on the Internet; the thoughts and opinions of a person or group posted online.

brief: A document submitted to a court that presents one side's argument in a case.

broadcast media: Media that is distributed over the airwaves.

Brown v. Board of Education of Topeka, Kansas: Supreme Court case that ended segregation and declared "separate but equal" to be unconstitutional.

bundling: The practice of lumping campaign donations from several donors together.

bureaucracy: An administrative way of organizing large numbers of people to work together; usually relies on specialization, hierarchy, and standard operating procedure.

buying power: One's ability to purchase things; it is undermined by inflation.

C

cabinet: A group, composed of the heads of federal departments and key agencies, that advises the president.

caesaropapism: The belief that the powers of church and state should be united in one person.

candidate-centered politics: Campaigns and politics that focus on the candidates, not party labels.

case law: The collection of court decisions that shape law.

casework: Work done by a member of Congress or his or her staff on behalf of constituents.

categorical grants: Money given for a specific purpose that comes with restrictions concerning how the money should be spent. There are two types of categorical grants: project grants and formula grants.

caucus: A gathering of political leaders to make decisions, such as which candidate to nominate for an office; set policy; and plot strategy.

census: Counting the population to determine representation in the House of Representatives; the constitution mandates one every ten years.

central bank: The institution with the power to implement monetary policy.

centralization: the process by which law- and policymaking becomes centrally located.

centrally planned economy: An economy where all decisions are made by the government.

charter: A document issued by state government granting certain powers and responsibilities to a local government.

checks and balances: The ability of different branches of government to stop each other from acting; designed to prevent one branch from gaining too much power.

chief of state: The ceremonial head of government; in the United States, the president serves as chief of state.

citizen: A legal member of a political unit.

civic education: Education geared toward training the young to be good citizens.

civil liberties: Individual freedoms that the government cannot take away, including free speech, freedom of religion, and the rights of the accused.

civil rights: The rights of equality under the law.

Civil Rights Act of 1964: The major civil rights legislation in the modern era, the Civil Rights Act banned discrimination and segregation in public accommodations.

Civil Rights Cases: Supreme Court decision in 1883 that said the Fourteenth Amendment only made discrimination by government illegal; private citizens could do as they pleased.

civil service: Government employees hired and promoted based on merit, not political connections.

Civil Service Commission: The first federal personnel agency.

Civil Service Reform Act of 1883: Law that established the federal civil service; also known as the *Pendleton Act*.

Civil Service Reform Act of 1978: Law that updated and reformed the civil service.

civil society: The network of community relationships that builds social capital.

civil war: A war fought within a single country between or among different groups of citizens who want to control the government and do not recognize another group's right to rule.

classical conservatism: A view that arose in opposition to classical liberalism; it claimed that tradition was very valuable, human reason limited, and stability essential.

classical liberalism: A view that arose in the early modern era in Europe; it argues for the value of the individual, the necessity for freedom, the importance of rationalism, and the value of the free market.

clear-and-present danger: A limit on free speech stipulating that speech that constitutes a "clear and present danger" can be banned.

closed primary: A primary in which the voter must belong to the party in which he or she participates.

closed rule: A rule on a bill, issued by the House Rules Committee, which limits or bans amendments during floor debate.

cloture: A motion to end debate in the Senate, it must be approved by sixty votes.

codetermination: A policy used in some states with strong social democratic parties that forces large corporations to have substantial representation from the workers on the board of directors

command economy: An economy where all decisions are made by the government.

commerce clause: A clause in Article I, Section 8, of the U.S. Constitution that grants Congress the power to regulate interstate commerce.

common-carrier role: The media's role as an intermediary between the people and the government.

common law: A system of law, originally from England, in which previous decisions guide judges in interpreting the law.

communism: An extreme form of socialism that advocates violent revolution to create a socialist state.

comparative politics: An academic discipline that compares states in order to understand how they work.

concurrent powers: Powers exercised simultaneously by the states and the federal government.

concurring opinion: An opinion issued by a judge who votes with the winning side but disagrees with the majority or plurality opinion.

confederacy: A loose relationship among a number of smaller political units.

confederate system: A system of government with a very weak central government and strong states.

conformism: A tendency for people to act the same way, watch the same television programs, read the same books, and so on.

constituency: The people in a district represented by a legislator.

constitution: A set of rules that govern how power will be distributed and used legitimately in a state.

constitutional democracy: A type of government characterized by limitations on government power spelled out in a constitution.

constitutional government: A regime in which the use of power is limited by law.

constitutional powers: Powers of the president granted explicitly by the Constitution.

continuing resolution: A measure passed by Congress that temporarily funds an agency while Congress completes its budget.

conventional participation: Political participation in activities deemed appropriate by most; includes voting, donating to a campaign, and writing letters to officeholders.

convention delegate: A party member or official who goes to the national convention to vote for the party's presidential nominee and to ratify the party's platform.

cooperative federalism: A term used to describe federalism for most of the twentieth century (and into the twenty-first), where the federal government and the states work closely together and are intertwined; also known as *marble-cake federalism*.

corrupt practices acts: A series of laws in the early twentieth century that were the first attempts to regulate campaign finance.

credentials committee: Party officials who decide which delegates may participate in the national convention.

critical election: An election that marks the advent of a realignment.

D

dealignment: The loosening of party ties as more voters see themselves as independents.

decision: A document issued by the court stating who wins the case.

Declaration of Independence: The document written by Thomas Jefferson in 1776 that broke the colonies away from British rule.

de facto segregation: Segregation that exists due to economic and residential patterns, not because of law.

defamation of character: Unfairly hurting a person's reputation.

deficit spending: When a government intentionally spends more money than it takes in.

de jure segregation: Segregation imposed by law.

delegated powers: Powers granted by Congress to help the president fulfill his duties.

demand-side economics: An approach to economic policy that stresses stimulation of demand by putting more money in the hands of consumers.

democracy: Rule by the people.

democratic socialism: A peaceful form of socialism that works within democratic governments to attain socialism gradually.

demosclerosis: The inability of the U.S. government to get anything significant done because interest groups block all major change.

denial of power: Declaring that a certain person or group does not have a particular power.

depression: A severe economic downturn that lasts a long time; more serious than a recession.

deregulation: The repeal or reduction of regulations in order to boost efficiency, increase competitiveness, and benefit consumers.

deterrence: Threatening to use military force to prevent another state from taking a particular course of action.

devolution: The process of the national government giving responsibilities and powers to state, local, or regional governments.

dictatorship: An absolute government in which one person holds all the power and uses it for his or her own self-interest.

diplomacy: The act of negotiating and dealing with other nations in the world, trying to achieve goals without force.

direct democracy: A government in which the people come together to vote on all important issues.

discharge petition: A measure in the House that forces a bill out of a committee for consideration by the whole House.

dissenting opinion: A court opinion written by the losing side that explains why it disagrees with the decision.

diversity: A mix of different cultural and religious traditions and values.

divided government: A situation in which one party controls the presidency, while the other controls at least one house of Congress.

divine right theory of kingship: The view that the monarch is chosen by God to rule with absolute power over a country.

division of labor: The practice of dividing a job into smaller component parts and assigning one person or group to do each part.

dual federalism: A term to describe federalism through most of the nineteenth century, where the federal and state governments each had their own issue areas, which rarely overlapped; also known as *layer-cake federalism*.

due process clause: Part of the Fourteenth Amendment, which declares that no person can be deprived of life, liberty, or property without due process of law.

duopoly: A term to describe the overwhelming power of the two major parties in American politics.

E

Earned Income Tax Credit: A federal welfare program that refunds all or part of a poor family's social security tax.

economic aid: Assistance to other countries designed to help the recipient's economy.

economic group: An interest group that seeks material benefits for its members.

economic growth: The expansion of the economy, leading to the creation of more jobs and more wealth.

effective tax rate: The actual percentage of one's income that one pays in taxes, after deductions and tax credits.

elastic clause: Clause in Article I, Section 8, of the Constitution that says the Congress has the power to do anything that is necessary and proper in order to carry out its explicit powers; also called the *necessary and proper clause.*

elector: A member of the Electoral College.

Electoral College: The body that elects the president of the United States; composed of electors from each state equal to that state's representation in Congress; a candidate must get a majority of electoral votes to win.

elitism/elite theory: The view that a small capable group should rule over the rest.

emergency powers: Inherent powers exercised by the president to deal with emergencies.

empire: A state that governs more than one national group, usually as a result of conquest.

enabling legislation: A law passed by Congress that lays out the general purposes and powers of an agency but grants the agency the power to determine the details of how it implements policy.

entitlement program: A program under which the federal government is obligated to pay a specified benefit to people who meet certain requirements.

enumerated powers: The powers specifically given to Congress in Article I, Section 8, of the Constitution.

environmental impact statement: A statement that must be prepared by the federal government prior to acting that describes how the environment will be affected.

environmentalism: The belief that humans have an obligation to protect the world from the excesses of human habitation, including pollution and the destruction of wilderness.

equality of opportunity: When all people are given the same chances to compete and achieve so that those with talent and diligence will succeed, whereas others will not.

equality of outcome: When all people achieve the same result, regardless of talent or effort.

equal protection clause: Part of the Fourteenth Amendment, which states that states must give all citizens the equal protection of the law.

Equal Rights Amendment: A proposed amendment that would end gender discrimination; it failed to be ratified.

equal time rule: A broadcast media regulation that requires media outlets to give equal amounts of time to opposing candidates in an election.

equity: When all parties to a transaction are treated fairly.

establishment clause: A part of the First Amendment that forbids government establishment of religion.

excess demand: An economic situation in which the demand for something exceeds the supply.

exclusionary rule: A legal rule that excludes from trial evidence obtained in an illegal search.

executive leadership: The view that the president should have strong influence over the bureaucracy.

Executive Office of the President: A set of agencies that work closely with the president to help him perform his job.

executive order: An order issued by the president that has the effect of law.

executive privilege: The right of officials of the executive branch to refuse to disclose some information to other branches of government or to the public.

ex post facto law: A law that declares something illegal after it has been done.

expressed powers: The specific powers given to Congress or the president by the Constitution; also called the *enumerated powers*.

F

fairness doctrine: A broadcast media regulation that requires a broadcaster that airs a controversial program to also provide airtime to people with an opposing view.

faithless elector: An elector who votes for someone other than the candidate who won the most votes in the state.

fascism: Ideology from Italy that stresses national unity, a strong expansionist military, and absolute rule by one party.

federal budget: A document detailing how the federal government will spend money during a fiscal year.

Federal Communications Commission: The federal agency that regulates the broadcast media.

Federal Election Campaign Act: A law, passed in 1971, that limited expenditures on media advertising and required disclosure of donations above $100; made more stringent following the Watergate scandal.

Federal Election Commission: The independent agency established in 1974 to enforce campaign finance laws.

federalism: A system of government in which power is shared by national and state governments.

Federal Register: A federal publication that lists all executive orders.

federal reserve bank: The name of the central bank of the United States; often called the Fed.

federal system: A system of government where power is shared between the central government and state and local governments.

feminism: The belief that women are equal to men and should be treated equally by the law.

filibuster: A Senate tactic; a senator in the minority on a bill holds the floor (in effect shutting down the Senate) until the majority backs down and kills the bill.

First Continental Congress: A gathering of representatives from all thirteen colonies in 1774; it called for a total boycott of British goods in protest against taxes.

fiscal federalism: The practice of states spending federal money to help administer national programs.

fiscal policy: How the government influences the economy through taxing, borrowing, and spending.

fiscal year: A twelve-month period (which does not coincide with the calendar year) used for accounting and budget purposes by the federal government.

527 groups: A political organization, not affiliated with a party, that can raise and spend soft money; named after a section of the Internal Revenue Code.

flat taxes: A taxation system in which everyone is charged the same rate, regardless of income.

food stamps: Coupons issued by the government that can be used to purchase food.

foreign policy: A state's international goals and its strategies to achieve those goals.

formalized rules: Another term for standard operating procedure.

formula grants: Grants in which a formula is used to determine how much money each state receives.

framers: The men who wrote the Constitution.

franking: The ability of members of Congress to mail informational literature to constituents free of charge.

free exercise clause: The part of the First Amendment that forbids the government from interfering in the free exercise of religion.

free rider: A person who benefits from an interest group's efforts without actually contributing to those efforts.

front-loading: Moving primaries up in the campaign calendar so that many primaries are held early in the campaign.

front-runner: The candidate perceived to be in the lead in an election campaign.

full faith and credit clause: A clause in Article IV of the Constitution that declares that state governments must give full faith and credit to other state governments' decisions.

fundamentalism: The belief that a religious document is infallible and literally true.

G

gag order: An order by a court to block people from talking or writing about a trial.

gender discrimination: Treating people differently and unequally because of gender.

general election: An election contest between all party nominees and independent candidates; the winner becomes a member of Congress.

general jurisdiction: A court's power to hear cases, which is mostly unrestricted.

gerrymandering: The term used to describe the process by which the party that controls the state government uses redistricting to its own political advantage.

Gibbons v. Ogden: An 1824 Supreme Court case that gave the federal government extensive powers through the commerce clause.

Gideon v. Wainwright: Supreme Court case of 1963 that ordered governments to provide an attorney to criminal defendants who cannot afford one.

globalization: The trend toward the breakdown of state borders and the rise of international and global organizations and governments.

government: The organization of power within a country.

Government Accountability Office: Congress's main investigative agency, the GAO investigates operations of government agencies as part of congressional oversight.

government bond: A promissory note issued by the government to pay back the purchase price plus interest.

government corporation: A federal agency that operates like a corporation (following business practices and charging for services) but receives some federal funding.

grandfather clause: A voting law that stated that a person could vote if his grandfather was eligible to vote prior to 1867; designed to keep blacks from voting.

grant-in-aid: A general term to describe federal aid given to the states for a particular matter.

grant of power: Declaring that a certain person or group has a specific power.

grassroots activism: Efforts to influence the government by mobilizing large numbers of people.

Great Compromise: The compromise plan on representation in the constitutional convention; it created a bicameral legislature with representation determined by population in one house and equality in the other; also known as the *Connecticut Compromise.*

gross domestic product: The total value of all economic transactions within a state.

guerrilla war: A war in which one or both combatants use small, lightly armed militia units rather than professional, organized armies; guerrilla fighters usually seek to topple their government, often enjoying the support of the people.

gun control: Policies that aim at regulating and reducing the use of firearms.

H

Hatch Act: A law passed in 1939 that restricts the participation of federal civil servants in political campaigns.

hierarchy: An arrangement of power with a small number of people at the top issuing orders through a chain of command to lower-level workers; each person is responsible to someone above him or her.

home rule: The granting of significant autonomy to local governments by state governments.

home style: The way a member of Congress behaves in his or her district.

honeymoon period: The first few months of an administration in which the public, members of Congress, and the media tend to give the president their goodwill.

horizontal federalism: How state governments relate to one another.

hyperpluralism: The idea that there are too many interest groups competing for benefits.

I

idealism: The view that states should act in the global arena to promote moral causes and use ethical means to achieve them.

ideology: A set of beliefs a person holds that shape the way he or she behaves and sees the world.

illegal participation: Political activity that includes illegal actions, such as sabotage or assassination.

impeachment: The power of the House of Representatives to charge an officeholder with crimes; the Senate then holds a trial to determine if the officeholder should be expelled from office.

implementation: The act of putting laws into practice.

implied powers: Powers given to the national government by the necessary and proper clause.

income distribution: The way income is distributed among the population.

income transfer: A government action that takes money from one part of the citizenry and gives it to another part; usually the transfer goes from the well-off to the poor.

incorporation: The practice of federal courts forcing state governments to abide by the Bill of Rights.

incrementalism: The tendency of policy in the United States to change gradually, in small ways, rather than dramatically.

independent: A person who does not feel affiliation for any party.

independent executive agency: A federal agency that is not part of any department; its leader reports directly to the president.

independent regulatory agency: A federal agency charged with regulating some part of the economy; in theory, such agencies are independent of Congress and the president.

individualism: The idea that all people are different and should be able to make their own choices.

inflation: The increase of prices.

informational benefits: The educational benefits people derive from belonging to an interest group and learning more about the issues they care about.

inherent powers: The powers inherent to the national government because the United States is a sovereign nation.

in-kind subsidies: Government aid to poor people that is not given as cash but in forms such as food stamps and rent vouchers.

inside game: Interest groups' efforts to influence government by direct and close contact with government officials; also known as *lobbying*.

interest group: An organization of people who share a common interest and work together to protect and promote that interest by influencing the government.

international agreement: An understanding between states to restrict their behavior and set up rules governing international affairs.

internationalism: The view that the United States should play an active role in world affairs.

international law: A set of agreements, traditions, and norms built up over time that restricts what states can do; not always binding.

international organization: An institution set up by agreements between nations, such as the United Nations and the World Trade Organization.

international system: The basic structures that affect how states relate to one another, including rules and traditions.

Internet media: Media that is distributed online.

interpretive reporting: Reporting that states the facts along with analysis and interpretation.

intervention: When a state sends military forces to help a country that is already at war.

iron triangle: An alliance of groups with an interest in a policy area: bureaucrats from the relevant agency, legislators from appropriate committees, and interest groups affected by the issue.

isolationism: The view that the United States should largely ignore the rest of the world.

issue advertising: Advertising, paid for by outside groups, that can criticize or praise a candidate but not explicitly say "vote for X" or "vote against X."

issue network: A collection of actors who agree on a policy and work together to shape policy.

J

Jim Crow laws: Laws passed by southern states that imposed inequality and segregation on blacks.

Joint Chiefs of Staff: A group that helps the president make strategy decisions and evaluates the needs and capabilities of the military.

judicial activism: A judicial philosophy that argues courts must take an active positive role to remedy wrongs in the country.

judicial implementation: The process of enforcing a court's ruling.

judicial philosophy: A set of ideas that shape how a judge or lawyer interprets the law and the Constitution.

judicial restraint: A judicial philosophy that believes the court's responsibility is to interpret the law, not set policy.

judicial review: The power of the courts to declare laws and presidential actions unconstitutional.

jurisdiction: A court's power to hear cases of a particular type.

justiciable question: A matter that the courts can review.

just-war theory: A theory of ethics that defines when war is morally permissible and what means of warfare are justified.

K

Keynesian economics: A demand-side economic policy, first presented by John Maynard Keynes after World War I, that encouraged deficit spending by governments during economic recessions in order to provide jobs and boost income.

kitchen cabinet: An informal name for the president's closest advisers.

Kyoto Protocol: An international treaty aimed at reducing greenhouse gas emissions.

L

laissez-faire capitalism: The economic philosophy that the government should not interfere with the economy.

lawmaking: The power to make rules that are binding on all people in a society.

layer-cake federalism: A term used to describe federalism through most of the nineteenth century, in which the federal and state governments each had their own issue areas, that rarely overlapped; also known as *dual federalism*.

legislative agenda: A series of laws a person wishes to pass.

legitimacy: Acceptance by citizens of the government.

***Lemon* test:** A three-part test to determine if the establishment clause has been violated; named for the 1971 case *Lemon v. Kurtzman.*

libel: Printing false statements that defame a person's character.

liberalism: A theory of international relations that deemphasizes the importance of military power in favor of economic power, trade, and international institutions.

libertarianism: The belief that government should be small and most decisions left up to the individual.

liberty: The freedom to do what one chooses as long as one does not harm or limit the freedom of other people.

limited government: A government that places few restrictions on its citizens' choices and actions, and in which the government is limited in what it can do.

limited jurisdiction: A court's power to hear only certain kinds of cases.

limited war: A war fought primarily between professional armies to achieve specific political objectives without causing widespread destruction.

line-item veto: A special type of veto that the president can use to strike the specific parts of the bill he or she dislikes without rejecting the entire bill.

line organization: In the government bureaucracy, an agency whose head reports directly to the president.

literacy test: Historically, a test that must be passed before a person can vote; designed to prevent blacks from voting.

lobbying: Attempting to persuade government officials through direct contact via persuasion and the provision of material benefits; also known as the *inside game.*

logrolling: A practice in Congress where two or more members agree to support each other's bills.

loophole: A part of a tax code that allows individuals or businesses to reduce their tax burden.

loose constructionism: A judicial philosophy that believes the Constitution should be interpreted in an open way, not limited to things explicitly stated.

M

machine: A very strong party organization that turns favors and patronage into votes.

Madisonian Model: A structure of government proposed by James Madison that avoided tyranny by separating power among different branches and building checks and balances into the Constitution.

majority leader: (1) In the House, the second-ranking member of the majority party; (2) in the Senate, the highest-ranking member of the majority party.

majority opinion: A court opinion that reflects the reasoning of the majority of justices.

majority party: In a legislative body, the party with more than half of the seats.

majority rule: The idea that the government should act in accordance with the will of the majority of people.

malapportionment: An apportionment of seats in Congress that is unfair due to population shifts.

mandate: When the federal government requires states to do certain things.

mandatory retirement: An employment policy that states that when an employee reaches a certain age, he or she must retire.

marble-cake federalism: A term used to describe federalism for most of the twentieth century (and into the twenty-first), where the federal government and the states work closely together and are intertwined; also known as *cooperative federalism*.

markup: When a Congressional committee revises a bill in session.

material incentive: The lure of a concrete benefit, usually money, that attracts people to join a group.

McCain-Feingold bill: The popular informal name for the Bipartisan Campaign Finance Reform Act of 2002; it is named after its sponsors, Republican John McCain and Democrat Russell Feingold.

McCulloch v. Maryland: A Supreme Court case that granted the federal government extensive power to carry out its enumerated powers.

means-testing: Basing benefits from a policy on a person's wealth so that poor people get more benefits than rich people.

media: Information and the organizations that distribute that information to the public.

media consolidation: The trend toward a few large corporations owning most of the media outlets in the country.

merit system: The practice of hiring and promoting people based on skill.

Merit System Protection Board: A board that investigates charges of wrongdoing in the federal civil service.

midterm election: A congressional election that does not coincide with a presidential election.

military aid: Assistance to other countries designed to strengthen the recipient's military.

military-industrial complex: The alliance of defense contractors, the military, and some members of Congress that promotes a large defense budget in order to profit themselves.

minority leader: In both the House and Senate, the leader of the minority party.

minority party: In a legislative body, the party with fewer than half of the seats.

Miranda v. Arizona: A 1966 case in which the Supreme Court ruled that police must inform suspects of their rights when arrested.

mixed economy: An economy that includes elements of the free market and central planning.

monarchy: A regime in which all power is held by a single person.

monetary policy: An economic policy that seeks to control the supply of money in the economy.

monopolistic model: A view of the bureaucracy that says bureaucracies have no incentive to reform or improve performance because they face no competition.

Monroe Doctrine: An American policy, set by President James Monroe in 1823, that claims America's right to intervene in the affairs of Western Hemisphere nations.

multiculturalism: The idea that Americans should learn about and respect the many cultural heritages of the people of the United States.

multilateralism: The idea that nations should act together to solve problems.

multinational corporation: A business that operates in more than one country.

multiple-member district: A legislative district that sends more than one person to the legislature.

multipolar system: An international system with more than two major powers.

N

nation: A large group of people who are linked by a similar culture, language, and history.

national convention: A convention held by a political party every four years to nominate candidates for president and vice president and to ratify the party platform.

national debt: Money owed by a government.

national interest: Things that will benefit and protect a state.

nationalism: A belief in the goodness of one's nation and a desire to help make the nation stronger and better.

National Security Council: A part of the White House Staff that advises the president on security policy.

nation-building: The task of creating a national identity through promotion of common culture, language, and history.

nation-state: A state that rules over a single nation.

Nazism: Political ideology from Germany that stressed the superiority of the German race, authoritarian rule by one party, military expansion, and a longing for a mythical past.

necessary and proper clause: A clause at the end of Article I, Section 8, of the U.S. Constitution that grants Congress the power to do whatever is necessary and proper to carry out its duties; also known as the *elastic clause.*

necessary evil: Something that is believed to be needed but is not good in and of itself; many Americans see government as a necessary evil.

negotiated rule-making: A federal rule-making process that includes those affected by the rules.

neoconservatism: A recent development in American conservatism that believes the power of the state should be used to promote conservative goals.

New Deal coalition: The supporters of Franklin Roosevelt's New Deal; the coalition included labor unions, Catholics, southern whites, and African Americans; helped the Democrats dominate politics from the 1930s until the 1960s.

new federalism: An American movement, starting in the 1970s, to return power to state and local governments, thereby decreasing the amount of power held by the federal government.

New Jersey Plan: A plan at the constitutional convention that gave each state equal representation in the legislature.

nihilism: The belief that in order to remake society, one must first destroy the current society.

Nineteenth Amendment: Passed in 1920, it gave women the right to vote.

No Child Left Behind Act: A law passed in 2001 that expanded federal funding to schools but required increased testing and accountability.

noneconomic group: An interest group that works on noneconomic issues; also called a *citizens' group.*

nongovernmental actor: A participant in the international arena that is not part of a government; such participants include nongovernmental organizations, multinational corporations, and international organizations.

nongovernmental organization: A political actor that is not affiliated with a particular government. Many NGOs are nonprofit institutions run by private citizens, such as the Red Cross, Doctors Without Borders, and the Catholic Church.

Nuclear Non-Proliferation Treaty: An international treaty, signed in 1968, that aims to prevent the spread of nuclear weapons.

O

objective reporting: Reporting only the facts with no opinion or bias.

office-block ballot: A ballot that groups candidates by office: All candidates for an office are listed together; also called the *Massachusetts ballot.*

Office of Personnel Management: The central federal personnel office, created in 1978.

oligarchy: Rule by the wealthy few.

ombudsperson: A person who investigates complaints against government agencies or employees.

open primary: A primary in which a person can participate in any party's primary as long as he or she participates in only one party's primary.

open rule: A rule on a bill, issued by the House Rules Committee, allowing amendments during floor debate.

opinion: A document issued by a court explaining the reasons for its decision.

opinion leader: A person whose opinion can shape the opinions of many others.

original intent: A judicial philosophy that states that judges should seek to interpret the law and the constitution in line with the intent of the founders.

original jurisdiction: The authority to be the first court to hear a case.

outside game: A term used to describe grassroots activism and other means to influence elections and policymaking.

overregulation: An excess of regulation that hurts efficiency.

oversight: Congress's power to make sure laws are being properly enforced.

P

pack journalism: The idea that journalists frequently copy and imitate each other rather than doing independent reporting.

paradox of participation: When many people vote because they wish to make a difference, but the actual chances of making a difference are infinitesimally small.

pardon: A release from punishment for criminal conviction; the president has the power to pardon.

parliamentary democracy: A regime in which the legislature chooses the executive branch.

partisan journalism: Journalism that advances the viewpoint of a political party.

party activist: A person who is deeply involved with a party; usually more ideologically extreme than an average party voter.

party-centered politics: Campaigns and politics that focus on party labels and platforms.

party-column ballot: A ballot that groups candidates by party; also called the *Indiana ballot.*

party identification: Feeling connected to a political party.

party in government: The role and function of parties in government, particularly in Congress.

party in the electorate: Party identification among voters.

party organization: The formal structure and leadership of a political party.

party platform: The collection of issue positions endorsed by a political party.

party reform: Measures aimed at opening up party leadership adopted by the major parties following the 1968 election.

patronage: Government jobs and contracts given out to political allies in exchange for support.

Pendleton Act: Another name for the Civil Service Reform Act of 1883.

per curiam: An unsigned decision issued by an appellate court; it reaffirms the lower court's ruling.

pigeonholing: The ability of a committee to kill a bill by setting it aside and not acting on it.

Plessy v. Ferguson: The Supreme Court case of 1896 that upheld a Louisiana law segregating passengers on trains; it created the separate but equal doctrine.

pluralism: The view that society contains numerous centers of power and many people participate in making decisions for society.

plurality: More votes than any other candidate but not a majority.

plurality opinion: An opinion written by the majority of justices on the winning side.

pocket veto: An unusual type of presidential veto: When the president neither signs nor vetoes a bill, after ten days the bill dies if Congress is not in session.

political action committee: An organization, usually allied with an interest group, that can donate money to political campaigns.

political appointees: Federal bureaucrats appointed by the president, often to reward loyalty.

political culture: The set of beliefs, values, shared myths, and notions of a good polity that a group of people hold.

political economy: The study of how politics and economics interact.

political efficacy: The belief that the government listens to normal people and that participation can make a difference in government.

political equality: Treating everyone the same way in the realm of politics.

political participation: Engaging in actions to achieve political goals.

political party: An alliance of like-minded people who work together to win elections and control of the government.

political science: The systematic, rigorous study of politics.

political socialization: The process by which political culture is passed on to the young.

politics: The process by which government decisions are made.

polling: Assessing public opinion by asking people what they think and feel.

pollster: A person who conducts polls.

poll tax: A fee for voting, designed to keep blacks and other poor people from voting.

popular sovereignty: A regime in which the government must respond to the wishes of the people.

Populists: A political movement in the late nineteenth century that fought on behalf of the poor workers and farmers; fused with the Democratic Party in 1896.

pork: Money spent by Congress for local projects that are not strictly necessary and are designed to funnel money into a district.

poverty line: The federal standard for poverty: Anyone below a certain income level is considered poor.

power: The ability to get others to do what you want.

power of the purse: The ability of Congress to spend money; all federal expenditures must be authorized by Congress.

precedent: A court ruling bearing on subsequent court cases.

preemption: The practice of the national government overriding state and local laws in the name of the national interest.

Presidential Commission: A body that advises the president on some problem, making recommendations; some are temporary, whereas others are permanent.

presidential democracy: A regime in which the president and the legislators must be entirely separate.

president pro tempore: In the vice president's absence, the presiding officer of the Senate.

primary election: An election within a party to choose the party's nominee for the office.

print media: Media distributed via printed materials.

prior restraint: Stopping free expression before it happens.

private bill: A bill that offers benefit or relief to a single person, named in the bill.

private good: A good that benefits only some people, such as members of a group.

privatization: The practice of private companies providing government services.

privileges and immunities clause: Part of the Fourteenth Amendment, which forbids state governments from taking away any of the privileges and immunities of American citizenship.

probability sample: A sampling technique in which each member of the population has a known chance of being chosen for the sample.

professional legislature: A state legislature that meets in session for long periods, pays its members well, and hires large support staffs for legislators.

progressive taxes: A taxation system in which the rich must pay a higher percentage of their income than the poor.

prohibited powers: The powers specifically denied to the national government by the Constitution.

project grants: Categorical grant programs in which states submit proposals for projects to the federal government and the national government chooses which to fund on a competitive basis.

proportional representation: An electoral system in which each party gets a number of seats in the legislature proportionate to its percentage of the vote.

prospective voting: Making a vote choice by looking to the future: Voters choose the candidate(s) they believe will help the country the most in the next few years.

proxy war: A war fought by third parties rather than by the enemy states themselves.

public administration: The task of running the government, and providing services through policy implementation.

public assistance: Another term for *welfare.*

public education: Informing the public about key issues and about what Congress is doing about those issues.

public good: A good that benefits everyone, not just some; also called *collective good.*

public opinion: The basic attitudes and opinions of the general public.

public policy: Any rule, plan, or action pertaining to issues of domestic national importance.

public representative role: The role of the media to act as a representative of the public, holding government officials accountable to the people.

purposive incentive: The lure of a desire to promote a cause.

R

rally 'round the flag effect: A significant boost in presidential popularity when a foreign crisis arises.

random selection: A sampling technique to ensure that each person in the population has an equal chance of being selected for the sample.

ranking member: The senior committee member from the minority party.

ratings game: The practice of organizations rating members of Congress based on votes that matter to the organizations and their members.

rational choice theory: An approach that assumes people act rationally in their self-interest, seeking to maximize value.

rationalism: The belief that human reason can find solutions to many of our problems.

realignment: A dramatic shift in the balance of the two parties that changes the key issues dividing the parties.

realism: A theory of international relations that stresses the importance of power (particularly military power) and claims that states act in their national interest.

reapportionment: The process of reallocating representation in the House of Representatives after a census; some states will gain seats, while other will lose them.

recession: An economic downturn; milder than a depression.

redistributive policy: A government action that takes money from one part of the citizenry and gives it to another part; usually the transfer goes from the well-off to the poor; also known as *income transfer.*

redistricting: Redrawing district boundaries after a state loses or gains seats in the House of Representatives.

regime: A word used to describe a particular government.

regressive taxes: A taxation system that costs the poor a larger portion of their income than it does the rich because the amount of tax gets smaller as the amount to which the tax is applied gets larger.

regulated federalism: The practice of the national government imposing standards and regulations on state governments.

regulatory policy: Government policies that limit what businesses can do; examples include minimum wages, workplace safety measures, and careful monitoring of stock sales.

remand: Sending a case back to a lower court for a new trial or proceeding.

rent voucher: A voucher issued by the government that can be used to pay all or part of a poor person's rent.

representative democracy: A system of government in which the people elect officials to represent their interests in the government.

representative sample: A sample that resembles the population as a whole.

reprieve: A formal postponement of the execution of a criminal sentence; the president has the power to grant reprieves.

republic: A regime that runs by representative democracy.

reregulation: Significantly changing government regulations on an industry.

reserved powers: The powers reserved to the states and the people in the Tenth Amendment.

responsible party: A party that is strong enough to carry out a specific platform if elected to office.

retention election: A state election, held in states using the merit plan for selecting judges, in which voters are asked whether a judge should keep his or her job.

retrospective voting: Making a vote choice by looking to the past: Voters support incumbents if they feel that the country has done well over the past few years.

revenue agency: A government agency that raises money by collecting taxes or fees.

revenue sharing: The practice of the federal government giving money to the states with no strings attached; started by the Nixon Administration and ended by the Reagan Administration.

reverse: When a court overturns a lower court's ruling, declaring it void.

reverse discrimination: Discrimination against majority-status people due to affirmative action policies.

revolution: A major event causing a fundamental change in a state.

rider: An amendment attached to a bill that has nothing to do with the bill itself.

right of rebuttal: A media regulation that requires broadcasters to give people an opportunity to reply to criticisms aired on the outlet.

rights of the minority: Rights held by the minority that must be respected by the majority.

Roe v. Wade: A 1973 Supreme Court case that legalized abortion during the first trimester.

rogue state: A state that does not follow international law or unspoken rules of the global arena.

roll-call vote: Occurs when each member's vote is recorded.

rugged individualism: A form of individualism that emphasizes self-reliance and ignoring what others want and think.

rule-making: The bureaucratic function of creating rules needed to implement policy.

rule of four: An informal rule in the Supreme Court: Four justices must agree to hear a case for the Court to issue a writ of certiorari.

S

sample: A group of people who are used to stand in for the whole population in a poll.

sampling error: Mistakes in polls caused by bad samples.

school vouchers: Government money given to parents to help pay for tuition at private schools.

Second Continental Congress: The governing body over the colonies during the revolution that drafted the Articles of Confederation to create the first national government.

selective incentives: The lure of benefits that only group members will receive.

selective incorporation: Forcing states to abide by only parts of the Bill of Rights, not the whole thing.

self-selected candidate: A person who chooses to run for office on his or her own initiative.

senatorial courtesy: A tradition in which a Senator, if he or she is of the president's party, gets input into nominees for federal judgeships in his or her state.

separation of powers: Dividing up governmental power among several branches.

sexual harassment: Unwanted and inappropriate physical or verbal conduct of a sexual nature that interferes with doing one's job or creates a hostile work environment.

Shays' Rebellion: A 1786 uprising of Massachusetts farmers against high taxes and debt.

signing message: A message attached to a bill the president signs, explaining his or her understanding of the bill.

single-member district: A legislative district that sends only one person to the legislature.

skewed sample: A sample that is not representative and leads to inaccurate polling results; a deceptive practice used to manipulate public opinion.

slander: Publicly stating things that the speaker knows to be untrue that hurt a person's reputation.

social capital: Mutual trust and habits of cooperation that are acquired by people through involvement in community organizations and volunteer groups.

socialism: Political view that the free market breeds servitude and inequality and should be abolished.

social security: A social insurance program that aims to keep retired people and the disabled out of poverty.

sociological representation: A type of representation in which the representative resembles the constituents in ethnic, religious, racial, social, or educational ways.

soft money: Unregulated money raised by parties and spent to influence elections indirectly; banned by the 2002 Bipartisan Campaign Reform Act.

solicitor general: A high-ranking Justice Department official who submits requests for writs of certiorari to the Supreme Court on behalf of the federal government; he or she also usually argues cases for the government in front the Court.

solidarity incentive: The lure of a social benefit, such as friendship, gained by members of an organization.

sovereignty: The right to exercise political power in a territory.

Speaker of the House: The leader of the House of Representatives, elected by the majority party.

special district: A type of local government designed to meet a very specific need.

special election: An election to replace a member of Congress who leaves office in between regular elections.

specialization: The practice of a group or person becoming extremely knowledgeable and skilled at one specific task.

splinter party: A third party formed when a faction from a major party breaks off and forms its own party.

split-ticket voting: Voting for candidates from one party for some offices and from the other party for other offices.

spoiler: A losing candidate who costs another candidate the election.

spoils system: The practice of an elected officials rewarding supporters and allies by giving them government jobs.

staffer: A person who works for Congress in a supporting capacity.

standard operating procedure: A set of rules established in a bureaucracy that dictate how workers respond to different situations so that all workers respond in the same way.

stare decisis: The legal doctrine of following precedent.

state: A political unit that has sovereign power over a particular piece of land.

statecraft: The exercise of power, guided by wisdom, in pursuit of the public good.

State of the Union address: A constitutionally mandated message, given by the president to Congress, in which the president lays out plans for the coming year.

statute: A law passed by Congress, a state legislature, or some other government body.

stewardship theory: A view of presidential power, put forward by Theodore Roosevelt, arguing that the president is uniquely suited to act for the well-being of the whole nation because he or she is elected by the whole nation.

straight-ticket voting: Voting for only candidates from one party.

strict constructionism: A judicial philosophy that argues that constitutional interpretation should be limited to the specific wording of the document.

subnationalism: Identification with small ethnic and regional groups within a nation.

suffrage: The right to vote; also called the *franchise.*

sunset provisions: Expiration dates written into some federal programs; Congress can renew the program if it is satisfied that the program is achieving its objectives.

sunshine laws: Laws that require government agencies to hold public proceedings on a regular basis.

superdelegate: A party leader or elected official who is automatically granted delegate status for the national convention; superdelegates do not have to be chosen in primaries.

Super Tuesday: A term used to describe primary elections held in a large number of states on the same day.

Supplemental Security Income: A federal program that provides a minimum income to seniors and the disabled who do not qualify for social security.

supply-side economics: An attempt to improve the economy by providing big tax cuts to businesses and wealthy individuals (the supply side). These cuts encourage investment, which then creates jobs, so the effect will be felt throughout the economy; also known as *trickle-down economics.*

supremacy clause: The part of Article VI of the Constitution that specifies that the federal Constitution, and laws passed by the federal government, are the supreme law of the land.

supremacy doctrine: The doctrine that national law takes priority over state law; included in the Constitution as the supremacy clause.

surplus: When a government spends less money than it takes in.

symbolic speech: Actions that are intended to convey a belief.

system of government: How power is distributed among different parts and levels of the state.

T

talk radio: A radio format featuring a host who interviews guests that is often very partisan.

tax credit: A reduction in one's tax burden designed to help certain people.

Temporary Assistance to Need Families: A federal welfare program that provides money to poor families.

term limits: Limits on the number of terms an elected official can serve.

terrorism: The use of violent tactics with the aim of creating fear and destabilizing a government; frequently targets civilians.

third party: In American politics, any political party other than the Democrats and Republicans.

Three-Fifths Compromise: A compromise on how to count slaves for determining population; slaves were counted as three-fifths of a person.

totalitarian government: A regime in which the government controls every facet of life.

total war: A highly destructive total war in which combatants use every resource available to destroy the social fabric of the enemy.

transnational: Something that lies beyond the boundaries of a nation-state or consists of several nation-states.

trickle-down economics: An attempt to improve the economy by providing big tax cuts to businesses and wealthy individuals (the supply side). These cuts encourage investment, which then creates jobs, so the effect will be felt throughout the economy; also known as *supply-side economics.*

trustee representation: A type of representation in which the people choose a representative whose judgment and experience they trust. The representative votes for what he or she thinks is right, regardless of the opinions of the constituents.

tyranny of the majority: When the majority violate the rights of the minority.

U

unconventional participation: Political activity that, although legal, is not considered appropriate by many people; it includes demonstrations, boycotts, and protests.

underemployment: When people who seek work can only find part-time jobs.

unemployment: When not everyone who wants a job can find one.

unfunded mandate: A mandate for which the federal government gives the states no money.

unilateral: A state acting alone in the global arena.

unipolar: An international system with a single superpower dominating other states.

unitary system: A system of government where power is concentrated in the hands of the central government.

unity: The idea that people overwhelmingly support the government and share certain common beliefs even if they disagree about particular policies.

user fee: A fee charged by the government to do certain things (e.g., paying a toll to use a tunnel).

V

veto: The power of the president to stop a bill passed by Congress from becoming law.

veto message: A message written by the president, attached to a bill he or she has vetoed, which explains the reasons for the veto.

Virginia Plan: A plan at the constitutional convention to base representation in the legislature on population.

voter turnout: The percentage of citizens who vote in an election.

voting behavior: A term used to describe the motives and factors that shape voters' choices.

Voting Rights Act: A law passed in 1965 that banned discrimination in voter registration requirements.

W

War Powers Resolution: Passed by Congress in 1973, the War Powers Resolution demands that the president consult with Congress when sending troops into action; it also gives Congress the power to force withdrawal of troops.

Washington community: The "inside the beltway" group that closely follows politics and constantly evaluates the relative power of politicians.

watchdog journalism: Journalism that attempts to hold government officials and institutions accountable for their actions.

Weberian model: The model of bureaucracy developed by sociologist Max Weber that characterizes bureaucracy as a rational and efficient means of organizing a large group of people.

welfare: The term for the set of policies designed to help those in economic need.

welfare state: The term to describe the government or country that provides aid to the poor and help to the unemployed.

whip: A member of the leadership of a legislative body responsible for counting votes and connecting the leadership with the rank and file.

whistleblower: A person who reports wrongdoing in a government agency.

White House staff: The people with whom the president works every day.

white primary: The practice of political parties only allowing whites to participate in their primaries.

winner take all: An electoral system in which the person with the most votes wins everything (and everyone else loses); most states have winner-take-all systems for determining electoral votes.

writ of certiorari: The legal document, issued by the Supreme Court, that orders a lower court to send a case to the Supreme Court for review.

writ of habeas corpus: A court order requiring that the government show cause for detaining someone and charge him or her with a crime.

Y

yellow journalism: Journalism that focuses on shocking and sordid stories to sell newspapers.

Index

INDEX

C

INDEX

INDEX

INDEX

D

E

INDEX

F

INDEX

G

INDEX

H

INDEX

INDEX

O

INDEX

INDEX

INDEX

R

S

INDEX

INDEX

T

INDEX

INDEX

Y